About the Author

Chris Daffy has over 35 years of sales, marketing and management experience. His early career was spent in the engineering, chemical and service industries, and in the 1980s he formed a marketing services and consultancy business that grew to have 14 offices throughout the UK.

In 1990 he embarked on a solo career and is now a successful business consultant and popular speaker at seminars, conferences and company meetings. Among the many companies he has provided consultancy services for are American Express, Bank of Scotland, Britannia Building Society, British Telecom, BBC, Hewlett Packard, JCB, JMC Holidays, Kingspan Group, Microsoft UK, Maersk Line, and the Whitbread Group.

Chris also presents seminars on a variety of management training programmes at the Manchester Business School and is one of the organisers of the MBS Study Tour of UK Service Excellence.

He is a founding member of The Marketing Group, which provides a wide range of business consultancy services, and a director of several small businesses in the North West of England.

Once a Customer
Always a Customer

How to deliver customer service
that creates *customers for life*

Chris Daffy

Oak Tree Press
Dublin

Oak Tree Press
Merrion Building
Lower Merrion Street
Dublin 2, Ireland
www.oaktreepress.com

A catalogue record of this book is
available from the British Library.

ISBN 1-86076-164-X
Second edition 1-86076-113-5
First edition 1-86076-034-1

Printed in the Republic of Ireland by Colour Books Ltd.

Contents

Preface to Third Edition

When I first wrote this book I had no idea how successful it would be. I obviously hoped it would make some kind of mark and become recognised as a good source of ideas and inspiration for people and organisations to achieve greater success through the delivery of exceptional customer service. But I never imagined that in just four years there would be three editions and several print runs, that it would become recommended reading for people studying for their Chartered Institute of Marketing Diplomas, that thousands of copies would be bought by organisations for distribution to their staff, or that it would be published and distributed in India. I certainly didn't expect to be sitting here this morning, writing the preface for a third edition, which will not only be distributed in the UK, Ireland and throughout Europe, but also now in the US.

I've therefore been surprised and delighted by the book's success and I'd like to thank all the people who've helped me to make this happen. But above all, may I thank you, my customer, for buying the book. If you've bought earlier editions, I hope you find that the new material in this latest edition helps you to continue improving the service delivery provided by your organisation. If this is your first copy, I hope it will give you the practical ideas and confidence to create that rare but special type of service that can set an organisation apart from all its competitors.

The main reason for writing this third edition is that we decided the book needed a chapter about e-service. The Internet and its impact on business are topics that are in the minds of many people. I therefore wanted to provide comment and thoughts about service and customer loyalty via this new medium. There is a great deal of volatility and hype surrounding the Internet. Many organisations are unsure about its effect on their competitive position and the delivery of customer service. But as you'll see in Chapter 16, I'm convinced that the same basic rules and principles that apply to all other means of communicating with customers also apply to the Internet. I therefore hope you will find this an interesting and useful chapter and that it will help you to plan and implement a successful e-service strategy for your organisation.

Chris Daffy
February 2001

Preface

There is no shortage of books on how to serve customers. I've just counted and I've got over 40 of them in my own collection, so there must be hundreds. "So why on earth have you written another one?" you may well ask. The main reason is simple. It's because I am committed to responding to the requests of my customers — they've asked me to so I have.

It's also because I believe that I have something different to say, and some new and different ways of explaining familiar things. You'll read later that the ideas and techniques I recommend are neither complicated nor difficult to use. In fact, if you find them to be either I shall have failed because I want to make them as simple as possible. You'll also discover that in isolation none of them are particularly earth-shattering. On its own, no one of them would make much real difference. But what I've found is that there is a tremendous synergy if you combine them in certain ways. The right combinations will result in an explosion in customer loyalty, business growth, profitability and the sheer enjoyment of work.

"So how do you know so much about this?" may be your next question. Well, I've been involved in sales and marketing for over 35 years, ever since I started selling crockery from a stall in Stockport market. All my working life I've been looking for ways to make the job of selling easier and more rewarding. I discovered a long time ago that if you give better service to customers, they come back for more and that makes the next sale a lot easier and a lot more profitable. During the 1980s I built a marketing services business around the simple concept of serving customers better than anyone else. In 1990, I became a freelance consultant and since then I've been fascinated by the topic of how to use service as a strategic differentiator in business. Most of my time, therefore, is currently spent studying, presenting ideas about and working with companies that want to be viewed by their customers as the best for service.

This means that I now do dozens of seminars, conferences and in-company presentations on this subject. After these events, people often come over to me to say things like, "You ought to write a book about that, Chris. You're the first person I've heard that can explain it in a way that means something to me." So I decided to do what they've been asking and try to put what I've learned into this book.

You'll find that the book contains a lot of graphics. I've done this so that you can, if you wish, quickly get the gist of what's on most pages by scanning the graphic. Then, if you see something that's of interest, you can read the text. But if you don't, you skip that page or section and move on to something more relevant to you. I hope you like this style; it should save you a lot of time.

I've also provided many checklists and places for you to record your own thoughts or business details. Please use them. This is a book you should write in. If it's in pristine condition when you've finished with it then it hasn't worked the way I hoped it would. It should stimulate you to make notes within it and then to take action after you've read it. In my experience, the former can trigger the latter. So if you really want to make service a differentiator for your business, if you genuinely want to change things so that customers will see you in a new light, please use this like a workbook. The more you write in it, the more you make it personal to you and your business, the more likely it is that you will then use the ideas and techniques to change things in your business.

The underlying principle of this book is that customer service is not an ordeal that we have to endure, but an opportunity that can produce huge benefits for any organisation. The experience of studying and working with hundreds of businesses, in most sectors, has taught me that little things can make big differences. This book is therefore crammed with lots of these little things that together can release those huge benefits — benefits like faster growth, more orders, bigger orders, and better profits.

So I hope you like my book and that you and your business benefit hugely from your time spent reading it.

Chris Daffy

Acknowledgements

I could not have written this book without a great deal of help and encouragement. I'd therefore like to record my sincere thanks to all those that contributed.

Graham Phillips has been my close friend and business partner for about 18 years. He's one of a very few people I've been involved with in business who I know I can totally trust. We've been through a lot together, good times and bad, and we both have a few scars to show for it. So, for all the help, fun, encouragement, inspiration, ideas, debates, and consistent support, thank you, Graham.

It was my friends at Manchester Business School who first made me believe that I was capable of writing a book. Thank you all for that encouragement and the opportunity of working in such a fantastic place of learning. My very special thanks must go to Tony Mosely of the Institute of Services Management at Manchester Business School. He's been a true friend and a great supporter of my work over the past few years to raise customer service standards throughout the UK. Thank you, Tony. I look forward to working with you on many more projects.

Finding a publisher for your first book is not easy. Finding one who you also really like working with is, I understand, close to being a miracle. I'm therefore very fortunate to be working with David Givens and his team at Oak Tree Press. From our first chance exchange on the Internet, throughout our negotiations and on to the finished publication, David has always been very patient, thoroughly professional and extremely supportive. He's also done what I think is a great editing job to help me get my ideas into a logical order and readable style. Thank you, David. I hope this will be just the first of many book projects that we work on together.

Most of the ideas and techniques in this book came from others. I've simply found the connections between them and some neat ways they can be used. My customers have taught me a lot of these ideas and techniques. They have also allowed me to develop a lot of the ideas with their staffs and customers. Thank you all for the unending flow of fresh ideas and for the opportunity to keep practising what I preach.

I have three sons, Nick, Simon and Andrew. They've all left home now and are a source of great pride to Jean and me as they find their own way in life and success in their chosen careers. While they were growing up, I moved around the UK quite a lot, moving home and family to wherever the next, better job seemed to be. The experience of working for loads of organisations was a great foundation for many of the ideas in this book. The nomadic life it created seems to have done more good than harm to my sons, but I'm sure there must have been times when they wished that I would settle in one place so they didn't have to keep making new friends. So thank you guys for putting up with your wandering Dad. Thanks also for the tremendous inspiration to succeed that having three eager and intelligent sons provides.

I've left Jean until last because she's the most important. I must be a very difficult person to live with. I love change, enjoy risk, thrive on variety, yet like things to be right and get annoyed when they go wrong. Life with me must therefore be something of a roller-coaster ride. Yet Jean's always there, hanging on, providing stability, support and encouragement, and rarely complaining. She's allowed me to risk our family's fortunes on my many business ventures and I know that there were times of potential problems when I may have slept well, but she didn't. We also work together so Jean has typed my endless drafts for this book, listened to my constant ramblings and rantings about customer service and accompanied me to numerous places I wanted to visit to experience a particular company's service first-hand. Jean is also my external con-science. She keeps my feet on the ground, stops me getting too full of myself and helps me to remember always to practise what I preach. So for your ceaseless love and support, thank you, Jean. This book is for you.

Chapter 1

Introduction: Back to the Future

What business needs today is customer service standards that were commonplace years ago, but are sadly all too rare nowadays.

The business climate of today is changing faster than it's ever changed before. Charles Handy has called it "the Age of Unreason" — the age when unreasonable people, who challenge conventional business thinking, are what is needed. Tom Peters called the last decade "the nano-second 90s" where things happened faster than ever before, creating the need for new, and perhaps crazy, ways of working. Well, one thing's certain: all this change is not going to come to a sudden stop during the 21st century. In fact, when you consider the rate at which technology is advancing, it's more likely that the pace of change which we all experience will continue to accelerate .. . forever more! This could suggest that many of the management principles that worked yesterday may not work today and will be completely out of place tomorrow. Yet in the area of customer service, for many businesses, I believe that what is really needed, now and in the future, is to get back to some of the basic principles that were commonplace years ago but are all too rare today. This is not to say that we shouldn't make the best use possible of the technology available to serve our customers because we obviously should. But we must ensure that the technology is there to serve us and our customer service goals. In all too many organisations I see that it's the technology that is being served and some basic yet essential customer service principles are being ignored or have been forgotten.

To be *market-led* you must be *customer-driven*. To increase market share individual customers must want to come back, time and time again, and spend more with you than with your competitors. This means that *share of customer* is for many businesses becoming more important than *share of market*.

I am therefore convinced that if many of the bigger, longer-established companies brought back a few of the basic principles of customer service that were employed by their founders, they would not have the problems many of them are experiencing today. The story below provides a good example of this.

Back to the Future — In the Life Assurance Industry

I was working with one of the UK's major life assurance companies. We were at the end of a few days of training for their senior managers. Something was needed for the final session that would make a lasting impression and leave them with ideas to start the process of change for the better in the business. I therefore used a summary list of 10 ideas that outlined the content of the training and indicated a few key actions that would help turn the ideas into actions. Having considered and debated the list for awhile it was generally accepted as a useful reminder of the training containing practical actions to implement the ideas.

I then revealed who had been the real author of the list. It was the founder of that business. The list was an extract from a letter he used to send to new insurance agents when they first joined the business . . . in the late 1800s.

Those basic ideas and principles of customer service, teamwork and leadership from over 100 years ago, that had made that business a success in the first place, were what was needed for today's highly competitive marketplace. In other words the company needed to go — Back to the Future.

The simple message in this story could be applied to many businesses and most markets. Things are changing. They're probably changing faster now than ever before. If you're going to keep up, or better still be ahead, you will need to be constantly changing many things in your business. But whatever change is going on, you shouldn't allow it to detract you from a core requirement for real success. That is the requirement to provide a level of customer service that will cause your customers to think (or better still, say):

"Wow! Now that's what I call service!"

The sorry fact is that service levels today in most industries are still low (even lousy) to mediocre. Most people find it difficult to list just five businesses where they get really good service. But when asked to list 10 where they would describe the service as poor they usually have no problem. (Try this yourself.)

The point is that there just aren't many businesses around that have realised the advantages of providing exceptional levels of service. The few that have are so rare that they stand out from the others. They are usually held in high esteem by their customers and competitors alike. They also generally have a number of characteristics that are common to all high-level service providers. Characteristics like:

✓ High staff morale

✓ Low staff turnover

✓ High repeat purchase levels

✓ Long customer retention levels

✓ Relatively low promotional costs

✓ Relatively low cost of sales

✓ High numbers of referrals and recommendations

✓ Middle to high prices compared with competitors

✓ Relatively high profit levels.

These are the type of rewards that can be created through providing exceptional levels of customer service. Therefore, making your customers go "WOW" about your service levels is not only great for them, but also good for your business.

Richer Sounds plc —
How to Make Money from Old-fashioned Service

Richer Sounds is a remarkable hi-fi retailer. Julian Richer established the business in 1978 and since then he has built it into Britain's biggest retail hi-fi chain. While companies like Dixons and Comet have average turnovers per square foot of around £600 to £650, Richer Sounds has almost ten times that at £5,800. It is also in The Guinness Book of Records for 1991, 1992, 1993, and 1994 because its London store is listed as the world's busiest retailer with turnover per square foot of £17,500 per year.

This has been created by simply delivering "old-fashioned service" and by cramming much more into its generally small, back-street outlets. It has more products, more Day-Glo price tickets, more hand-written signs, more special offers, more discounts, more guarantees, more fun, more bargains and more friendly and helpful staff.

Julian has five basic principles on which the business operates:

- *Work should be fun*

- *People should get recognition*

- *Service rather than sales should be rewarded*

- *You should tell people what's going on and listen to their ideas*

- *You must show people loyalty.*

Richer Sounds has proved that even in today's highly competitive world of hi-fi retailing, simple techniques and superior service can win big rewards.

So things may be changing faster than ever before, new technology may be making it possible to do many things quicker or better than in the past, but what is needed in many businesses is to get back to some of the basic values of customer service which were common in the past but are all too rare today — in fact, so rare that the companies that have them have generally created for themselves a distinct, sustainable and profitable competitive advantage.

Business Success through Strategy

"People are always blaming their circumstances for what they are.
I don't believe in circumstances. The people who get on in
this world are the people who get up and look for the circum-
stances they want, and if they can't find them, make them."
— George Bernard Shaw, from Mrs. Warren's Profession

Your business will obviously be affected by circumstances like the state of the economy or the state of the market you trade in. But it's your state of mind that will have most impact on the success or failure of the business. It's no good blaming the things over which you have little or no control. You must create success through the things you can control.

Business Success is All About Strategy

A Managing Director I know returned from a course at London Business School bubbling with enthusiasm to apply what he had learned and eager to share his new ideas. I was keen to listen and learn what I could from him. One of the most important things he felt he had learned was the following:

> **Business Success is:**
> **20% Situation**
> **80% Strategy**

His new understanding of this confirmed my belief that it's not the circumstances or situations that determine your success or failure, it's what you do about them. The circumstances have some influence but it's your reaction and what you do that is decisive.

Over the last few years I've been fortunate to have the opportunity to work with dozens of organisations — from one-woman businesses to major plcs, in manufacturing and service sectors, charitable and for profit, in the UK and internationally. In almost every sector there have been businesspeople who have been complaining about the effects of recession, the shortage of orders, the downturn in trade, the high costs of borrowing, the lack of skilled people, the rising cost of raw materials, etc., etc. Yet in the very same markets, sometimes literally just down the road, I have found people in similar but thriving businesses making comments like:

> *"We've never grown so fast or made so much profit as over the past few years. So if these are supposed to be hard times, please can we have more of them."*

They have realised that in any market or business climate there are opportunities for those who can recognise them and are prepared to make the changes necessary to take advantage of them.

The boom times of the 1980s created arrogance and complacency amongst many businesspeople. Some believed that the success they had enjoyed was as a result of their skills rather than as a result of the boom climate. For some it was their skill that created the success, but for many it wasn't. With its new and very different climate the 1990s provided challenges which some have found difficult to overcome. So the 2000s, with an even faster pace of change and new, never before experienced situations, must inevitably provide even greater challenges to management.

This book is about a strategy that many businesses have found to work successfully in the 1990s' markets and will, I believe, continue to provide success into the 2000s. It explains how many different businesses have discovered that they can use superior customer service as the basis of a strategy for success. Illustrations and diagrams have been used wherever possible to make it quicker to read and easier to understand the key points.

My hope is that it will inspire you to start a programme to raise the level of customer service in your organisation and convince you of how simple, natural, logical and above all how profitable it would be for you and your colleagues to do so. And perhaps also how reassuring it is to know that some of the "good old" principles of business and service to customers still work today.

Daffy's Laws

Having a name like Chris Daffy can be both a blessing and a curse. One of the blessings is that once people know it's Daffy, not Duffy, Datty or Dassy, but Daffy, and we've got past the inevitable Daffy Duck stage, people remember it. This is very useful during the many seminars and conferences I do. I have developed a number of Daffy's Laws, and find that because people tend to remember the name Daffy, they also remember the Daffy's Laws.

Daffy's Laws are based around some odd or interesting facts or relationships that I've found apply in most businesses. One such relationship is in the area of strategy. My Daffy's Law about this is:

> **CHANGE IS THE CONSTANT.**
> **The only thing that seems to be constant for most businesses nowadays is the need to be constantly changing almost everything they do.**

I shall pick up on this theme of constant change (for the better) throughout this book and, as appropriate, give you a few more of my Daffy's Laws to remember.

Chapter 2

The Need for Customer Obsession

The only way to embed customer service into the culture of a business is through a management-led obsession.

Our business schools and management training programmes keep churning out people who can read a balance sheet or understand statistical analysis, but many of these graduates still don't seem to have grasped the fact that it is customers, not products or services, but *customers* that are the only source of sales, profit, growth and pretty well anything else that really matters to a company.

One of my customers, a director of one of the UK's major banks, sent me this list of ten golden rules of customer care a few years ago. I've since learned that it originated from Mahatma Gandhi. Apparently it was what he used to advise Indian Government employees about how they should view and serve the general public. It also serves as a good way to establish a few of the core principles of customer service that will be expanded upon in this book.

Customers are:

♦   The most important people in any business.

♦   Not dependent upon us — we depend upon them.

♦   Not an interruption of our work — they are the purpose of it.

- Doing us a favour when they call — we do not do them a favour by serving them.

- Part of the business — not outsiders.

- Not a cold statistic but flesh-and-blood human beings with feelings and emotions like our own.

- Not someone to argue or match wills with.

- People who bring us their wants — our job is to satisfy them.

- Deserving of the most courteous and attentive treatment we can provide.

- The life-blood of every business.

Who Needs Crystal Balls When You've Got Customers?

Over the past 20 years or so I've been involved in organising or monitoring many market research programmes. The brief often is "help us find out what's in our future" or "find us some new markets". With all these projects the basic approach is simple: *Ask your customers and prospects.*

Anyone who has studied marketing will know the name Philip Kotler. His books are the basis of many marketing courses. One of his simple gems of wisdom is:

> **"Figures are your history, customers are your present and future. "**

So you don't need a crystal ball to know where a business is heading or could go in the future. You just have to ask your customers.

- If they are growing, you might.
- If they are diversifying, you might need to.
- If they have tight cash flow, you probably soon will have.

> ◆ If they're pleased (or better still, *delighted*) with what you provide, they'll probably take you along with them into their future.
>
> ◆ If they're not pleased with you, they'll probably take one of your competitors along instead.

Yet many businesses seem to operate as if customers are something which are bolted onto a business at the end of a process rather than the vital core element, without which the business would not exist.

An example of a company that demonstrates an obsessive approach to providing exceptional customer service levels is Nichols Foods Ltd. Gary Unsworth, its Managing Director, has successfully used customer service as a key element of its competitive strategy for many years. He commits substantial budgets to providing quality products and industry-leading service levels. He also invests in an ambitious training programme for his customers and their employees.

Case Study — Nichols Foods Ltd.

Nichols Foods Ltd. is part of the J. N. Nichols Group, which is best known for its soft drink VIMTO. Nichols Foods manufactures packs and distributes supplies for the food and drink vending industry.

Gary Unsworth, its co-founder and Managing Director, has always recognised how important delivering exceptional customer service is to the success of his business.

Nichols Foods has a customer service strategy that is based on the following key elements:

- *Ensuring that every employee is focused on the need to provide exceptional customer service.*

- *Encouraging employees to get closer to customers in order to develop their own customer obsession.*

- *Empowering employees to act on behalf of the customer.*

- *Establishing a series of basic standards and key measures of customer service.*

> • *Investing in training for the management and employees of customers to help them become more knowledgeable and skilful.*
>
> *This commitment to the provision of knowledge and training for customers' employees has been a key part of the strategy for a long time. Gary states that "we realised a long time ago that we needed to invest in our customers to ensure our own success".*
>
> *This investment began with an ambitious education and training programme to take customers to the coffee-growing regions of Colombia to see for themselves where and how coffee is produced. This programme was so successful that it has been developed over the years to the situation today where Nichols Foods is one of the main providers of management, sales and customer care training programmes for the UK vending industry.*
>
> *Nichols Foods has invested in a subsidised programme of training courses to help the management and employees in their customer companies to improve their knowledge and skills.*
>
> *The success of this strategy is seen in the excellent reviews Nichols Foods gets from its customers through the feedback it continually gathers. Also in the fact that over the past three years, in spite of recession in the vending industry, Nichols Foods has grown by over 50 per cent. In 1998 Nichols Foods also won the Service Excellence Award from* Management Today *magazine in the Business to Business category.*

The Nichols Foods Ltd. case study demonstrates the following:

1. Satisfied customers, who purchase again and again, are worth investing in.

2. A strategy should be developed to involve every employee in exceptional customer service delivery.

3. Employees need to be empowered to act on behalf of the customer.

4. The basic standards of customer service need to be agreed and some simple measures established to ensure they are met.

5. Your success is dependent upon the success of your customers.

Like Nichols Foods Ltd., the businesses that have gained a reputation for providing high service levels generally have an obsessive approach to customer service. They have core values which are understood and practised by all employees. Core values like these on the following list.

Core Values Needed to WOW Customers

♦ Customers are the business.

♦ Customer Relationship Values must influence decisions.

♦ Customers' reactions to service are predictable and therefore manageable.

♦ Customer satisfaction is no longer good enough — nowadays you need *delighted* customers.

♦ Customer perceptions usually differ from reality.

♦ Customers know what they want — you just have to ask.

♦ Employees are also customers.

♦ Customer care needs simple strategies, standards and systems.

♦ Customer care needs great leadership.

♦ Customer service success can easily lead to failure.

♦ Customers repay every investment in service.

Each of these core values and the way it is applied in a business needs to be clearly understood if you are to gain maximum benefit from them. The following chapters are therefore devoted to these core values.

Chapter 3

Customers *Are* the Business

To provide world class levels of service the customer must be placed at the centre of all business activities.

The language of many businesses needs to change. We use phrases like "profitable products or services", "return on capital", "utilisation of resources", etc. These are phrases which can easily mask the simple truth about business success and lead people up a wrong path.

To survive and grow a business must make a profit. In order to make a profit it must find people who are prepared to pay more for the products or services provided than they cost to have available. Up to the point of finding such people, the products or services are a *cost* to the business. *Profit* is only made when someone pays more for them than they cost. Therefore, the profit does not come from the products or service. They are the vehicle through which it is created, but the profit comes from whoever is found to pay more for them than the cost. That obviously is the customer. The simple truth, therefore, is this:

> **All profit comes from customers**
> So if no profit = no business
> and no customers = no profit
> then no customers = no business
> **Therefore customers ARE the business**

This may be a bit simplistic, but the implications are quite far-reaching. If all profit comes from customers, then it must make sense to focus the business on and around this source of profit. The business should be structured to make the flow of profit as easy as possible. The main requirement must be to ensure that the source of profit is the key driving force in the way the business is run. In other words, the business must be customer-obsessed.

There is an excellent book on this subject called *The Loyalty Effect* written by Frederick Reichheld, a consultant with Bain and Co. In it he explains how his 20 years' experience and research have shown that the companies that have long-term financial success are the ones able to create long-term employee, customer and investor loyalty. One way they do this is by making the delivery of "superior customer value" the nucleus around which their whole business enterprise revolves. This creates a simple and worthwhile goal that all employees generally agree makes sense and should therefore be keen to achieve. I sadly come across far too many businesses that have made "superior shareholder value" the nucleus of their business. This rarely provides the worthwhile goal that employees need to get them to commit their best efforts. (You don't need an MBA to work out that it's not going to be very easy to get people to work really hard and with enthusiasm in order to make somebody else even richer.) It therefore may produce good financial results in the short term (perhaps for the few years' term of the typical transient CEO who introduces it), but it rarely provides consistent growth and profitability for the organisation over the long term. (The transient CEO has usually left and is doing the same to another business by the time the long-term effects of the policy hit home!)

What is needed is an *outside-in* view. One that starts with what the customers and prospective customers want and then brings that into the business. The alternative is an *inside-out* view, which starts from what the business wants, and/or what it's already got, and takes that out to customers. These alternative views tend to cause the following:

The Customer-focused Business *(outside-in)*

👍 Customers are the focus of all activities.

👍 Customers find it easy to do business with you.

👍 Customers' views influence business decisions.

👍 Customer-friendly systems and structures are used.

👍 Customers are the focus of all business plans and activities.

👍 Customers appear at the top of the organisational chart. (If you really must have one.)

The Management-focused Business *(inside-out)*

👎 Customers are treated like an afterthought.

👎 Customers are expected to comply with the ways management wishes to run the business.

👎 Management views dominate business decisions.

👎 Systems and structures are developed and used to make life easy for management and employees.

👎 Investors, directors and managers are the focus of business plans and activities.

👎 Customers appear at the bottom of the organisational chart. (Are you really sure you need one?)

Many organisations have even created names for customers to ensure that they are kept as outsiders to the business. Some names even suggest that customers aren't really people at all but things to be used by the business as and when it pleases.

Names that Make Customers Seem Less Human:

Banks	⇨	Account holders
Credit cards	⇨	Card holders
Various	⇨	Consumers
Taxis	⇨	Fares
Utility suppliers	⇨	Householders
Building societies	⇨	Home owners
Airlines	⇨	Passengers
Hospitals/opticians	⇨	Patients
Bookmakers	⇨	Punters
Insurance	⇨	Policy holders
Local authorities	⇨	Rate payers
Holiday companies	⇨	Tourists
Computer suppliers	⇨	Users

These words have the effect of turning people (customers) into things or items. They de-humanise the act of serving them. It makes it easier then to accept the loss of a few (or maybe a lot!).

There is also the technique amongst marketers and statisticians to group customers together into what are called "segments" or "profiles" — groups of people who have similar habits or attributes and thus can be grouped together as being the same or similar. This again causes people to view customers as "things" or groups of "things" rather than individuals with needs, wants and expectations which generally are very similar to their own. Viewed *en masse* we tend not to care so much about the odd losses, certainly not as much as we would if we personally knew every customer we were losing.

This de-personalisation of customers is widespread and very damaging to a company. It can encourage staff to think that individual customers don't matter, that it doesn't make any if the odd one or two are lost. "There are plenty more," they say. You can even find people who then say and believe things like:

> *"My job would be much easier if it*
> *wasn't for all these customers."*

These people don't appear to see any connection between the service they give customers today and whether or not they have a job tomorrow. They perhaps think that wages are created in a wages department, that the people in that department simply conjure up the money to pay the wages each week or month. They don't see that a wages department merely distributes some of the profit that comes from customers. So they must continually be adding value to the products or services, so that customers will pay a price, that makes a profit, to create the income, to pay their wages.

But it's not the fault of employees if they think this way. It's the fault of the company and its leaders for creating an environment and a way of working which either encourages or allows it. It's the fault of managers and directors who don't set the right examples to all employees, who don't demonstrate by their actions that serving customers is the prime responsibility of everyone in the organisation.

Jan Carlzon, when he was the chief executive of SAS, told all the employees:

> **"If you're not directly serving**
> **customers, you need to be**
> **serving someone who is."**

It can't be put better than that. There should be just two roles in an organisation: either directly serving customers, or serving the people who do so that they can serve customers better.

This thought leads to an idea for an organisational structure that is totally customer-focused, with just two internal layers, as shown in the following diagram.

The Customer-focused Company

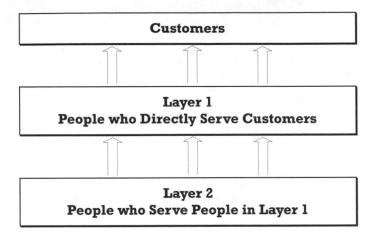

NB: There are no other layers!

The following example is of a business that not only adopted this two-layer approach but took it one stage further to reinforce the customer service message.

Management by Button-badge

A manufacturing business with about 60 employees adopted the two-layer structure and then took it a stage further. People in Layer 1 were given red button badges to wear, people in Layer 2 blue ones. Then they were all told the following:

"When a customer asks someone with a red badge for something, their job is to find a way to say 'Yes' to that customer.

"When someone with a red badge asks someone with a blue badge for something, their job is also to find a way to say 'Yes' to that colleague."

That simple idea quickly got the message through to the whole workforce and helped them to understand better the real purpose of their work and the need for everyone in the business to focus on the job of serving customers.

If you want to test how outside-in or inside-out your business is you can use the list of questions in the Customer Focus Questionnaire on the following page. They cover a few areas which I have found useful in assessing how customer-focused any business is.

First do the questionnaire yourself. Then take a few copies of it and get your colleagues to do it also. Their views will probably be different from yours. Remember that if their jobs keep them closer to your customers than yours does, their views are likely to be more accurate than yours.

You should also get a few customers to answer these questions. Yet again, their views will probably differ from yours or your colleagues'. Obviously your customers' views are the most important.

Customer Focus Questionnaire

	Usually	Some-times	Rarely
1. Company executives show *by their actions* that customer satisfaction and delight are important.			
2. Serving our customers' needs *takes precedence* over serving our internal needs.			
3. We *do not* make promises to customers that we know we cannot deliver.			
4. We use information *from customers* to design or improve our products or services.			
5. We *welcome* complaints from customers.			
6. We provide opportunities for employees *from all levels and departments* to regularly meet customers.			
7. We *regularly* ask customers to give us feedback about our performance.			
8. Our key managers *clearly understand* and broadcast the needs of our customers.			
9. Our employees at all levels are *encouraged and empowered* to exceed customers' expectations.			
10. We try to resolve all complaints to the *complete delight* of our customers.			
Totals			

The differences in opinions about your service levels that you will find are known as *perception gaps*. These are the gaps between how you, your colleagues and your customers view your products or services. Research has shown that the most common perception gaps are the following.

The Five Most Common Perception Gaps

♦ The gap between what you think the customer wants and what they actually want.

♦ The gap between what you think the customer has bought and what they perceive they have received.

♦ The gap between the service quality you believe is being provided and what the customer perceives as being provided.

♦ The gap between the customer's expectation of service quality and the service quality you actually deliver.

♦ The gap between the marketing promises and your actual delivery.

Knowing where these gaps are in your business will help you focus attention on the areas that matter most to customers.

The more ticks you have in the Usually column on the questionnaire, the more customer-focused your business is. The really top service providers around the world would score 8, 9 or 10 in this column. However, there are very few companies that can truly justify a score that high. Smaller companies generally find it easier to get more ticks in this column. One reason for this is that more of their employees are closer to customers and therefore are able to see more clearly the link between service delivery and business success.

If you have a lot of ticks (6 or more) in the Rarely column you need to get to work on the ideas in this book. I would suggest that survival in your current state will be very difficult. You therefore need to act quickly.

The typical score for this questionnaire is to have a spread of ticks across all three columns or to have a score of 6 or more in the

Sometimes column. This suggests that the business has the capability to provide great customer service, but that this does not happen consistently. The goal in this case should be to use the ideas in this book to move as many as possible of the ticks into the Usually column.

Having gathered all these views, scored your business and discovered the perception gaps, you need to decide how to react to them. What changes need to be made? How could you reorganise the business so that it is truly focused on the fact that "customers are the business"? The following chapters will provide you with lots of ideas for doing just that.

Recommended Actions	✓
♦ Make sure all employees realise that customers create wages.	❑
♦ Don't allow the use of any de-personalising names for customers.	❑
♦ Make the provision of "superior customer value" the nucleus around which your whole organisation revolves.	❑
♦ If you must have a formal organisational structure, make sure that customers are at the top of it.	❑
♦ Complete the Customer Focus Questionnaire. Get your staff and customers to do it as well. Then analyse the results to identify the perception gaps.	❑

Chapter 4

Lifetime Customer Value and Loyalty

If you really want your existing customers to become customers for life, start treating them as if they already were.

It's easy to overlook that customers have a lifetime of purchasing at their disposal. Someone working in a supermarket may view a man or woman with a trolley load of shopping as just worth the cost of the goods in that trolley. Someone selling a car could easily just focus on the value of that sale. Someone quoting for a new piece of manufacturing machinery could easily become obsessed with the profit on that one order.

But the man or woman shopping in the supermarket probably buys groceries every week. Over a lifetime the average person probably buys 10 to 20 cars. A manufacturing business buys machinery for as long as it is in business. What is needed, therefore, is a lifetime view of customer worth. All employees should understand precisely how much satisfied customers could potentially spend with their company if they chose to purchase for life, that is, for as long as they need what the company supplies and has it available. The single purchase is the Transaction Value. The lifetime of purchasing is the *Relationship Value*.

This is easy to calculate. You just multiply these two elements:

| Average Annual Purchase Value (expressed as sales value or profit) | X | Potential Lifetime of Purchasing (expressed in years) |

One easy way of calculating the average annual purchase value is to take the total annual sales and divide it by the number of customers. Some businesses may need to work out different figures for different types of customers, but this should not be difficult. This figure then needs to be multiplied by an estimate of the number of years in the customer's potential lifetime of purchasing.

This is easier for some companies to estimate than for others. The following examples show how it might be done in different industries.

Car Sales

Someone selling cars could say that the average car buyer will be in the age range of 17 to 70. This gives 53 years of potential purchasing. They could then say that the average person buys a car every 2 to 3 years. Therefore the potential lifetime of purchasing for a car buyer is:

53 years divided by one every 2 to 3 years
= 17 to 26 cars in a lifetime

They might then choose 20 cars in a lifetime as a safe, low potential.

Holiday Providers

A provider of holidays could say that the average person goes on holiday once per year. However, they probably will want to go to different places so it would not be reasonable to expect them to return to the same holiday location every year. They might, therefore, say that a visit once every 5 years was safe. If we then assume that people purchase holidays between the ages of about 17 to 70, we get the following:

53 years divided by once every 5 years
= 10 to 11 holidays.

A Computer Supplier

A computer supplier may know that the average company will re-place or upgrade a computer once every 5 years. Therefore, if they also know the number of computers a particular business has or could have, say 10, then the potential is as follows:

Say 50 years of purchasing
÷ replacement every 5 years x 10 computers
= a total potential of 100 computers.

I've helped dozens of companies work out this figure. They usually choose somewhere between 10 and 50 years. For example, I've already been using the same insurance broker since the year I got married (30 years ago) and the same accountant for as long as I've needed one (22 years). So somewhere between 10 to 50 years is probably right.

I thought an interesting exercise would be to calculate the life-time potential worth of a family like mine to a supermarket. Here's how it worked out.

The Daffy Family's Lifetime Potential Spend on Groceries

Jean and I have been married for 30 years. We have three sons. They're growing lads so they eat a lot. (One of our friends once suggested that they should be called "food disposal systems".)

This has meant that Jean has always had to buy large stocks of food, almost every week. We estimated that on average, over our first 25 years of marriage, we must have spent at least £100 per week in the local supermarket (allowing for the odd bottle of wine or spirit). The calculation therefore goes like this:

£100 per week for say 50 weeks per year = £5,000 per year
£5,000 per year for 25 years = £125,000.

I hope we shall be married for at least another 25 years. This therefore gives a potential lifetime spend on groceries for my family of £250,000 — £125,000 spent in the first 25 years and an-other £125,000 over the next 25 years.

When we first calculated this we were astonished by the size of the figure: £¼ million spent in the local supermarket during our married life. No wonder we're always broke!

When I've calculated figures like this with different companies I've worked with, they, too, are usually surprised at the size of the figure. Here are a few examples of figures we've arrived at:

- Fast food restaurant £2,500
- Cinema operator £3,000
- Shoe retailer £6,000
- Electronic components £150,000
- Car dealer £200,000
- Chain manufacturer £10,000,000

Returning to my family's lifetime spend on groceries, I wonder how many staff in our local supermarket say to themselves as they see me or Jean pushing the trolley around:

**"There goes a £¼ million potential customer.
We'd better give incredible service."**

I wonder if they see £¼ million over a lifetime or just £100 in the trolley? My guess is that most just see the trolley value.

But what if they all knew that we have the power to spend £¼ million in their store over our lifetime? I wonder if it would make any difference to the service we get? I've asked that question many times over the past few years during seminars. There is occasionally the odd cynic who says that they don't believe it would make a difference. But most people seem to agree that, provided the staff are helped to understand how the figure was calculated, and what it means or could mean to them, then they would be encouraged to provide £¼ million service levels to £¼ million potential customers.

I've often thought I could make a fortune if I could create some products that would do the job of keeping staff fully aware of the real potential worth of every customer. Products like:

- **Daffy stamps** — These are a bit like the stamps some people use to record the date and time of all letters coming into a business. A Daffy stamp would still record the date and time but would also display the potential worth of that customer to the business. This way people would be reminded that the way they deal with that letter could have that much financial impact on the business.

- **Daffy telephones** — These would be telephones with a special tone. They wouldn't ring or beep like most phones do today, they would go £40,000, £400,000, £40,000,000, or whatever was the potential worth of the customer that was telephoning. I doubt whether you would need silly rules like "all calls must be answered in three rings" if the phone was announcing the worth of the customer whenever they phoned (I'll explain later in the book why I think rules like this are silly).

- **Daffy scanners** — These would be like the doorframe things we have to walk through at airports, but these would not scan for metal but for potential worth to the business. They would then be installed in the entrance doors so that as customers passed through the scanner would be able to calculate their potential worth. Then a laser beam on the adjacent wall would be triggered to lightly engrave that figure on the customer's forehead so that all staff could see it when they met the customer.

I'm afraid I haven't been able to create these products yet so other means must be used. These have differed from business to business but have included:

- Getting the workforce to work out for themselves what they think the relationship value of an average customer is.

- Working it out in advance and having meetings with the workforce to explain how it was done.

- Publishing the figure at regular intervals to keep it at the forefront of everyone's minds.

- Management making regular use of the figure and reference to it in company information and at company meetings.

The companies I have worked with that have gone through this exercise with their staff have found that it does make a difference. Of course, money is not the only reason why we may wish to deliver great service. But a focus on potential customer worth can help to keep the need for great service at the forefront of people's minds. So this may be something that is used in isolation, but it is valuable as a key element of any programme designed to improve service levels throughout a business.

Knowing this figure provides an extra dimension to the everyday actions and decisions people take. It enables them to weigh the long-term potential against any short-term gain or cost. It provides a more balanced view between present and future needs. And provided people are properly empowered and trusted to make decisions, they then will make better decisions for customers and for the business.

It's therefore worth going through this exercise in your own business. Involve all the staff. Encourage them to work out what they think is the Relationship Value of an average customer. Then agree with them the figure to be adopted for the business. Discuss the implications of this to everyone and agree any actions that need to be taken as a result.

When you have calculated this figure, record it in the box below. You will be making further use of it later in the book.

Average Customer Relationship Value
£_____

Customer Loyalty

I think the best way to begin this section is with another Daffy's Law:

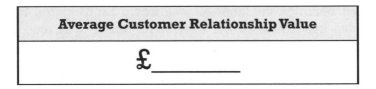

What matters is not how satisfied you keep your customers . . . it's how many satisfied customers you keep.

You will realise, I'm sure, that service alone may not trigger long-term customer loyalty. So even if you do all that is required to satisfy your customers you still may not be able to get them to commit to a lifetime of spending with you. (Don't get too depressed here because I'll show you how you *can* get them to do this later.) There have been many research studies on this subject and they all seem to agree that satisfied customers are rarely loyal, especially in highly competitive markets. In fact there was even an article in the *Harvard Business Review* that was entitled "Why Satisfied Customers Defect". The graph below indicates how loyalty is affected by the degree of competitiveness in a particular market.

The Loyalty/Service Relationship

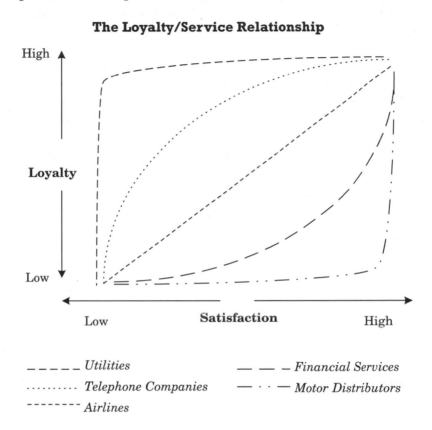

This graph shows various markets with their different degrees of competitiveness and how it affects the relationship between customer loyalty and satisfaction. As you can see, the more competitive the market, the more difficult it is to make customers loyal through service satisfaction. And in the highly competitive markets, there is little or no loyalty until you reach the really high extremes of satisfaction. So if satisfaction alone doesn't trigger loyalty, the obvious question is "what does"?

This Thing Called Loyalty

There's an awful lot of time and money being expended at present in attempts to create what is called "customer loyalty". There's even now a magazine called *Loyalty* solely devoted to it. But the more I've looked into and thought about the topic, the more obvious it has become that different people or organisations mean different things when they refer to customer loyalty. It's also clear that the different techniques and devices that organisations use to create customer loyalty each cause loyalty to different things — and these things may not be the company, its product or service.

I think there are seven basic types of loyalty. I'm sure there will be people who claim there are more than just these seven and could add to my list (I'd love to hear from you if you can), but for this chapter I will work with the seven that I am familiar with. They could have many names, but I've called them

1. Incentive Loyalty

2. Inertia Loyalty

3. Lazy (Habitual) Loyalty

4. Monopoly Loyalty

5. Price Loyalty

6. Trend Loyalty

7. True (Lifetime) Loyalty.

So let's look into each one of these and see how they work.

Incentive Loyalty

Having some form of incentive (bribe?) or reward for customers to remain loyal creates this type of loyalty. There are many examples of this, such as

*   Retailer loyalty cards

*   Motor manufacture credit cards

*   Credit or charge card points schemes

*   Petrol points cards

*   Hotel bonus schemes

*   Airline points schemes.

They obviously work. If they didn't, schemes like British Airways Airmiles, American Airlines AAdvantage Scheme, the Tesco loyalty card or the Marriott Hotels Rewards would have been scrapped long ago. But my question is, "what is it customers become loyal to with schemes like these?" I fear that these schemes don't always create a direct loyalty to the company, product or service, they often simply create loyalty to the scheme. The following two examples are evidence of this.

Diners Card. Whenever I can I use my Diners Card to pay for any purchases. I guess from this that Diners might conclude that I'm a loyal customer. But I'm not. It's not the Diners Card that I'm loyal to, it's the profile points I get for using it. (I think they have the best "profile points" scheme of all the cards.) Therefore, if Diners were to end or substantially worsen their points scheme, I'd no longer be the loyal card user that I am.

Motor manufacturer credit cards. I have a business partner who uses his Vauxhall credit card whenever he can. Why? Because his wife likes Vauxhall cars and he can accumulate automatic discounts off them by using this card. So, here again, we have an example of someone who is not loyal to the core product but to the incentive that goes with it. So if his wife goes off Vauxhall cars, or if the discount off Vauxhall cars reduces or disappears, my colleague will stop using that card.

So this type of incentive loyalty does work, but remember that it often only creates a loyalty to the incentive.

Inertia Loyalty

This type of loyalty occurs when an obstacle exists (or is created) that makes it difficult or inconvenient to change suppliers. Again there are many examples of this, a good one being the high street banks.

High Street Banks. A form of inertia loyalty was created by the attitudes and practices in many UK banks not long ago. If you have ever tried to move your bank account you will have learned just how effective inertia loyalty can be. They seemed then to work together to make it really difficult to move from one to another at will. We often got poor or flawed service, but when we tried to move it was very difficult to find an alternative bank that would welcome us. (Maybe *welcome* is a bit too strong a word to use for many of the old-style banks; *accept* would be nearer the mark.) If you wished to move your account, the potential new supplier seemed to view you with great suspicion. It was as if you were a *bad* customer because you wished to exercise your right to change your supplier. You had to be prepared to undergo a major interrogation (even if you only wished to be a depositor) with an amazing list of questions being asked, often about things that were nothing to do with them, before they were prepared to be so gracious as to accept you as a customer. Many people have told me that it's still much the same nowadays, even though the banks have tried to become more "customer friendly".

I'm sure that the difficulty many people experienced in moving their accounts from one bank to another was a key reason why many customers stayed (and maybe still stay) with banks they would leave were it not for the inertia involved.

Lazy (Habitual) Loyalty

Some people become loyal to a particular product, service or supplier simply because they can't be bothered to find or try an alternative. They have got themselves into a habit or routine and, so long as nothing goes wrong, or no substantially better alternative comes along, it's just not worth the trouble to change.

These customers are great to have, but it's important not to allow this situation to lead to complacency. There are many examples of companies that were in this situation, became complacent and then lost these customers to a smart competitor who recognised the situation and came along with a substantially better offer.

Marks & Spencer and Kendals vs. John Lewis. This has happened in my local area when a new John Lewis superstore arrived. My wife Jean and her mother had always been loyal customers of our local Marks & Spencer and Kendals (Manchester's premier department store). They were firmly entrenched in the habit of visiting Marks & Spencer weekly and Kendals about monthly.

But when John Lewis arrived in the area they were suddenly presented with a new and, in their view, much better alternative. So they broke their old habits and now visit John Lewis weekly, Marks & Spencer occasionally and Kendals rarely.

Monopoly Loyalty

The origin of this type of loyalty is obvious. If you want or need what a particular supplier provides and there is no alternative supplier you have no choice but to use that one and only monopoly supplier.

There are fewer examples of this nowadays but some that still exist include:

- The privatised local water companies
- British Gas (at least until recently in many parts of the country)
- Many of the privatised train operators
- Most of the local authority services
- Some airline routes.

In these instances we have no choice but to be loyal to the monopoly supplier if we want what it is that they provide.

Local water companies. If you wish to take a bath or shower tonight, unless you wish to arrange for a truck-load of Evian or Perrier to be shipped to your home, you're going to take your bath in whatever water comes through the tap from your local water company. You may not like them, you may think they're overcharging you for what they provide, you may even think that their product or service is lousy, but you really have no alternative. You therefore must be loyal by default.

Privatised railways. If I want to travel by rail, from my nearest railway station (Macclesfield) to London, I have no choice but to use the Virgin Rail service. I don't rate it as good. Their first class service is, to my mind, far from "first class" and I have experienced other rail operators that in my view provide a better (and cheaper) service, but from Macclesfield to London I have no alternative choice. I therefore must keep booking with Virgin Rail.

But these monopoly providers need to think long and hard about how they treat their customers. (I actually think that "customers" is the wrong word, "hostages" would be more accurate.) They should consider what normally happens when hostages are released. (Someone in one of my seminars once said, *"they write a book, don't they?"*). I have in mind that when released, hostages usually run in any direction that takes them away from their previous captors.

This happened when other companies presented themselves as alternatives to BT. Many people immediately switched, just to get away from BT. Perhaps they also switched just to get some revenge for the way they had been treated when they were a hostage BT customer. (However, many then found that the service from the competitors was actually no better, and in some cases worse, than BT and therefore switched back as soon as they could.)

The same has happened with the alternative suppliers to British Gas that have sprung up. I'm sure that many of the old British Gas customers will jump at the opportunity to try an alternative. (But they too may jump back later if they these alternatives are worse.)

Price Loyalty

In any market there will be some customers that are loyal to the supplier with the lowest price. This means that so long as they maintain the lowest price, these customers will stay loyal. The danger is that if a lower-price competitor comes into the market, then these customers will go where they get the better prices.

Kwik Save. Kwik Save is a good example of this. They built their UK reputation on being the lowest-price provider of grocery products. This worked well as a strategy for many years and attracted many loyal customers.

But as soon as the likes of Aldi, Netto, Costco and Lidl started to appear in the UK with some prices that were considerably lower than Kwik Save, these price-loyal customers then switched there allegiance to the lower prices they could get from the new suppliers.

Direct Line Insurance. The same happened with Direct Line Insurance. When they appeared on the UK market with their very low, direct prices, people in their thousands flocked to them for the cheapest prices. But then other companies, like Admiral and Churchill copied the basic concept and were able to offer the same or better prices. When this happened, Direct Line lost its price advantage — and market share, too.

Trend Loyalty

There are people who will become loyal to whatever is the latest trend. Many young people are so inclined and must have the latest designer shoes or clothes, or eat in the latest "trendy" restaurants or drink the latest "in" drink. They are both a marketing person's dream and nightmare. They're a dream when you can make your product or service the "trendy" one to have, but a nightmare when a competitor beats you at it. Examples which come to mind include:

- Nike sportswear and shoes

- Rayban sunglasses

- Sol lager

- Louis Vuitton luggage

- Rolex watches.

With many of these it is possible to keep the product trendy and so keep customers loyal (e.g. Rolex or Louis Vuitton). But others find this more difficult and, as new brands become more "in", they then lose favour and custom (e.g. Sol lager and Foster Grant sunglasses).

True (Lifetime) Loyalty

True loyalty is where a customer will be loyal to your company or product or service or brand even when you have lots of competitors who make it easy to switch to them and perhaps even offer incentives or advantageous prices to do so. Does this exist? Of course it does! And how is it created? I think The Loyalty Equation can help us find the right path.

The Loyalty Equation

To create an enduring loyalty, of the type I call "true loyalty", you obviously need something more than just good service. What this extra ingredient is has intrigued me ever since I realised that you might have a service that customers rate highly, but those same customers could still switch to a competitor without a second thought. I've therefore been doing lots of research and reading about this over the past few years and I came to an important stage in this when I was reading a recent issue of *Management Today*. In it was a short piece entitled "Loyal Yes, Staying No". It referred to some research done by Jan Hofmeyr, who is described as a South African religious psychologist-turned-market researcher. He has been researching the subject of loyalty and has concluded that it is made up of three core elements: affinity, satisfaction and involvement.

I once heard Tom Peters describe great management ideas as "a blinding flash on the obvious" because they're so right, so simple and so obvious. Reading this article was to me one of those blinding flashes of the obvious. It tied together all the research I'd been doing into loyalty and matched with my experience of working in this area of customer service. So let me try and explain how I think this loyalty equation works.

The diagram below provides a useful graphical reference for these three elements of true loyalty.

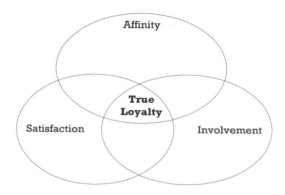

The actual loyalty equation is, I believe, as follows:

Loyalty = Affinity x Satisfaction x Involvement

I'm suggesting that the relationship between the elements is one of multiplication, rather than addition, because I believe that a zero score in any area can neutralise the others. You therefore need to have all three together to have any chance of generating the type of enduring customer loyalty that pays real dividends. So let's now consider these elements to highlight what you might do to make the most of the opportunities they present.

I'll begin by defining what I mean by "true loyalty". True loyalty is the kind of loyalty you might describe as irrational because it goes beyond logic. I often call it "emotional loyalty" or "lifetime loyalty". It's rather like the kind of loyalty one has to family, friends or country. Somebody at one of my seminars once suggested that what I was describing was perhaps "blind" loyalty. I suppose that wouldn't be a bad definition: a loyalty that may become blind to logic because it is based equally on emotion.

Let's then look into these elements of "true loyalty" to see how they interact and combine.

Satisfaction

Satisfaction is the starting point. If customers are not satisfied with the product or service they are getting then loyalty cannot follow. They must perceive that what they are receiving is what they were promised, what they expected, and is at least as good as they could get elsewhere. It's therefore vital to ensure that you do all the work that is necessary to ensure that your product or service is high quality and offers absolute reliability.

Sewell Village Cadillac in Dallas, Texas has the reputation of being the highest service motor dealers in the world. Carl Sewell, the owner, explained the importance of this element perfectly when he said,

> *"No amount of smiles will overcome lousy systems*
> *or inadequate skills."*

You must first, therefore, get your basic service right. However, simply being able to deliver a service or product that customers view as satisfactory will not create true loyalty. You could say that it's an essential to get you into the race, but it's no longer enough to make you a winner. For that you need to add the other two essential ingredients of true loyalty.

Involvement

Hofmeyr describes involvement as "a reflection of how much the customer has invested (financially or emotionally) in the relationship and how difficult it would be to sever the links". Involvement, therefore, requires you to build strong links with your customers that they value, rely upon and would not wish to break. This means that you must treat your customers as if they were part of your business. (This really shouldn't need to be said because no customers = no business!) I've described this in Chapter 14 as "treating customers like colleagues". It means that if you wish to create true loyalty you cannot treat them like outsiders. You must treat them like insiders or colleagues; involved with the business and connected to it through the role they feel they play in its development.

Customer Involvement at Tesco

I remember attending a lecture at Manchester Business School given by Terry Leahy, the Chief Executive of Tesco. He had been invited to talk about the key elements of Tesco's success and it was interesting to note how much importance he put on the way Tesco has involved its customers in the development of the business. At one point he said: "We've learned that if management will just shut up for awhile and listen to what their customers have to say, they'll write their business plans for them." He then explained the many ways that Tesco continually involve their customers in the development of the business. He ended his presentation by telling us: "When we stopped chasing Sainsburys and chased our customers instead, we started beating Sainsburys." There are more details about what Terry told us in the case study at the end of this chapter, but it's clear that the degree of involvement that customers have had in the business has been a key element in the success of Tesco over the past few years.

Involvement, therefore, means creating links (that they value) and being keen (not just willing) to include your customers in your management decision-making processes. It means asking their opinions and acting on them. It also means continually checking with them to make sure that you have got it right.

Affinity

Affinity can follow once satisfaction and involvement are in place. Hofmeyr describes it as "how customers feel emotionally about the brand and the would-be alternatives".

This final element is where our emotions must come to the fore. If we're going to get customers feeling emotional about us, the only way I know to do this is to find ways to show that we feel emotional about them. This means that you must be prepared to encourage everyone in your organisation to do those little but important things, for colleagues and customers, day in and day out, that demonstrate they have their wishes and wellbeing at heart. (Maybe just to show that they have a heart and don't leave it at home when they come to work.)

The more I've studied great service in action, the more obvious it has become that the actions that have the biggest impact on customers tend to be these little things which people do that show that they care. They are things that generally can't be anticipated or planned for, and therefore only happen consistently in an environment that encourages and rewards high service, personal initiative and spontaneity. However, although these things may be small and, in isolation, a single one will not make much of a difference to a customer's overall perception of service, their sum definitely does. So if you can encourage everyone throughout your business to do these little things that make such a big difference you should then trigger this third element called affinity. (The kind of things I have in mind, the +1s and WOWs are explained fully in Chapter 6.)

When this happens customers start to recognise that they are dealing with an organisation that is genuinely interested in them, one that delivers at least what they expect and involves them in the process of continually learning about their needs and wants. One of those rare companies that is designed with customers in mind, with people that care and are genuinely there to serve their customers. It is not surprising that what follows is that the customers of such an organisation feel a closeness, an emotional bond, and therefore true (lifetime) loyalty to it.

The following case studies about Hewlett Packard, Tesco, and Co-op Travelcare all provide further evidence of how these three elements can work together.

Hewlett-Packard

I had been asked to give a couple of presentations to the Business Managers and Customer Care Managers at Hewlett-Packard. Between the presentations I had the chance to compare notes with David Straker from their Quality Department who had also been investigating the subject of loyalty. We were both very pleased and surprised to find that, although we had come at it from different perspectives and had each used different reference sources, we'd come to pretty much the same conclusions.

David too had defined three elements of loyalty (he also called it "preventing the desire for escape"). His three were value proposition, involvement and relationship. We then discussed what he meant by value proposition and I meant by satisfaction and agreed that we were just using different words to describe the same thing. Relationship and affinity were also virtually the same.

Tesco

I briefly referred to Terry Leahy, the Tesco Chief Executive, and his presentation at Manchester Business School earlier in this chapter. I think that the story Terry told also provides evidence to support the loyalty equation. Here is more detail about what he told us:

Satisfaction — Tesco spends amazing amounts of time, effort and resources to get to know their customers' requirements for products and services and then to deliver exactly what they say they want.

Involvement — Tesco customers feel involved in the development of the company and its offering. For example:

- *It was customer requests that got Tesco to take the sweets away from the checkouts*

- *It was customer requests that got Tesco to provide the many types of trolleys that are now available*

- *It was customer requests that got Tesco to pledge to keep opening checkouts if there are queues until every one is manned*

- *It was customer requests that got extra people into the stores to help with bag and car boot packing*

- *It was customer requests that got Tesco to stop putting in the revolving entrance doors (and to start ripping them out where they already existed).*

Affinity — Tesco are working at an incredible pace to build a "cradle-to-grave" affinity with their customers. From the Tesco baby club, to the Loyalty Card, to the "Goof" programme, where customers are invited to report any service "goofs" (and be rewarded with loyalty card bonus points for doing so). These are all the type of things that will build the emotional bond that creates affinity.

Co-op Travelcare

I've been working with Co-op Travelcare and they too provide an excellent example of what can be done.

Satisfaction *— Co-op Travelcare make extensive use of questionnaires for customers to report on how satisfied they are with the booking procedure, the holiday, etc. They also use the dreaded "mystery shoppers" to check the performance of all outlets.*

Involvement *— Customers are now asked to write their own reviews of holiday locations and hotels and these are made available for other customers to read. Customers are shown the relevant "trade reviews" of locations and hotels so that they know the basic facts as well as the sales descriptions from glossy brochures. Customers are encouraged to tell the shop staff about their holiday experiences and any complaints are seen and dealt with as an opportunity to build the relationship with the customer. A customer newsletter has been produced to let customers know what is going on in the business and the industry.*

Affinity *— Customers are now telephoned both before and after their holiday to check that all is or was OK. There is a "Kiddies Corner" in many shops so that customers can book their holiday without being pestered by their children. The staff even now fill in the luggage labels for their customers.*

These projects are all part of a "Target 2000" programme that has produced remarkable results for Co-op Travelcare. Turnover has doubled in four years. Profit is up by £1.25 million. Their market share has increased in summer, winter and late-booking markets. Individual productivity is up, staff retention is up and the company's profile in the industry has improved substantially with the result that recruitment of the best people is now much easier. The final "icing on the cake" came when the latest staff survey revealed that over 99% of the staff felt "proud" to be working with the business.

So What Does All This Mean?

There are, therefore, many types of loyalty. I've listed above the ones that I'm familiar with but, as I indicated earlier, there may well be others. The important thing to note, however, is that different loyalty initiatives create different types of loyalty. So when you're thinking of creating some form of loyalty initiative or programme, always ask yourself what kind of loyalty you want. You need to consider precisely what it is you want your customers to become loyal to.

As I hope I've demonstrated, in many instances customers may become loyal to a particular situation or attraction that is attached to your product or service but that does not mean that they will also be loyal to your organisation. There's obviously nothing wrong with this kind of vicarious loyalty, but you must realise that if the situation or attraction is lost, then you may also lose those apparently loyal customers.

The loyalty that I think is most likely to last, regardless of competitive influences on the customer, is what I have called true or lifetime loyalty. It requires the three elements of satisfaction, involvement and affinity. Somebody once said that the best things often come in threes. (My three sons, of whom I'm really proud, have shown to me how true that phrase can be.) And if you think about it, wouldn't Freeman have been lost without Hardy and Willis, Snap without Crackle and Pop or Goldwyn without Metro and Mayer? Well, I hope that this chapter has convinced you that it's the same with lifetime loyalty. It needs the combination of all three elements, working together, to create the desired effect. Each element alone is quite powerful, but when all three are present, the loyalty equation starts to work, synergy clicks in and the results are then lifted to a new, higher level. I suppose the bad news in this is that true loyalty is the most difficult kind of loyalty to create. But the accompanying good news is that it is also the most difficult to compete against.

Recommended Actions	✓
◆ Calculate the Relationship Value of your average customers.	❏
◆ Involve your colleagues in the calculation of the figure.	❏
◆ Help them to understand what influences they have on whether or not customers will use your business for life.	❏
◆ Update the figure regularly to keep attention focused on it.	❏
◆ Check how good you are at providing the three key elements of satisfaction, involvement and affinity.	❏
◆ Make sure you're as focused on creating true loyalty as you are on satisfaction.	❏

Chapter 5

Predictable — and Manageable — Customer Reactions to Service

Customer reactions to service are mainly governed by emotions — what you get is determined by what you give.

Customer service works like a boomerang. You pitch a particular level of service in the direction of your customers. Then, like a boomerang, something comes spinning back. What you get back depends upon the service you give.

There has been lots of research into this over recent years to learn what are the reactions of customers to different levels of service. The most extensive and informative has come from Technical Assistance Research Programmes (TARP). By bringing together various bits of TARP research we can learn the predictable customer reactions, which depend upon the service levels they experience.

To understand the results of the research it helps to categorise customers into three basic levels of satisfaction.

Categories of Customer

Satisfied customers are taken as the midpoint. Delighted customers are somewhere above this and dissatisfied somewhere below. This does not signify that delighted customers are the pinnacle of success in customer service. There are levels above delight. Academics give them names like advocates or apostles. I prefer the name chosen by Ken Blanchard in his book of the same name, *Raving Fans*. We'll consider these higher levels in later chapters. Similarly, there are levels below dissatisfied. There are lots of names for these, too, but I think the best one is "terrorists". These are ex-customers who have decided to "get you back" for your bad service to them. We'll consider these later as well.

Satisfied Customers

Satisfied customers occur when you provide them with what you promised or they expected. The following diagram shows this.

Satisfied Customers Occur When:

What You Provide	Is Equal to	What You Promised and/or What They Expected

This should not be something to get excited about — just doing what you promised. Yet it's amazing how many companies seem to have made it their *raison d'être*. There are many company mission statements that use phrases like the following.

Mission Statement

Our life-long ambition is to satisfy our customers by actually doing for them all that they think we should and all that we promise to.

The belief seems to be that if you can achieve this, you can be pleased with your day's work and sleep soundly at nights. But this only creates satisfied customers. And when you ask a typical customer, as many researchers have, what they think about a supplier they are satisfied with, they use words like:

> *"Oh they're really ... er ... really ... em ...*
> *really ... ah ... OK."*

Or perhaps:

> *"Oh them ... they're all right I suppose."*

So is this something a company could be proud of? Being an "OK" or an "all right" supplier? Well how would it look on a letterhead?

Bloggs & Company Ltd.

Your local "OK" supplier

Or how about:

Smith & Jones Ltd.

Buy from us ...
our service is all right !

Obviously this wouldn't work very well as an advertising slogan. So why do so many companies have this goal of merely satisfying customers?

Another phrase used by satisfied customers about their suppliers is:

> *"Well they're about the same as our other suppliers.*
> *No better or worse. Just about the same."*

Perhaps this is something else that could be used for promotion, maybe on the flags flying outside the building.

This is the place to shop ...
We're no better or worse
than our competitors!

Obviously that wouldn't make many people stop and shop either. So companies should stop telling their staff that satisfied customers are the goal. The truth is that in most markets customers will view a satisfactory service as *bland* or *boring*.

The fact is that **satisfied customers just aren't good enough**. You need to do much better than create satisfied customers to compete successfully in today's marketplace.

People do not thumb through the Yellow Pages to find "OK" or "all right" suppliers or ones that are "no better or worse than their competitors". Satisfied customers do not nowadays create the best business rewards like increasing market share, premium prices or longer customer retention.

However, the research indicates that there are some small re- wards for having satisfied customers — rewards for simply doing what your customers expected or you promised.

These are shown in the diagram below.

> **Satisfied Customers**

> Continue to purchase from you (so long as nothing better comes along).

> Are likely to provide you with three to five referrals over their lifetime of purchasing.

This means that so long as competitors don't start offering better or cheaper things to your customers, they're likely to keep buying from you. But as soon as they do your customers will defect. This is why research has also shown that in most businesses, over 50 per cent of a company's satisfied customers will be customers of the competition within about four years.

Also, for the period of them buying from you they could refer you to three to five other potential customers. So if you chose a lifetime of purchasing of say 30 years, you would probably get a referral from each satisfied customer about once every six to ten years (three to five times in 30 years). This is obviously not very good. You're not going to build much of a business from this. You will therefore have to spend large amounts of money on sales and marketing activities if you want the business to grow. (You'll also have to spend large sums replacing all those satisfied customers who are defecting to your competitors.) But at least this, as you will see later, is better than what happens with dissatisfied customers.

When we talk about customer referrals we should always also consider one of my Daffy's Laws of selling:

> **If you can't convert most of the referrals you get into orders, you can't sell — so get out of selling and let someone else have those referrals.**

This rule may seem a bit harsh but I've asked hundreds of sales people if they agree with it. The only ones who don't seem to be those who shouldn't be in sales because they themselves aren't much good at converting the referrals they get into orders. So I think it's safe to say that it applies in most businesses. Therefore, you should be able to turn most of these three to five referrals into customers. Let's say four.

So let's use my local supermarket example to do a bit of "Daffy" maths with these figures. I think these figures suggest that my family could be worth a lot more to them than the £¼ million we would spend in our lifetime. We could also provide three to five referrals (say four), which could each be worth another £¼ million. Therefore our total potential worth, if we were just kept satisfied, is our £¼ million plus the four referrals, each also potentially worth £¼ million, which gives a total of £1¼ million over a lifetime.

Just think of it. Potentially £1¼ million revenue, from one family's spend on groceries and the referrals they could create. All that, just for making sure that what is provided matches what is promised or expected by that customer.

So what might this be in your business? Having already calculated the average Customer Relationship Value we considered in Chapter 4, you can easily now work out the total potential satisfied customer gains from the referrals they could create. It will help to give yourself a constant reminder by inserting the figure in the box below.

Potential Satisfied Customer Gains
Relationship Value X 5   (4 referrals + original customer)
£ _____

Now that you've calculated this figure, it is another one that you need to make all your colleagues aware of and to discuss with them the major implications that this could have on your business.

Dissatisfied Customers

If satisfied customers occur when what you provide is equal to your promise or their expectations, it follows that dissatisfied customers occur when what you provide is less than your promise or their expectations. Again this can be shown by a diagram.

Dissatisfied Customers Occur When:

This means that it's not at all difficult to create circumstances that will dissatisfy a customer.

Simple Ways to Create Customer Dissatisfaction:

☹ Promise delivery on Wednesday — and deliver on *Thursday*.

☹ Promise to call back this morning — but leave it until this *afternoon*.

☹ Claim that what you sell is reliable — *knowing* that it regularly goes wrong.

☹ Say that you'll have an answer in two days — and then take *three*.

☹ Promise to replace or repair defects with no questions asked — *but always hold an inquest.*

☹ Advertise a helpful friendly service — and then employ *unhelpful, discourteous people*.

☹ etc., etc., etc.

All of the above will create dissatisfied customers. It's that simple. You just don't do what you promise or what the customer expected.

There are, of course, degrees of dissatisfaction. There is extreme dissatisfaction which can have the effect of creating not just a dissatisfied customer but a "terrorist". This is someone who wishes to inflict whatever damage they can on your business. There is also tolerable dissatisfaction (perhaps this could be called disappointment), where the customer is not happy but decides that it's easier to do or say nothing about it. In other words, *to suffer in silence*. But these minor dissatisfactions or disappointments have a cumulative effect. So, if they keep happening, eventually one minor irritation becomes the final straw that loses you the customer and potentially creates another terrorist.

So what do dissatisfied customers do? Research shows that dissatisfied customers do much the same kind of things that you probably do when you're dissatisfied with a supplier.

The diagram below shows the research findings:

Dissatisfied Customers

Stop purchasing (or start looking for an alternative supplier)

Tell 9 to 10 people about their bad experience (2 to 3 times more than the satisfied customer referrals

Exaggerate the bad stories (like we all do sometimes)

Tell your competitors (who then spread the news to your other customers)

Usually don't tell you (only 1 in 25 causes of dissatisfaction get reported)

Generally don't come back (up to 90% NEVER return)

This clearly shows that the effects on a business of dissatisfied customers are much worse, more far-reaching and much longer-lasting than generally realised. It means that for every dissatisfied customer you've got, you can expect some or all of the following to happen:

1. They will stop purchasing from you, if not immediately, then as soon as they can find an acceptable alternative supplier. You've therefore lost their Relationship Value you calculated in Chapter 4.

2. They will tell nine to ten existing or potential customers about the causes of their dissatisfaction. They will also probably exaggerate these stories. You will therefore potentially lose a further nine or ten customers (along with their potential Relationship Value) as a result of this.

3. When they have found a new supplier, they are likely to tell that supplier (one of your competitors) the reason why they stopped purchasing from you. Again, they will probably exaggerate the story. Your competitor can then spread the exaggerated story to even more of your existing and potential customers.

4. The majority (up to 24 out of 25 [96 per cent]) of causes of dissatisfaction will not be reported to you. This is the SILENT majority. You could, therefore, be losing customers without knowing why and without any opportunity to do something about it.

• No matter what you later do, most (up to 90 per cent) of these lost customers will never come back. They are lost to you forever.

This is a devastating list of damaging effects resulting from just one dissatisfied customer. It's therefore no wonder so many companies choose to ignore it or pretend it doesn't happen. It proves that a sure way to destroy a business is to accept that a relatively high level of dissatisfied customers is either inevitable or unavoidable.

The bigger the company and the longer the company has been in existence, then the slower the destruction takes. But it's happening just the same. If you have a small or new business you will feel the effects of dissatisfied customers very quickly.

Beware of Being a Hypocrite!

I've been an advocate of the thinking of Stephen Covey ever since I read his book The Seven Habits of Highly Effective People. *One of the phrases from that book that really made me think is: "We tend to judge others by their actions but ourselves by our intentions".*

This phrase relates to the habit of exaggerating dissatisfaction. I ask people how they know that this happens and they always reply, "Because we do it ourselves".

You probably do too. So never patronise your customers for exaggerating dissatisfaction if, in the same circumstances, you would probably do just the same.

The Power of Negative Word-of-Mouth Advertising!

I believe that word-of-mouth advertising is the most powerful form of advertising that exists. And negative word-of-mouth advertising is much more powerful than positive. If you want confirmation of the power of negative word-of-mouth advertising, just ask Gerald Ratner! His business was ruined by a few careless words that spread via word-of-mouth and caused customers to stop buying.

Similar things happened to Hoover over their air travel promotion fiasco. Even Perrier lost and never recovered their previous market share following the scare about impurities in their bottled water that never were present but which the UK consumers "thought" might be there.

You should, therefore, never underestimate the power a dissatisfied customer has to damage your business.

So what would be the impact of this on my family's local supermarket? They would lose my family's business (£¼ million). Then we would tell nine to ten more people and they would potentially either lose them if they were existing customers or not attract them if they were potential customers (say nine x £¼ million). That means that the total potential loss of revenue from dissatisfied customers like my family could be ten times the lifetime customer value. This would give a potential loss of £2½ million worth of grocery sales. Just for a rude employee in the car park or an unhelpful checkout person? Maybe yes!

This is (or should be) a frightening prospect for any business. You should, therefore, work out what this figure could be for your business and record it in the box below. Then make sure the whole workforce knows this figure, how you calculated it and what it means or could mean to them.

Potential Dissatisfied Customer Losses

Relationship Value X 10
(say, 9 negative referrals + original customer)

£ _____

Whatever this figure is, I'm sure you don't want to lose that much business.

We can't leave this section without also considering in more detail the other points about dissatisfied customers.

Most Causes of Dissatisfaction Don't Get Reported to the Supplier

Research has shown that it can be as few as 1 in 25 (4 per cent) causes of dissatisfaction that get reported. The key reasons why it is so few are usually:

+ **Embarrassment** — Many customers don't feel comfortable complaining.

+ **Expectation** — Customers do not think the supplier will do anything about their complaint.

+ **Fear** — Customers fear the supplier might make things more difficult for them in the future if they complain.

+ **Inertia** — It's often easier for the customer to just go somewhere else in the future and not bother complaining.

+ **Indifference** — The customer doesn't care enough about the supplier's product or service to make the effort to complain.

+ **Ignorance** — The customer isn't aware of how to complain or that the supplier wants them to.

Yet research also shows that customers who do complain typically spend *twice as much* with their suppliers as the customers who don't. Customers who complain are, therefore, obviously our friends and allies. So why is it that in so many organisations they are treated like enemies?

Complaining Customers — Enemies or Allies?

Why do we keep treating our friends as if they were enemies? I often ask groups of people I'm speaking to, "Are customers who complain our friends or our enemies?" The answer I always get is "Friends!" This is obviously the right answer, the enemies are the ones who don't complain to us but tell anyone else who is prepared to listen, but it leads me to ask this next question. "So why is it that in most organisations our allies, the customers who complain, are treated as if they were our enemies?" What I mean is that we often do the things to complaining customers that are normally done to enemies, for example:

- *Put up defences and barriers that will make it difficult for them to complain.*

- *Provide resistance to their complaints to reduce the impact on ourselves.*

- *Take an opposing stance to them and their complaint so as not to be taken advantage of.*

- *Do everything we can to "limit our losses" as a result of the complaint.*

If we truly thought of complaining customers as allies or friends we wouldn't do any of these. We would welcome and support them and their complaint, see it from their perspective and do everything we could to put it right. You might like to test yourselves against these criteria to see if your complaining customers are treated as allies or enemies.

So the messages to your customers should always be:

"We *want* your complaints."

"Bring us *all* your niggles and gripes."

"Let us know if you are unhappy with *anything.*"

Marks & Spencer:
Proof that Complaints Can Be Profitable

For years I've been asking people at seminars if they can think of a company which has a good complaints or returns policy. The answer I almost always get is Marks & Spencer. It has (or at least had) a reputation for being one of the UK's best retailers for this. It was also one of the UK's most profitable retailers. I think these two things are closely linked. In fact, it's interesting to note that as Marks & Spencer's reputation for complaint handling has become less outstanding, their profitability has fallen too!

So it's good to have complaints. Most businesses, therefore, don't need fewer complaints — they need more. They may wish to reduce the *causes* of complaints, but to do this they need to increase the *number* of complaints. The latter is a way to achieve the former. A challenge, therefore, is to create a very unusual type of business, one where the following applies:

A Very Unusual Business

✓ Customers do not feel embarrassed to complain.

✓ They believe it's worthwhile complaining.

✓ They care enough about you as their supplier to want to tell you.

✓ They expect you to do something about their complaints.

✓ You have shown them how to complain.

✓ They have no fear of complaining.

If you can achieve all this, you're on your way to creating a remarkable reputation amongst your customers as one of the best in the business for complaints. Very few companies have achieved this, so if you can, you will have created something which sets you apart from and ahead of your competitors.

I've got a Daffy's Law for this:

> **Even the best companies occasionally get things wrong. The real measure of a company's service is how it reacts to being told things have gone wrong — and what it then does about it.**

You obviously don't want things going wrong. But when they do, what's most important is how you then react. We will consider in detail what to do about things going wrong in the section about recovery in Chapter 6.

Most Causes of Dissatisfaction Do *Get Reported to Competitors*

Your customers may not wish to tell *you* about their dissatisfaction, but they do want to tell *someone* so they often tell your competitors. This is not surprising when you consider they often get a more sympathetic reaction from a competitor.

It's crazy but true that many customers find that there is more interest and concern from the competition about a problem with a supplier or product than from the original supplier. So make sure your customers are not being driven to your competition whenever something goes wrong.

Also consider who your competitors may then tell. It may be anyone who will listen, but in particular they are likely to tell your existing and potential customers. And so the negative word-of-mouth advertising spreads, far and wide, and to the worst possible recipients.

This all further confirms the need to make certain that it is you who your customers will most want to tell about dissatisfaction. Remember, if it's not you it will probably be your competitors, so there's really no choice!

Remember:

Up to 90 per cent of dissatisfied customers are lost forever.

Why is this? Why don't they return to you if you improve? The answer usually lies in the phrase "damaged relationships".

When a customer becomes dissatisfied, the key thing that is damaged is the relationship the customer had with that supplier. The customer then finds a new supplier and creates another, hopefully (for the customer) better relationship. If sometime later the original supplier returns with claims like:

"We now deliver on time."

"We don't break our promises any more."

"Our new products now do what our old ones wouldn't."

"We now don't threaten to take you to court for bills you've already paid."

Or whatever other claims are thought will win the customer back, it's really no wonder they aren't impressed. They rarely respond with:

"Oh I'm so pleased. I will immediately revert back to dealing with you. Where do I sign?"

They more usually say:

"No, thank you!"

Or words to that effect. That's because they are likely to have formed a new relationship with a new supplier. Claims to the effect that "we're no longer as bad as we used to be" won't make the customer jump for joy and return with glee. They'll stick with the supplier they now have who is doing what they want, rather than one who had a chance, couldn't do what they wanted, but now promises that they can.

Turning the Tragic into the Magic at Superquinn

I first heard the phrase "turning the tragic into the magic" at Disney. They use it to describe how they believe that customer dissatisfaction should be dealt with. I think it's a brilliant way of expressing it and the following examples from Superquinn in Ireland show how it can be done.

Many of the things that are appearing in UK stores like Tesco, Asda and Sainsburys were invented by Feargal Quinn, the founder of the Superquinn stores in Ireland. He was first to:

- *Reward customers for finding goods close to their "sell-by" date by offering them at a lower price.*

- *Reward customers who find wobbly or difficult to drive trolleys with extra bonus points for their loyalty cards.*

- *Have people at checkouts to pack goods for customers (he often does this himself).*

- *Show on displays and till receipts the amount of Irish produce they sell and customers have bought.*

- *Have a crèche for children to play in while their parents are shopping.*

These are all small things but they help to make shopping in a Superquinn store a more pleasurable experience than in most of the competitors.

Turning the Tragic into the Magic at Bank of Scotland

Staff at Ibrox Branch arrived one Friday morning to find that overnight flooding had caused devastation to the premises, which meant the branch would be unable to open. The staff immediately went into action. Their prime concern was to minimise the disruption to customer service. Here's what they did.

- *Most staff were sent to nearby branches where arrangements had been made to service Ibrox customers. Business customers who were known to regularly call for wages, change, etc. were then contacted and requested to go to these other branches.*

- *Saturday saw football activity at nearby Ibrox Stadium. This meant that the nearby pubs would be extremely busy and require significant amounts of coins. Fortunately, the coin safe could still be accessed so staff phoned all the pubs concerned and arrangements were made for them to uplift their coin although the branch was closed.*

- *Arrangements were made with a local contractor to provide two buses that were used to shuttle Ibrox customers to the nearby branches.*

- *The local police, when hearing the plan, arrived with traffic cones to place in the street in front of the branch, which is normally a no-waiting area. This enabled the buses to park and wait for customers.*

- *Although notices were placed on the windows explaining the situation this was not considered good enough. Two young members of staff therefore took it in turn to spend a* dreich *(Scottish for cold, damp and miserable) Friday, outside the branch, greeting customers as they arrived, advising them of what had happened and personally offering them the services of the bus.*

The result was that not one customer was disgruntled that day because they felt the staff really cared and were going out of their way to help. (On hearing what had happened, Gavin Masterton, the Bank's Treasurer, telephoned the branch to personally thank all the staff.)

So beware:

Most lost customers end up lost for good!

Dealing with Difficult Customers

I thought I should include in this chapter some basic principles for dealing with difficult customers. Anyone working in a front-line position will have to do this at some time so it's worth mentioning the way the real professionals go about it.

In the next chapter you will learn about Whole Brain Service and how we basically have two parts to our brain: the left, logical side and the right, emotional side. It's most important to keep this in mind when you're dealing with difficult customers. You need to match your approach to whichever side of the brain seems to be in use by the customer. In most cases of difficult customers this will be the right side. Complaining or difficult customers are generally annoyed, angry, upset, disappointed, afraid (yes, some are actually afraid when they have to complain) or in some other emotional state. When this happens, the worst thing that you can do is to respond with a totally logical approach (even though you may feel this may appear to be the "professional" way to deal with it). If you

provide a logical response to an emotional appeal the odds are
that you will worsen the situation and heighten the emotion in the
customer.

An emotional approach from a customer needs an emotional response from the server. This obviously does not mean that you
should match anger with anger or annoyance with annoyance.
What it means is that you respond with empathy. Show you care. Try
to see it from the customer's point of view. Even if the complaint is
unreasonable or wrong you could at least say that you understand
why the situation could have caused annoyance or irritation to the
customer. By providing an emotional or empathetic response to an
emotional customer you generally defuse the situation, which allows a sensible and logical problem-solving approach to follow.

In his book, *Dealing with Demanding Customers*, David M. Martin
refers to someone he calls "Sharp end SARAH". SARAH is basically
a formula for dealing with difficult customers that works well and is
easy to remember.

- **Stop talking**. Never interrupt or try to "talk over" a customer
  who is complaining. You will annoy the customer even more, it's
  very rude, and you'll not learn properly about the complaint
  and/or the reasons for it so you won't be able to deal with it
  properly.

- **Adopt active listening**. This means that you focus your full attention on the customer. Don't allow anything to distract you.
  Look the customer in the face. Make eye contact. Ask questions
  if you're not clear about anything. Take notes if necessary.

- **Reflect content or feeling**. The best way to do this is to repeat or
  paraphrase the key things that the customer says. You could say,
  "Let me just make sure I've got this right and haven't missed anything" before you do. By repeating back to the customer the key
  things they told you, you put yourself on their side of the situation, it
  ensures that you understand the situation from the customer's
  viewpoint, it lets the customer know that you were listening and
  understand their position and it helps build a rapport between you
  and the customer that can be used to help find a solution.

- **Act with empathy**. Here's where you match feelings with feelings, emotions with emotions. If you have an approach from a
  customer that is very logical or clinical then you should respond
  in a similar manner. If your customer is displaying some emo-

tion then bring your own emotions into your early responses. Let your style of reaction be dictated by the customer's approach.

- **Handle the subject matter.** Now you can use your knowledge of your product or service to find a mutually acceptable solution. You will find the section about "Recovery" in Chapter 6 and the piece about "Dotty Logic" in Chapter 15 useful in this regard.

I thought I would end this section with one of my Daffy Laws that puts this simply:

> **When handling complaints,**
> **deal with the person first**
> **and the problem won't last.**

Recommended Actions	✔
◆ Calculate the potential worth to your business of satisfied and dissatisfied customers. Broadcast the figures to all staff.	❑
◆ Seek out and remove all possible causes of customer dissatisfaction.	❑
◆ Make yours a very unusual business and create systems to gather all customer complaints.	❑
◆ Teach all your front-line staff the SARAH formula to help them deal professionally with difficult and complaining customers.	❑
◆ Make sure you're not one of those organisations that treats its allies (complaining customers) as if they were enemies.	❑

Chapter 6

Delighted Customers

"Customer satisfaction is no longer good enough to survive today's competitive market place. What is needed is customer delight."
— *Tom Peters*

These words from Tom Peters should be part of your business culture. They should be written into all your business plans or missions. They should be incorporated into all your company meetings. You should be telling everyone in the organisation:

> **What we need are delighted customers.**
> **Satisfied customers just aren't good enough.**

The "D" Word Problem

Many managers (especially male ones) seem to have a problem with the word "delight". They have difficulty using it with their staff and about their customers. I am convinced that the main reason for this is because they're only comfortable using half their brains at work. Let me explain.

Whole vs. Half-Brain Service

Let's say that the diagram below is of a typical customer. Although I've met some people who would wish to claim otherwise, it's a medical fact that all customers have a brain. I've split that brain into two halves, the left and the right. This is because we now know that our brains are in two halves and that each half is responsible for different functions.

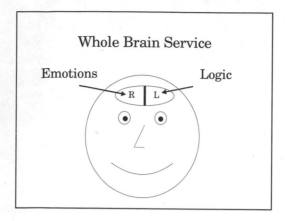

We know that the left side generally deals with what could be called the hard or logical functions, such as mathematics, organisation, planning, etc. (psychologists call these the cognitive functions). The right side deals with what could be called the "soft" functions such as emotions, creativity, feelings, etc. This means that to appeal to the whole brain of our customers (and our colleagues) and deliver what I call "Whole Brain Service" we must engage both right and left halves — logic and emotion. But many managers seem only comfortable with the logic half. They get very uncomfortable if you ask them to introduce emotions into the working environment. Delight is an emotional word so that makes them uncomfortable with its use.

I have therefore invented a new word, especially for those people who are uncomfortable with emotional words like delight. (I've had to invent a new one because I couldn't find a suitable one that already existed in the English language.) My new word is "PLUSSATISFIED". I've chosen this as my new word because I figure that if the existing, logical word for a customer who is less than satisfied is dissatisfied, then the new, logical word for a customer who is more than satisfied should sound like the opposite — therefore — "plussatisfied". So now, those people who are uncomfortable with "all this emotional stuff" can focus on creating plussatisfied customers. (While those of us who aren't afraid to bring our right brains to work and don't mind admitting to emotions can still talk about delighted customers.)

How delighted (or plussatisfied) customers are created is something that seems to baffle many people, yet the basic concept is really simple.

The definitions that were used for satisfied and dissatisfied customers were that satisfied customers occur when what is provided is *equal* to what is promised or expected and dissatisfied when it is *less*. Therefore, delighted customers occur when what is provided is *more* than what is promised or expected.

Again this can be shown graphically:

Delighted Customers Occur When:

What You Provide	Is Greater than	What You Promised and/or What They Expected

It really is this simple. If the customer gets more than they were promised or expected, then that will be a cause of delight. Perhaps only a small or short-lived delight, but delight just the same.

A logical question that usually follows this argument is:

> By how much must delivery exceed promise to create delight?

Again, the answer is simple. Consider this similar question: By how much does a sprinter have to beat a competitor to the tape to become the world's fastest man or woman? The most logical answer to that is: By any amount that can be measured!

The same type of answer can therefore be used for the question about delight. To create delight, delivery must be greater than expectation:

> By any amount that the customer will notice and value.

So if what you provide exceeds what you promised to provide, or what the customer expected you to provide, by any amount that the customer will notice and value, that will be sufficient to create delight. It may be only a small delight, a short delight or a fleeting delight, but delight it will be.

The Power of +1

In Ken Blanchard's book *Raving Fans*, he explains how to create delight with the following simple equation:

$$Delight = Expectation + 1$$

This is an excellent, simple way of expressing how to create delight. I sometimes change it slightly to:

$$Plussatisfaction = Expectation + 1s$$

This now makes the "left-only brainers" a bit happier and it emphasises that what is needed is a number of *+1s*. A single one will probably have little or no lasting effect.

But what is a *+1*? Delight needs expectation *+1* what? +1s could be any or all of the following:

+1s
+ 1 %
+ 1 more smile
+ 1 additional item
+ 1 more personal contact
+ 1 bit more thoughtfulness
+ 1 extra minute of your time
+ 1 telephone call to ensure that the customer's happy
+ 1 anything else that will delight your customers.

These extra items, the +1s, are what I sometimes call the WOW factors. The little extras you provide, that cause your customers to think:

"WOW, that was great!" or **"WOW, that's what I call service!"**

The best WOW factors meet the following three criteria:

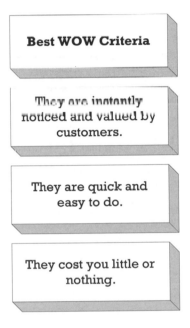

Best WOW Criteria

They are instantly noticed and valued by customers.

They are quick and easy to do.

They cost you little or nothing.

Here are just a few examples of WOW factors that I've experienced.

WOW — We Even Get New Letter Paper

Britannia Building Society is keen to focus attention on what matters to customers (buying a new house), and not on what matters to them (selling a mortgage). They have lots of little things that help to show this. One that I really like is that they print a small quantity of letter paper with the customer's new house address on it so that the customer can write to friends to let them know they have moved.

WOW — They Valeted my Car

I was thinking of buying a new car and was having test drives of the ones on my short list. One of the cars I was considering was the Lexus. I had already had drives in the equivalent vehicles from BMW and Jaguar and was looking forward to seeing how the Lexus compared. I was really impressed with the Lexus, but when I took it back after the test drive I was even more impressed with the +1 that I wasn't expecting. I returned to find that the dealer had fully valeted my old car for me while I was trying their new one. It made me think, "If the service is this good when I'm not even a customer, how good must it be when I am?"

WOW — The Room Privacy Card Made Me Smile

I was attending the Southampton Boat Show and stayed overnight in a small hotel in Winchester called Hotel du Vin & Bistro. It was a great hotel for many reasons, but one simple little thing that I remember it for are the cards they provided to hang outside the door of your room because they were so different to the boring ones you get in most hotels. On one side of the card it said:

DON'T COME IN.
We're either sleeping or having too much fun.

On the other side it said

DO COME IN.
We've now messed up your room,
ready for you to tidy again.

This is a WOW to me because it demonstrates that the owners are "human" and have a good sense of humour.

WOW — They Even Gave Me the Coin for the Call

I was a speaker at the Association of Independent Tour Operators (AITO) conference in Madrid. AITO arranged all the travel and accommodation for me and booked my car in at a firm called Autostrong near Manchester Airport for safe-keeping while I was away. As I was leaving Autostrong to be driven to the airport for my flight they gave me a small envelope which had printed on it the number to phone to summon the car to collect me when I landed back in the UK. They also then explained that the envelope contained a 10p coin for the call in case I had no change with me on my return. This little bit of thoughtfulness was much appreciated.

WOW — They Even Sharpen Our Pencils

I've run lots of seminars in many locations throughout the UK. I've found very few places that really know how to give great service to their conference or seminar guests. One I have found that does is Mere Golf and Country Club in Cheshire. When I was involved in the organisation of a series of seminars for Manchester Business School at Mere, we spent some time with the staff, developing a number of +1s that would WOW our delegates. One that had a surprising impact was to sharpen all the delegates' pencils at every break. This simple little service used to get numerous comments of praise on the delegate evaluation forms.

WOW — There are Crocodiles on the Bed

I was told of the following experience one of my customers had on a recent Nile cruise. Each evening when they returned to their bedroom, the cabin staff had not only cleaned and prepared the room for them but they had also created interesting or amusing sculptures from the bath towels. They ranged from a crocodile or swan on the bed to a cobra in the bathroom. They never knew what would be waiting for them each night in the room, but they were always keen to find out.

WOW — The Porter Changed the Wheel for Me

I was staying at the Moat House Hotel in Liverpool and traveling there in a car that was on loan while mine was in for service. This car seemed to be pulling slightly to one side as I was driving, but it wasn't very serious and I wasn't too concerned. When I arrived at the hotel it was difficult to find anywhere to park because construction work was taking place and the car park was full of contractor's vehicles. Because of this, the hotel had arranged valet parking for guests' cars. After the car was parked the porter brought back my key and asked when I would like the car to be returned. I explained that I needed it on the next morning by half past eight to be able to leave in time to speak at a conference. "Leave it to me," said Steve the porter.

At quarter past eight on the next morning there was a telephone call in my room. It was Steve. He explained that he had brought the car back and that it was outside waiting for me. But the real reason for his call was that he wanted to tell me that he had noticed that one of the back tyres had a puncture and was only half inflated. (This obviously explained why it had been pulling to one side the previous day.) He then said, "You have to be away by half past eight, don't you? You'll not want to get your hands dirty so would it be OK if I change the wheel for you?" I was both surprised and delighted that he was prepared to do this for me. "You don't have to be in a 5-star hotel to get 5-star service," I thought.

WOW — The Virgin Atlantic Special Service

On a recent Virgin Atlantic flight from New York to London, a passenger asked the attendant selling the duty-free goods for a special type of pen that includes a small voice recorder. (He had intended to get one while in New York but had been told by a fellow passenger that he could buy one, duty free, on the plane.) The attendant told him that unfortunately it was something Virgin didn't sell. She then noticed that he was really disappointed about this and asked why. He told her that he had promised to get one for his son, as a birthday present.

> *"No problem," said the attendant, "Give me the money and your address and I'll get you one on my next flight to New York and post it to you when I get back to the UK."*
>
> *He therefore gave her the money and just a few days later the pen arrived in the post with a "best wishes and happy birthday" note from the Virgin attendant.*

WOW — The World's Best Airport

Manchester Airport won the 1996/97 award for the world's best airport. There are a number of categories that are used for assessing potential award winners and service to passengers is one of them. Service is a high priority to the people who work in the airport and there are many +1 things that take place every day. Some great examples are the things done by the coach drivers, who take passengers to and from the long-stay car parks.

When it's raining they try to bring the coach to each car as it pulls into a parking bay. This is so that passengers won't get wet walking across the car park to the coach. They also try to help any passenger who is having difficulty with their luggage, either at the car or when they get to the terminal. They will not leave a lone woman who they've returned to her car at night until she has got in and started the car. They even carry de-icer, windscreen scrapers, etc. in winter so that they can help any passenger who is having difficulty getting a frozen car started.

WOW — They Have an International Pillow Menu

At the Melia Hotel in Madrid, they want their guests to feel as much "at home" as possible. They realise that their guests come from different parts of the world and in different countries people use different types of pillows. They therefore offer a choice of 10 different types of pillows, of the types used in different countries, so that you can have one that is just like the one you have at home.

WOW — You Don't Even Have to be a Customer to Receive Service the Richer Way

At Richer Sounds, Julian Richer, the owner, wants his staff to provide levels of service and a caring attitude towards customers and potential customers that far exceed customers' expectations. An article that appeared in Venture *magazine provides one example of how they achieve this.*

An elderly lady had come into the shop to ask for directions to the local hospital. She was going to visit her husband and had got lost because the bus had been using a different route due to road works and diversions. The staff member didn't give her directions to the hospital — he drove her there.

Julian commented, "I would hope that any member of my staff would have the same decency to help out an elderly person in trouble. I think it's worth doing just to be a good neighbour. And I also know it's good for business."

These are all examples of small, inexpensive things, which were unexpected and registered a "WOW, that was great!" I'm sure you could think of some examples where you have had a similar experience.

The following are the main categories of things that make customers think "WOW, what a great business!"

- **Banish the Bland** — Take something that you have to provide for customers that is usually presented in a standard, boring, bland, logical, "left brain", way. Now add some "right brain" thinking and turn it into something different, unusual, amusing, special or grand.

- **Excel with Grace** — Think of things that customers will value that are easy for you but may be difficult for customers and then make them part of your standard service.

- **Mesmerise with Anticipation** — Think about circumstances or situations your customers will face that they probably won't be prepared for but you can anticipate because of your experience or knowledge. Now make something unexpected happen to them or have something ready for them in those situations that will demonstrate your customer-focused forethought.

- **Be a Star** — Demonstrate any special skills in ways that will WOW customers.

- **Be a Friend** — Be there for customers in times when they would least expect it.

- **Melt Away Problems** — Remove problems from customers by taking ownership of them and making them your problem instead of theirs.

- **Charm with Care** — Do the spontaneous little caring things for customers that surprise and delight.

Everyone in the business can contribute to these if you encourage them to think about how they could surprise, amuse, impress, touch (emotionally), delight and WOW their customers.

But the occasional, small WOW isn't enough to create a seriously delighted customer, the type that will keep coming back for more, the ones that Ken Blanchard calls Raving Fans. To do that, you need to develop a barrage of WOWs. At every possible opportunity, with every "moment of truth" contact, you need to find ways to WOW and so delight your customers. That's quite easy, too. Here's how it's done.

Creating Corporate WOWs

It's mainly *people* who create WOWs — you and your colleagues. The things you and they do, the way you act, the decision you take. What you need is as many opportunities as you can create for you all to WOW your customers. This can be achieved by considering all the points of contact between your company and your customers, all those "moment of truth" opportunities, and creating ways to WOW the customer with +1s at every one.

You can use a matrix, like the one below, to create a corporate WOW chart. This is something that will focus the minds of you and your colleagues and help you to consider and develop ways to delight your customers at every stage of your business process.

Corporate WOW Chart							
	Mgmt	Admin	Sales	Prod	Accts	Engin	Etc
Advertising	+1s		+1s				
Sales visits		+1s	+1s				
Telesales calls	+1s		+1s				
Product demos	+1s		+1s	+1s		+1s	
Factory visits	+1s	+1s	+1s	+1s	+1s	+1s	
Installation		+1s	+1s			+1s	
Invoicing	+1s	+1s	+1s		+1s		
Service visits	+1s	+1s				+1s	
Etc.							

Note: The shaded boxes are those where there is no contact between the customer and that part of the company.

If you create a chart like this, you will see all the "moment of truth" contacts in your organisation where the opportunities to create WOW experiences exist. Each point of contact between the customer and your organisation creates opportunities for people in the various departments to create little WOWs. You should aim for at least one at every point.

Try to get your whole workforce involved in coming up with WOW suggestions. Then test all their ideas to find the best ones (they aren't always the ones you think, so don't pre-judge). They won't all work, but that doesn't matter. You can build on the ones that do and improve or discard the ones that don't.

When you've got the first batch working, repeat the whole process at regular intervals. Eventually you could have hundreds of ways of making your customers go WOW, at all points of contact with your business. Just think of it. Doesn't just the thought of it make you go WOW? It should, because what this creates is a continuous improvement process for customer service. Here is a simple overview of this process:

- Get every member of staff involved in generating WOW ideas.

- Test them all to find the best ones.

- Embed the best ones into your systems and processes to make them habitual.

- Repeat the whole process again and again.

This concept is simple but extremely powerful. I shall refer to it again in Chapter 14 on how to create a winning pace.

A Note for the Cynics

"Just a minute," the cynics say, "if you keep doing more than people expect, they eventually start to expect the 'extra' things. Then to delight them, you will have to do even more. That's a vicious circle, a road to ruin that we don't want to get onto."

But it's not a vicious circle, it's a virtuous one. It is the beginning of a continuous improvement programme for customer service. One that will enable you to move your business further and further in front of your competition, in ways that they will find hard to notice and difficult to compete with. In other words, it's a process that can provide a business with a distinct and sustainable competitive advantage. It's not a road to ruin, it's a road to riches!

Corporate WOWs at Clarks Shoes

I was involved with a programme to help improve the already good service levels at Clarks Shoes. Having spoken at a management conference we had to find a way to roll the ideas of +1s and WOWs out to the hundreds of shops around the country. It was also important to make whatever means we selected one that would be fun for the staff. The way chosen was to create WOW walls in every shop. Each staff room had in it a large poster that was stuck on the wall showing an illustration of what was called the WOW wall. The staff were then issued with dozens of cardboard bricks on which to write any +1 or WOW ideas that they'd developed, tested and found to work. These WOW bricks were then stuck on the wall. Everyone could then see everyone else's ideas and try them. They could also see how well they were doing as a team at filling the wall with bricks of WOW ideas. The object was to fill every space. When this happened they were presented with a reward from their area manager, who then collected the bricks of ideas to be typed and circulated around all the shops, and issued new bricks to fill the wall again. This simple idea resulted in thousands of WOW ideas being generated by front-line staff.

Corporate WOWs at the Churchill Inter-Continental Hotel

I spent some time working with the team at the Churchill Inter-Continental Hotel in London. They're a 5-Star hotel so the service was great already. But the General Manager, Chris Cowdray, was keen to keep service continually increasing to new levels and we agreed that a constant stream of new +1s and WOWs would do it. After introducing the concept of +1s and WOWs to the whole workforce the management then created a team of people they called "The Excelerators".

These were people who were responsible for making sure that everyone in the hotel contributed to the goal of accelerating excellence. They therefore organised regular idea-generating sessions and events and then facilitated the introduction of the ideas so as to get them working as well and as quickly as possible. This team has been extremely successful in getting lots of ideas generated and implemented.

Yet More WOWs through Dazzling Recovery

There is another major opportunity to create customer WOWs. One that again is really easy, yet which happens so rarely that for most people it is a "once in a lifetime" experience. This one is called recovery.

Recovery happens when something goes wrong, or perhaps a mistake is made, with the result that a customer is upset or disappointed, and this is then dealt with in such a way that the customer becomes delighted. So recovery takes place when a complaint is used as an opportunity to WOW the customer.

The diagram on the following page shows the recovery process graphically. As this diagram shows, a customer is not recovered by simply putting right whatever went wrong. You have to do more than that. You must neutralise the OUCH (which is always remembered) that comes from the mistake with a WOW (which will erase the bad memory) that comes from doing something extra. It's the something extra, the WOW, that creates recovery.

Recovered Customers

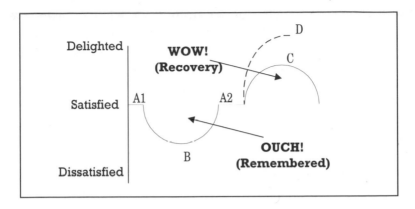

The blow-by-blow account of recovery goes like this. Up to point A1 in this diagram the customer was satisfied. But at point A1 something went wrong to cause the customer to plunge into dissatisfaction. At point B the customer is dissatisfied or unhappy. Now we're assuming that this is one of those rare customers who makes the effort to complain, perhaps because of the previous period of satisfaction. So they telephone, or write, or visit to let you know about their dissatisfaction.

Faced with this situation, most businesses believe that the task then is promptly, efficiently and politely to fix what is wrong. What is needed, they believe, is to get the customer quickly back to the position they were in before the dissatisfaction occurred — back to position A2 in the diagram. Once they've done that, they can then breathe a long sigh of relief and rest easy that night.

But doing that just isn't good enough. You cannot recover a customer by eventually doing for them what should have been done in the first place. That won't create a customer for life. In many cases it will not even recreate a satisfied customer, as the following example shows.

Case Study — The Faulty Furniture Story

We had built a new office at our home (I am a home-based tele-worker) and decided to treat ourselves to some new furniture. If you've dipped into the office furniture market recently you will know that you can choose from an amazing range of worldwide manufacturers. We decided to support British workers and so chose what appeared to be the best available from a prominent Northwest manufacturer. In the brochure it describes the range we chose as furniture "to reflect the status of senior management and their support staff". We were therefore really keen to see our new office fitted out with this super "status-building" furniture.

Delivery was six weeks. We could have had delivery of furniture from most other places in the world in six days, but we wanted to buy British so we decided to wait the six weeks. When the furniture arrived we could not have been more disappointed. Every single piece of furniture had something wrong with it. The faults ranged from missing rails in the filing cabinets (so there was nothing on which to hang files) to what appeared to be grit under the lacquer on the desk top. They even omitted to include the leather key wallet that was promised in the brochure as a complimentary gift to every purchaser.

We were obviously dissatisfied with what had been supplied and very disappointed because this was a British company, in a highly competitive world market, showing it couldn't even get the basics of its business right. I therefore faxed a letter to the chief executive of the company. The letter told him of our disappointment but explained that our view of a company is mainly determined, not by whether it gets things wrong, but by what it does when it gets things wrong. We therefore hoped it would act in a way that would restore our faith in its products and service.

The initial response to my letter was pretty good. Although the chief executive didn't reply in person, we had a telephone call within an hour from the sales representative of its local agent who visited that afternoon to inspect the furniture. He agreed with our complaint and left promising action. The next day the quality control manager from the manufacturer was in our office. He also agreed with the complaint, fixed what he could there and then and agreed to get the rest done as soon as possible. We then received a really nice letter from the sales director, who apologised for the problems we had incurred and enclosed the leather key wallet which we had been promised in the brochure.

About two weeks later we were informed that the replacements were ready so we cleared the desks so that the new parts could be fitted and then put everything back when they had gone.

When all this corrective action was complete and we eventually had the furniture we had originally ordered we waited with interest and anticipation to see what would happen next.

Some weeks later nothing else had happened so I wrote again to the sales director to check if that was it. I just wanted to know if what I had experienced was the full extent of their customer recovery system. As he didn't reply to my letter, I must assume that was it.

So their programme was:

* *Respond quickly*

* *Agree with the complaint*

* *Apologise*

* *Eventually deliver what was originally promised.*

But we're not recovered customers. We're not even satisfied customers. Although they eventually got there and provided what we were expecting in the first place, all we remember of the transaction is the problems.

The problem of the original disappointment; having to complain; the stream of unwanted people who arrived at our office; having to clear the office for the replacement desks and then put it back together again. That all adds up to one big OUCH which we will always remember. We wouldn't buy from them again and certainly wouldn't recommend them to anyone else.

Yet if they'd taken the trouble to recover us properly we could have been customers for life and a source of many referrals and recommendations.

What a lost opportunity!

I've told this story at many seminars and in every case people agree that we have cause to remain dissatisfied. If only the company had known or cared enough to recover us properly, it could easily have turned us into customers for life — perhaps even one of Ken Blanchard's Raving Fans of their business. But all we remember is the hassle. It's the OUCH that sticks in our minds.

Yet it would have been simple and inexpensive to WOW us with a little extra — to provide something more than we were expecting. Something that would have created delight. Something which would have removed that OUCH from our memory and replaced it with a WOW.

The earlier diagram shows this clearly. You need to take the customer up to the point of delight at position C to recover from the point of dissatisfaction at position B.

There are a few, very rare organisations that recognise that they can use this as an opportunity to take their customer way beyond the level of satisfaction they were at before the problem and create a delighted customer from a dissatisfied one. Perhaps even get the customer to point D.

As with +1s, I have suggested criteria for recovery WOWs:

Best Recovery Criteria

The WOW must be at least equal to the OUCH (it may need to be far in excess to have the desired effect).

Focus on the Relationship Value of the customer (do not consider the single transaction value).

The WOW action must be noticed and valued by the customer.

How is this done? Well, it depends upon the circumstances, the type of business, the degree of dissatisfaction, the amount of inconvenience, etc. However, here are a few examples of good recoveries:

Good Recovery Examples — See How Easy It Is

Example 1 — Tesco

David Cotterill is Chief Executive of Renold plc. He told me this story about a Tesco recovery.

David usually has a box of Tesco wine at home for whenever someone fancies a glass. One day he opened a new box and after tasting it decided it was not up to the high standard he was used to. He therefore telephoned Tesco to inform them and they asked him to return it.

When he did, the woman in the wine department tasted the wine and agreed with David that it was not as good as it should have been. She therefore exchanged the box immediately but also gave him a bottle of fine wine for the inconvenience he had been put to. David was delighted, and recovered, and Tesco has another customer for life.

Example 2 — David M. Robinson, the Jewellers

When David started his retail jewellery business 25 years ago, he admits he began with less stock to show customers than most of his competitors. Yet his business was successful and grew. A key reason for this was that he recognised that he could overcome the problem of lower stock levels by compensating for this with superior service levels.

Nowadays he has as much stock as any other jeweller but the superior service levels are still as important to him as in the early days. David says that "the real business in retailing is the relationship between the shop staff and the customers. If the staff treat customers like family or friends then they will come back. It's as simple as that."

But even a business as customer-focused as David M. Robinson occasionally makes a mistake which results in a customer complaint. But here again David has a simple, effective policy. He views a complaint as both a compliment and an opportunity. A compliment because the customer is trusting them to deal with it properly. An opportunity for them to show that customer just how much their business is valued.

David simply tells his staff to do what they know he would do when faced with any complaint. They know that he would view it from the customer's situation. He'd have an empathy with, and concern for, the customer. He'd do whatever was right and fair to deal with the complaint and then add something extra to delight the customer. So that is what they do, knowing that they will have David's full support for doing so.

David knows that a well-handled complaint can trigger a lot of free advertising. "I just like the idea of my customers, in a pub or restaurant with friends or relatives, telling positive stories about my business." And as he knows, word-of-mouth advertising is the most powerful advertising there is.

Example 3 — CareerTrack

CareerTrack is one of the world's biggest providers of business and personal development seminars, tapes and videos. It offers a 100 per cent, one-year guarantee on everything it provides. This means that if for any reason you're not happy with a CareerTrack seminar you attend, you can ask for a refund, up to a year later, and it will provide it immediately.

It also then provides you with a voucher entitling you to attend any other CareerTrack seminar of your choice, free of charge, as an apology for your lost time on the one you didn't like.

Example 4 — Mothercare

John Negus is a senior manager with Clarks International, the shoe manufacturers and retailers. He told me this recovery story about Mothercare. John and his wife have a new baby son. When he was a few weeks old they decided it was time for him to start sleeping in a cot, rather than the crib he had spent his first few weeks in. They therefore went on a Saturday afternoon to Mothercare to buy a cot. For ease of transport the cot was flat packed, so when they got home they opened the box to assemble it. You can imagine their disappointment when they discovered that the cot had a large mark on one of the side panels.

John telephoned Mothercare straightaway to report the fault. The person he spoke to apologised and asked him to hold while she checked if they had another cot in stock. Having established that they had one, she asked John for his address. He thought she was planning to arrange some form of delivery. But she wasn't. She wanted the address because she intended to immediately get a taxi to John's home to exchange the cots.

About half an hour later she arrived at John's front door. She assembled the new cot for John to check and be sure he was happy with the replacement. This done, she then presented him with a Mothercare voucher to spend on his son, apologised again and left.

You could have knocked John down with a feather. He was really impressed by this tremendous service. The cost to Mothercare was relatively small, but they gained a boost in reputation, numerous referrals from John and his wife, an employee who must be proud to be part of a company that gives her the authority to deliver such fantastic service and the lifetime spend on baby and child goods from John and his wife.

Example 5 — Slaters Menswear

I bought a new dinner suit from Slaters Menswear in Manchester. It was on a Saturday near Christmas so, although they can usually make any alterations necessary at the time of purchase, they were really busy that day and I agreed to collect it in a week. Jean collected the suit for me and when I looked at it I was disappointed to find that they had not put the tape around the inside bottom of the trousers that I like. I therefore took it back the next morning.

When I showed them the trousers and explained my disappointment they took them straight into the alterations department for correction. They then invited me to choose any silk tie in the store, with their compliments, and apologies for the inconvenience.

I then spent an enjoyable time choosing my FREE tie, then an equally enjoyable time choosing a shirt or two to wear it with. I was a happy, recovered customer who immediately started purchasing again at the store.

Example 6 — Mandarin Hotel, Hong Kong

The Mandarin Hotel in Hong Kong has won the World's Best Hotel award more times than any other. I regularly quote Mandarin Hotel stories in my seminars. When Jean and I last visited Hong Kong we therefore stayed at the Mandarin to sample their world class service for ourselves.

In one respect Jean was dreading the visit because she knew that I would be hoping they would get something wrong just so we could experience their version of world class recovery first hand. Both she and I were therefore delighted when an error occurred immediately after we arrived.

We had booked a harbour view room. When we were shown to our room it did not have a harbour view. I therefore showed the receptionist who had shown us to the room our booking confirmation which clearly stated harbour view.

She apologised for the error and invited us to visit their rooftop bar to relax and have whatever we wanted, with their compliments, while they sorted out the right room. We soon forgot the small problem over the room as we sat in the bar enjoying the view and the free drinks.

Example 7 — The 5-star Service Caravan Park

Aberconwy Park is a holiday caravan park in Conwy, North Wales. In the spring of 1997 the North Wales coastline was hit by freak, hurricane-force winds. Hurricanes and caravans (even the 30-40-feet-long fixed caravans they have at Aberconwy Park) don't mix. So when Ken, the owner of the park, learned that these winds were coming, his first concern was the safety of the caravan owners.

He therefore booked rooms in the best hotel in Llandudno for the 30 or so caravan owners that were on site at the time. He then also arranged a bar account and booked dinner for them in the restaurant. He then asked all these owners to go to the safety of the hotel, have a good time and forget about the hurricane winds.

During the night he and his staff did all they could to minimise the damage to the caravans (there are almost 300 caravans on the site so it was a challenge). By morning the winds had gone and they had managed to save all the caravans except just seven that had been written off.

When the owners returned, many broke into tears when they saw the damage the winds had done to the park and the caravans. Ken asked them to go home and leave it to him and his team to sort out. He promised that within a week it would all be resolved.

When they came back the next week the whole park had been restored to normal. All the people who had damaged caravans found a brand new one waiting for them, and it had been upgraded, at no cost to them, to an even better one. This amazed and delighted the owners, who couldn't believe that such a level of service and care could be available from a UK caravan park.

When Ken was later asked why he had done all this, he gave the following explanation:

"1. I wanted the people who were in the park that night not to remember the storm but to remember the dinner and party they had in the hotel, on me.

2. I wanted the people who had their caravans damaged that night not to remember their damaged caravan but to remember the better caravan they came back to the following week.

3. Finally, I wanted the people who didn't have their caravans damaged that night to wish they had!"

These examples show how easy recovery is and that there are companies, in all industries, already committed to it. They also highlight some important points about recovery, which are:

☞ A complaining customer provides you with a golden opportunity to show him or her just how important their custom is to you.

☞ The cost of recovery need not be high to create delight. It's more about being thoughtful than being lavish. (However, remember that the cost should be considered in relation to the Relationship Value of the customer.)

☞ Putting yourself in the customer's position, and doing what *you* would then like to be done, is important.

☞ Deal with the customer first and the circumstance second. First resolve the human, emotional situation, then the practical one.

☞ Speed and spontaneity are essential. The quicker it's dealt with and the fewer people involved the more chance you have of delighting the customer.

So it is also possible to create delighted customers, even when you start with dissatisfied ones. This is done by having a good recovery programme.

What Are the Rewards from Delighted Customers?

So what does the research show delighted customers do to their suppliers? The rewards for creating delighted customers are shown on the diagram below.

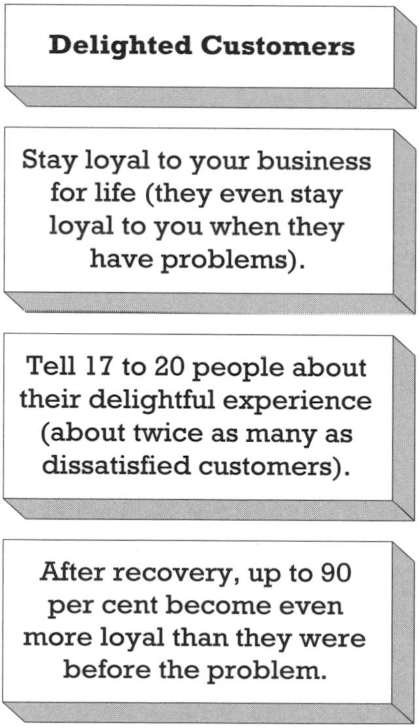

Delighted Customers

Stay loyal to your business for life (they even stay loyal to you when they have problems).

Tell 17 to 20 people about their delightful experience (about twice as many as dissatisfied customers).

After recovery, up to 90 per cent become even more loyal than they were before the problem.

Delighted customers are extremely loyal. The period of delight builds up credits for you. You can then draw on these credits during problem times. Provided you then repay and rebuild the credits these customers remain delighted and loyal for life.

Look at the number of recommendations from delighted customers — 17 to 20. If it were, say, 19 recommendations, plus the original delighted customer, this means that a delighted customer has a potential value to your business of 20 times the Relationship Value.

So for my family's local supermarket we've used in the previous examples, that would be 20 x £¼ million which is £5 million. An average family like mine could, if kept delighted, spend in and attract to that store £5 million sales over a lifetime. I wonder how many have a strategy to give £5 million worth of service to people like us? Too few, I'm afraid.

So what could delighted customers be worth to your business? I recommend that you calculate the figure and place it in the box below to serve as a constant reminder of the value of delighted customers to your business.

Potential Delighted Customer Gains
Relationship Value X 20 (19 positive referrals + original customer)
£ _____

One place that's world-famous for the way they delight their customers at every visit is a dairy store in America called Stew Leonard's. Stew has built his business into one which has made the *Guinness Book of Records* as the world's highest turnover per square foot in food retailing.

Stew Leonard's — One Place Where the Customer *Is* Always Right

Stew Leonard may not be world-famous as a guru of customer service, but he certainly is a practising expert. He's been dedicated to customer service ever since the day, soon after he opened in 1969, when he learned a valuable lesson about customer service that caused him to change his whole business philosophy.

A woman had returned a carton of eggnog to Stew, complaining that it tasted sour. He tasted it and was convinced that it was fresh. He therefore proceeded to convince her that he was right and she was wrong. He eventually won the argument, but lost the customer. Once he realised that he had lost a customer over a 99 cent carton of eggnog, he pledged thereafter to always put his customers first and never again attempt to prove them wrong.

To demonstrate his commitment to this he placed, at the front of his store for all to see, a 6,000-pound piece of granite on which is engraved:

Rule 1 — The customer is always right.

Rule 2 — If the customer is ever wrong, re-read Rule 1.

He also developed some basic principles based on the name STEW:

S	*stands for service to the customer.*
T	*is for teamwork that gets it done.*
E	*is for excellence, quality and cleanliness.*
W	*is for WOW — things done to make the customer go WOW and want to come back.*

These simple techniques have turned his business into a veritable gold mine. His dairy store has grown from a seven-item store with seven people to one that employs 700 people, carries 800 lines, serves 100,000 customers a week and has sales of $100 million a year ... WOW!

But places like Stew Leonard's are extremely rare. I regret that I cannot think of an equivalent example in UK food retailing (if you know of one please write and tell me).

This brings us to another interesting point: the rarity of companies that create delighted customers. I often ask delegates at seminars how many of them have experienced, more than once in their life, a recovery similar to the stories in the earlier examples. Occasionally the odd hand goes up at that stage, but that's rare. Then I ask how many have experienced it just once in their life. Usually about 10 per cent to 25 per cent of the audience hands then go up.

So just think of what this means. According to my rough survey, of what must now be a few thousand people, for most people recovery is something that is never experienced and for just a few, it happens once in their life. It's very rare to get service that delights, yet it's so easy to do. What a missed opportunity for many businesses. And what a tremendous opportunity for you if you can become the first and best in service in your area, or your industry.

Recovered Customers Are More Loyal

One final point about delighted customers. Those who are properly recovered usually become more loyal after the recovery than they were before the problem occurred. (Research shows that up to 90 per cent of recovered customers become more loyal.) This does not suggest that you should rush out and dissatisfy as many customers as you can so that you may then later recover them. What it does suggest is that you should go searching for all the customers who are already dissatisfied. Remember that the research indicates that it could be as low as 1 in 25 (4 per cent) who report any dissatisfaction. So you need to go looking for the other 24 (96 per cent) so that you can recover them. (We'll cover how you can locate them in Chapter 8 on gathering customer feedback).

So make delighted customers your goal. Welcome complaints. Go looking for them. Recover your dissatisfied customers. And watch your business grow.

Review Time

I think it would be a good idea just to stop for a minute or so and review the potential impact to your business of the details and calculations from the last three chapters. In Chapter 4 we considered and calculated the true potential value of a lifetime customer relationship. In Chapter 5 we considered how you can create satisfied and dissatisfied customers and the financial impact they could have on your business. In this chapter we have considered how you create delighted customers and what their potential financial impact could be. When I work out these kind of figures with my customers I always find that having got to this stage, it helps to bring these figures all together. I think you too would find it valuable so I suggest that you transfer to the box below the figures you have calculated in the previous three chapters:

Potential Customer Values
Every average customer is potentially worth £_____
Every delighted customer is potentially worth £ _____
Every satisfied customer is potentially worth £ _____
Every dissatisfied customer potentially costs £ _____

Now that you have all these figures in one place you can clearly see the potential profits and the often unseen losses that can accrue from customer service. You will also find that it helps to focus your mind on the potential of these figures if you consider the following.

Moments of Truth Meet Aladdin's Lamp

A problem I find during seminars and in workshops is that the potential figures are often so big, and the time scale so long (the potential lifetime of purchasing, which may be 10, 50 or perhaps more years), that people find it difficult to appreciate the real impact and the effect they can have on it. However, I have found that the "moments of truth" concept first used by Jan Carlzon of SAS, coupled with an Aladdin's Lamp, helps with this.

A "moment of truth" occurs every time a customer comes into contact with the company. Whether it is in person, over the telephone, by letter, or through some other media, all these contacts are "moments of truth" opportunities. At each of these contacts there is an opportunity to please or displease the customer. The result of the contact could be a satisfied, a dissatisfied, or perhaps even a delighted customer.

These "moments of truth" are happening in every business, throughout each day. Every employee is responsible in some way for their outcome. As we've already seen, the results of these "moments of truth" opportunities can be financially very beneficial or very damaging to the business. Yet it can be very difficult for everyone in a company to realise the real impact of these "moments of truth" actions or decisions that they do or take. But an Aladdin's Lamp can help.

Imagine you owned an Aladdin's Lamp which you could use to change things, perhaps just for one day. What if you used it to compress time, so that the impact these figures have on your business, for that one day, will not be over 10 to 50 years, but 10 to 50 minutes?

During that day, every time you or a colleague does something to create a satisfied customer, 10 to 50 minutes later your bank balance will increase by the amount in the Satisfied Customer Gains box. Every time something is done which will cause customer dissatisfaction, 10 to 50 minutes later your bank balance will reduce by the amount in the Dissatisfied Customer Losses box. And every time something is done which will cause customer delight, 10 to 50 minutes later your bank balance will increase again by the amount in the Delighted Customer Gains box.

The questions to consider now are:

- Would you still be in business at the end of that day?

- Would you be worth a fortune or bankrupt?

- Would you and your colleagues want to buy as many shares as possible in your business if you knew this was going to happen?

- Would you even mortgage your homes to raise the money?

- Or would you want to quickly sell any shares that you've already got? ... Perhaps at any price!

- Above all, if you had such a lamp, would you make that wish?

The answers to these questions will tell you a lot about the confidence you and your colleagues have in your ability to give good customer service. If you or they would choose to sell rather than buy, or if you would not be prepared to make that wish ... worry!

After all, the odds aren't that bad. If you create twice as many reasons for satisfaction as dissatisfaction you stay even. If you create any more than that, you win. And if you create delight you will make a fortune! That should be fair odds in any business.

Yet I've asked this question of many a seminar audience and it's remarkable how few say they would be keen to buy shares. The majority just don't believe enough in their own or their colleagues' ability to satisfy customers. They fear there is more dissatisfaction than satisfaction being created by their company.

The key point of all this is that all that was changed was the time frame. Whatever you imagined would happen *is* happening, but it's happening very slowly, so slowly you can easily miss it. However, it must surely have an effect on the business over time. If your customers are satisfied, then your business and your profits will grow. If they're dissatisfied, then your business is in decline. In fact, I believe that whatever flashed through your mind as you were considering what might happen on that day was a picture of the future of your business. So if you don't like what you saw — change things now!

You therefore need to ensure that the actions you and your colleagues are taking, and the decisions that are being made by you all, are those that will satisfy or delight and so build, rather than dissatisfy and so destroy, the business.

Giving the Business Style

Someone at one of my seminars once commented that if all the companies in a particular market concentrated on these ideas, wouldn't they all end up very much the same? It was a good point but it doesn't actually work like that. The reason is because of the key, extra unique ingredient — people. We're all different. We see and do things differently. So even though we may concentrate on the same things, as different people we end up with different results.

Service with Style in the Construction Industry

I had a strong example of this when I was working with the building and maintenance contractors Mansell plc. Geoff Bell, one of their directors, was convinced that service could help them differentiate themselves from their many competitors. He and I therefore held workshops throughout the UK until every employee had been on one. During these workshops we held +1 projects to get the attendees thinking up ideas to WOW their customers. These generated hundreds of ideas that eventually formed the basis of a small booklet that Geoff called "The Book of WOW!"

> *What we found both surprising and interesting was that although the people involved in these sessions were all from the same company and they all served the same type of customers, in every session some +1 ideas were generated that we hadn't had in previous similar sessions. So different people always came up with different results — even in the same business.*

In service this means that although people in different organisations may focus on the same ideas because of the different people with different perspectives and approaches, the results will all be different. I like to think of this as different styles of service. They may all be high, but each will have their own style, made up of the different and unique contributions from different people.

Having your own style of service is really important. The following example indicates just how much impact your style of service can have on customer actions.

Service with Style

I was hosting one of the Manchester Business School study tours of UK service excellence. We were nearing the last day of the tour and I was asking different people for their thoughts and observations about what they had seen and experienced. One person said she had noticed some major, interesting differences between the various hotels we had stayed in. (They had all been chosen for the high level but different style of service they provide.) She contrasted one of London's top hotels, with a worldwide reputation for service (to save embarrassment, I won't name them), with One Devonshire Gardens in Glasgow, that is less well known, but which also has a reputation for its quality and style of service.

She said of the London hotel that she found it to be "large, exclusive, lavish, luxurious, a bit elitist, with high service, of their style, that was slightly snooty — and she therefore wouldn't have forgiven them anything!" In comparison she described One Devonshire Gardens as "small, exclusive, lavish, luxurious, also with a high service, of their style, which was warm, friendly and welcoming — and she would therefore have forgiven them anything!"

So it was the style of service, not the level of service, that determined her reaction to service errors.

I spoke at a sales and customer service conference for Elida Fabergé awhile ago and Simon Marshall, their Sales and Customer Development Director, had chosen for the conference theme the following quotation from Jerry Garcia, the late singer from the band The Grateful Dead:

> **"You do not merely want to be considered just the best of the best.**
>
> **You want to be considered the only ones who do what you do."**

Service style can do this. It can make you unique — the only ones who do what you do. So make sure that you have the right style of service, one that will attract the type of customers that you want.

Recommended Actions	✓
◆ Calculate the potential worth to your business of satisfied, dissatisfied and delighted customers. Broadcast the figures to all staff.	❑
◆ Try the Aladdin's Lamp test on your staff. Would they sell or buy? If it's sell, change things . . . fast!	❑
◆ Create a corporate WOW chart. Start a +1 programme. Involve every employee in it.	❑
◆ Check to ensure that complaining customers are not being treated like enemies of your organisation.	❑
◆ Develop a recovery programme for the business. Encourage and empower all staff to use it. Broadcast all the stories of success to inspire others to do the same.	❑
◆ Get to know the style of service your organisation delivers. Make sure it's right to attract the type of customers you want.	❑

Chapter 7

Managing Customer Perceptions

No two people ever see the same thing exactly the same way. What one customer views as delightful could be viewed as just OK by another. What is unacceptable to one customer may be perfectly acceptable to another. It's all down to the way each customer perceives the service they are receiving.

We also know that a customer's perception of a product or service usually differs from the reality. My Daffy's Law about this is:

> **The customer perception of your product or service will probably differ from reality. But to a customer, perception *is* reality.**

This means that it can be just as important for you to manage your customers' perceptions about your product or service as it is to manage the reality of the actual product or service. For some businesses it can be more important.

But if we are to manage perceptions, we need to understand what creates them. We need to know how our customers form their views about our particular product or service. What are the things they use to create an overall impression of our business? These can be very difficult questions to find answers for. It could therefore be a worthwhile investment to organise some research into this.

However, extensive research has already been done that provides useful general answers to these questions. This is called the

SERVQUAL research. It was done by Valerie A. Zeithmal, A. Parasuraman and Leonard L. Berry in the US and is explained in detail in their book *Delivering Service Quality: Balancing Customer Perceptions and Expectations*. This book provides details of how the research was done, the results and the researchers' conclusions. Some of the findings are summarised in the following diagram:

Customer Perceptions of Service are Determined by:				
32%	Reliability	⇨ *Trust*		
22%	Responsiveness	⇨ *Help*		
19%	Assurance	⇨ *Belief*	+	Intangibles
16%	Empathy	⇨ *Care*		*Feel*
11%	Tangibles	⇨ *Basics*		

The first column gives the researchers' words for each element, but I think the words in italics are more important. They are the words I have found customers tend to use to interpret each element. The percentage weightings for each element are also shown. They may not be spot on for your particular business, but that doesn't matter. They are there merely to show the *relative* importance of each of the elements.

So let's consider each of these elements and how they might be managed.

✿ *Reliability — Your ability to perform the promised service dependably and accurately*

The most important element is reliability. In my experience, customers interpret this as *Trust*. Can you or your business be trusted to do exactly what you say you will?

There is an excellent book about customer service by David Freemantle called *Incredible Customer Service*. In this book David has listed what he has found to be the 14 tests of customer service. He then presents them in the order of importance that customers would choose and suggests that you equip your company to pass them one at a time, starting with Test 1 and then working on through the 14 tests. It's a very logical approach and one which I recommend to many of my customers.

However, problems often occur when a company is confronted with Test 1. It states:

Test 1
Keeping the service promise
"All declarations of intent made by the organisation,
corporately or by individual employees and thus
perceived by customers as promises, must be met."

Having read this I've had a few people say, "That's very interesting. And are there any other books or approaches you could recommend, Chris?" This always makes me smile because they obviously realise that they currently have little or no chance of passing this first test, so would prefer to start with something easier.

Yet, as the research shows, it's the most important. It's the measure of your company's reliability. That's why it is Test 1 in David's book. That's also why it's top of the list of elements that create customer perceptions. Your customers *must* know that they can *trust* your company and all its employees to do whatever is promised.

This leads me to two more of my Daffy's Laws:

To customers, your most
important *ability* is
***reliability*.**

Always *under*promise
and *over*deliver.

What you must do now should be obvious. You must impress on everyone in your business that any commitments made to customers *must* be honoured. Make them aware that when they let down a colleague who has passed on their promise to a customer, letting down that colleague is the same as letting down the customer. It therefore must not happen.

What About Unreliable Suppliers?

I am regularly asked, "But what if you have unreliable suppliers who let you down and make it difficult for you to keep your promises to customers?" My advice is first to try to help these suppliers understand the need for reliability and encourage and help them to improve. If they can't, or won't, improve, then try to find other, more reliable suppliers. If you cannot find suitable, alternative suppliers then always tell your customers the truth. Explain that you have no alternative but to use these suppliers but you have found them to be unreliable and must therefore warn that their promises can't be relied upon. You will then be perceived by your customers as giving reliable information about the unreliable supplier you have to use.

The Direct Link between Reliability and Trust

In an article in *Customer Service Management* magazine Ron Zemke suggested that Total Customer Trust was the new goal many American organisations were striving for. There are many components that combine to create this Total Customer Trust but the foundation must be reliability. You could express this simply with the following equation.

Absolute Reliability = Customer Trust

🐾 *Responsiveness — Your willingness to help customers and provide prompt service*

Next comes *responsiveness*. Are you there, ready, willing and able to respond when the customer needs your *help*? (Even if the problem they need your help with was not of your making!)

It's interesting to note that one of the ways competitors are able to create an opportunity to develop business with a new customer is to do for them the things that their existing suppliers won't — for example, to help them with the awkward or small jobs that existing suppliers, who have the more straightforward or bigger jobs, don't want to help with.

Isn't this crazy? A potential new supplier, with no track record, no relationship, no sales and no profit as yet, being prepared to do more to get some business from a potential customer than the existing supplier is prepared to do to keep the business they've already got. It sounds completely nuts to me but I'm sure you'd agree it's not unusual.

So take a long, hard look at all your customers, your sales practices and your systems. How responsive are you to customer needs? Is it you they know they can turn to when they need help? Are you and your staff ready, willing, able and hopefully *eager* to get them out of a fix?

If you're not, change things now! If you don't, it may not be long before one of your competitors is doing this for your customers. And once they're in and have demonstrated their responsiveness, if they're any good they will be on a steady path to success and you will be on the slippery slope to failure.

🔲 *Assurance — The knowledge and courtesy of your employees and their ability to convey trust and confidence*

The third most important element is *assurance*. It's the degree to which customers have any *belief* in what you tell them. Do they believe you and feel confident about what you say you can do? If you say you can do something for a customer, will the way you tell them make them confident and assured that you can? A key element of this will be the level to which you train and trust your front-line people to deal with the many questions and situations presented to them by customers.

**The Leaky Radiator Story —
Gary, the Plumber with Assurance**

We had a radiator in our sitting room that developed a leak. I tried everything I could to fix it. I bought the epoxy stuff that you just spread over the leak. That didn't work. I tried carefully soldering over the hole. That didn't work either. So eventually I accepted that I would have to get a new radiator. I therefore called three plumbers to give me a price for the job.

The first didn't turn up on the appointed time. When he did turn up I was out so we never met. The second was the type who sucked his teeth when he saw the radiator. "That's one of the old imperial ones," he told me. "You can't get them any more you know." "So what do I do then?" I asked. "Oh you'll have to get a metric one and bend the pipes," he said. "It's a devil's own job to do." He then left, tutting and shaking his head and promising to send me a quotation.

> *The third had a sparkle in his eyes. He looked at the radiator and said, "That's one of the old imperial ones. You can't get them any more. But that's no problem. You just buy the nearest imperial size and use a special adapter to match them up. You'll never notice the difference."*
>
> *When the three prices came in they were all about the same. But I chose the one from the third plumber, Gary. He gave me confidence in his ability to do the job. I believed he could do it . . . and he did, with no problems.*

As this example shows, Gary gave me assurance. I believed he could do the job. It may be that the other plumbers were just as able, but their way of responding and their manner was such that I felt unsure. So I chose Gary because I felt assured by the feeling of confidence he gave me in his ability.

It's interesting to note that, since then, Gary has fitted a new central heating boiler, a new bathroom and has extended our whole heating system to keep up with the various extensions we have made to the house. All this work from a leaky radiator . . . it's powerful stuff, this customer service perception!

Providing Absolute Assurance through Guarantees

Some businesses have recognised the importance of customer assurance and therefore developed worthwhile guarantees that prove to customers that they mean what they say. Some examples of this are:

- *BT now guarantees the dates of installation or repair and provide a free month's rental if they fail.*

- *TNT guarantees the times of deliveries with no charge if they're late.*

- *First Direct Bank guarantees accuracy on your account with money paid into it if they ever make an error.*

- *When Douwe Egberts launched their new Cafinesse product they backed it up with a money-back taste guarantee. Anyone not completely satisfied with the taste could claim a full refund.*

So make sure your front-line staff are properly trained and can give your customers and prospects confidence and assurance so that they believe in their and your organisation's ability to deliver what they need. And, if necessary, be prepared to back this up with worthwhile guarantees that prove you mean it.

✤ *Empathy — The caring and individualised attention the organisation provides*

The next item is *empathy*. Are you and your staff on the same side as your customers? Do you and they try to see things from the customer's perspective, or do you really want customers to see things from your perspective? The key question here is, do you and your staff really *care* about your customers?

I've had some interesting and often quite heated debates about this subject of *customer care*. I believe that it has very little to do with things like instructing staff to smile, say "please" and "thank you" and answer the phone in three rings. These are the things managers get their staff to do that make them (the managers) feel that they are inspiring good customer service, but which the staff and customers know don't make much of a lasting difference. (This is where the heated debate often begins.) I think these are not customer care issues but customer courtesy, or cosmetic, issues. They are the things on the surface — a kind of thin gloss on top, like a bit of face powder.

The Three Ring Epidemic

Take, for example, this "answer in three rings" epidemic that's sweeping through so many businesses nowadays. I have lists of telephone numbers for people to call where the staff have obviously been instructed to answer the phone in three rings, and they do. But all this means is that customers are now getting their lousy service a bit quicker than they used to. It hasn't made the service any better, it's just made the telephone answering quicker. In some cases this actually makes the service worse because the phone is answered in three rings but you are then put on hold because the staff aren't there to deal with the calls. Then you're left listening to some awful music . . . and you're paying to hear it!

Customer care is something that must be deeper than these superficial things. It is something that must come from inside people. The question is, do they really care about their customers? Is it in their hearts to do it? Do they actually want to treat customers in a caring way? It's not whether they are compliant with instructions and do it because they're *told* to, but whether they are committed to the concept and do it because they *want* to.

You should ask yourself:

Do you employ the type of people that *want* to care for customers?

American Express recently ran a series of advertisements on television and in the press using famous business people who recommend their card. Sir Terence Conran, Anita Roddick and Richard Branson were all involved with the TV campaign. But the advertisement in this series that I liked most was the one used in national newspapers. It featured Ken McCulloch, the proprietor of One Devonshire Gardens.

One Devonshire Gardens is a fantastic small hotel in Glasgow which is renowned for its superb food, great rooms, and excellent service levels. It won the Egon Ronay Hotel of the Year Award in 1993. I've stayed there a couple of times and it's one of the best hotels I've ever stayed in.

The ad features a photograph of Ken McCulloch with the following caption:

"Good service isn't a mystery — employ nice people."

Ken does employ nice people, people who have empathy for their customers, and it shows in the service levels at One Devonshire Gardens. They are people who care about their customers and want to give good service. They have an empathy with customers that you can feel as a guest.

They need to. In her book *Quality: Sustaining Customer Service*, Lynda King Taylor quotes these words from Ken:

"With all our guests we never say 'no'. Whenever the customer comes to our reception area or speaks to any member of staff, the brain is automatically clicked into 'yes'. Before we even know what the customer — our guest — wants, we are saying 'yes'. That is the way it has to be in this business."

WOW! The answer is "YES" even before the question is asked. You need to be a special type of person, one who really cares about customers, one with a lot of empathy for customers, to live up to that requirement.

So how about you and your colleagues, particularly those who have regular dealings with customers? Are they nice people? Do they care about customers? Do they have empathy with them? Would they look for ways to say "yes" rather than "no" to them?

Always remember that no training course will turn a nasty person into a nice one, and no company procedures manual will make someone that hates dealing with customers become someone that loves to. Also note that one person that doesn't care can ruin the efforts and the morale of a whole team of people who do. So try to start with the right type of people, and act swiftly to remove any who are wrong.

As the research shows, this is something which is important now (16 per cent of customer perception is created by it) but it is something that I believe will get even more important, for all business, in the future.

There is an American firm called Brain Reserve that was created and is run by a woman named Faith Popcorn. In her book called *Clicking*, Faith lists what her organisation has found to be the top 16 trends for the late 1990s. One of these trends is something she has named:

Vigilante Consumerism

I love that phrase: Consumers (customers) acting in a vigilante manner. Not accepting shoddy goods or services. Being better informed, more demanding, expecting higher quality, more reliability and better service.

Since this trend is likely to strengthen in the years ahead, you'd better make sure you've got staff who have empathy with your customers. Nice people, who really care. I think that this too can be expressed as a simple equation:

Empathy = Type of people x Internal culture x What they're encouraged to do.

✎ *Tangibles — The performance of the products, and the appearance of physical facilities, equipment, personnel and communication materials*

The final determinant is the *tangibles*. I call these the *basics* of your business offer. They are the things that your customers expect you to get right. Things like:

✓ Does the car start when you turn the key in the ignition?

✓ Are the restaurant toilets immaculate?

✓ Does the photocopier produce clear copies without the paper getting mangled inside?

✓ Can you sleep in your hotel room without being disturbed by noise?

✓ Does the person serving you know all that they should know about what they are trying to sell?

✓ Do the premises and staff look clean and smart?

✓ Does the feature-rich telephone do the basic things it's supposed to do?

✓ Is the hotel room the same as shown in the holiday brochure?

(These are all very personal examples because for each one I've been exposed to products or services that were not what they should have been and would never deal again with these suppliers as a result.)

The above list includes things that you may spend a lot of time and money to get right, yet customers are rarely very impressed when you do. They expect these things to be right. That's why they're known as the *basics*. It's also why they're at the bottom of the list with only an 11 per cent score.

But don't imagine this means that they are not important. They are extremely important. This why I call them the *essential* basics. They must be there and they must be right. The point is that you may not win or keep many customers for getting them right but you will certainly lose many customers if you get them wrong.

The Optician's Tale

I do a lot of work with retailers. At a conference for one of the Northwest's major optician chains I explained to the workforce that whether or not their customers returned was probably more in the hands of the receptionists than the opticians.

Their customers expect the opticians to be able to prescribe the right lenses. So when they do, the customer will not be surprised or delighted but just satisfied that what they expected to happen did so.

But if the receptionist is particularly helpful, if he or she opens the door for customers laden with bags, takes wet coats off customers coming in from the rain, offers refreshments to customers having to wait, etc, that may be unexpected and so create delight. That could cause the customer to return and perhaps even recommend it to their friends.

So prescribing the right lenses is a basic tangible that is expected. The provision of special care or thoughtfulness can be an unexpected extra that makes you different and worth another visit.

So getting the basic tangibles right will only get you onto the starting blocks in the customer perception race. You obviously have to be there, but to win the race you will need a lot more besides. You will need to get right all the other items that make up the customer's overall perception.

🐾 *Intangibles — The things that make it feel good to be a customer of some businesses*

If you combine all the previous five items into one you get a sixth. It's what I call the *intangibles*. In my experience this is the most important thing for many businesses. It's the overall *feel* of doing business with an organisation. Does it *feel* good to do business with them? Do they make me *feel* like I'm an important customer? If the answer is "yes", I may come back. If it's "no", I probably won't.

These intangibles will vary a lot from one business to another. They are more important in some types of business than others. For example, the *feel* of a restaurant or hotel will probably have a much bigger influence on whether you return than the *feel* of a manufacturer may have on the choice of your next machine. However, the intangibles will always have some effect on customer perceptions so you need to find ways to learn exactly what it feels like to do business with your organisation. You must make sure that the *feel* is one which will bring customers back for more.

Good Feelings Build Loyalty

I'm a salesman at heart. More than 20 years of my career were spent as a salesman and recruiting, training and managing other sales people. I therefore know how hard it is to get a prospective customer to switch suppliers if they are already using one who treats them in a way that makes them feel good to be a customer. It usually takes a vastly superior offering to tempt them away when this intangible thing, which results from good management of customer perceptions, exists.

You could check yourself on this by asking customers the following questions:

- Do we make you feel as though you're important to us?

- Do we make you feel special as one of our customers?

- Does it feel great doing business with us?

Finally, just consider this list of the words customers use:

◆ Can I **trust** you?

◆ Can I **believe** what you tell me?

◆ Will you **help** me when I need it?

◆ Do you really **care** about me?

◆ Have you got the essential **basics** right?

◆ Does it **feel** good to do business with you?

These six items make an extremely potent cocktail — the cocktail of elements that make up the customer perception of your business. And remember my Daffy's Law, "perception *is* reality to a customer". You must therefore learn how to manage these six elements to create the perception you need if you want your customers to keep coming back.

Everyone Can Make a Difference

I have one last point on this, which is that everyone in an organisation has the power to make a difference that will affect customer's perceptions. The following stories, all from a trip I made to America, show how individual people can influence customers' perceptions of their whole business.

The American Eagle Baggage Bashers

I took an American Eagle flight from Las Vegas to Los Angeles. The one thing that sticks in my memory from this flight was what I observed from the terminal whilst waiting to board the flight. I'd not long finished the brilliant book about Herb Kelleher of Southwest Airlines called Nuts *so I was keen to observe how slick the American Eagle turnaround was, compared to what I'd read about Southwest. The actual turnaround time was quite good (about half an hour) but that wasn't what I remember.*

As I stood watching the aeroplane being serviced, my attention was drawn to the people unloading and reloading the baggage. Having now seen what goes on, I understand why my luggage often ends up so damaged after some flights. The baggage handling staff were actually appearing to throw (rather than place) the bags on the conveyor and then into the vehicle or the aeroplane hold.

At times they even seemed to be having some fun seeing who could drop the luggage with the biggest bang! And all this was taking place in front of the terminal where any passenger who cared to could watch what was occurring.

Knowing that my luggage was somewhere amongst this, you can imagine how I felt. It made me think, "If the baggage staff care so little about the passengers' personal belongings, how can the airline claim to care about them in other ways?"

I think that this is an excellent example of what I keep telling the staff in all the organisations I work with. It doesn't matter what you're job is, front line or back office, it's all the same. We all have the ability to influence a customer's perception of overall service and must therefore always act with the customer's best interests at heart. Everyone makes a difference. The American Eagle baggage staff certainly did. They made me decide to use a different airline for internal American flights whenever I had a choice!

Night Flight Nancy of American Airlines

Nancy was one of those rare people who are brilliant at service and who know instinctively what to do to make an ordinary experience extraordinary. Her full name is Nancy Lewis and she was a flight attendant on an American Airlines internal flight between Los Angeles and New York. It was an overnight flight so people were tired and some a little grumpy. But Nancy was superb at handling every circumstance with charm, courtesy and calmness. She made what was a potentially unpleasant flight as pleasant as possible.

Nancy yet again proved that everyone makes a difference. I'd previously thought that internal flights with American Airlines never match the service on their international flights. But she showed that this was not so. The service she provided was as good, and in many areas better, than the service on their international flights. My perception has therefore now changed. So yet again, just one person made a significant difference!

Simon the Supermarket Star

(This is a story I heard told by Ken Blanchard.) Simon worked in his local supermarket as a customer assistant helping with bag packing, boot loading and in any other ways he could. He had Down's Syndrome and was much liked by staff and customers alike. One day a customer service trainer finished a session by saying, "Every one of you is capable of making a difference to what customers think of this store. Tonight I want you to think of what you could do to make this place special for customers".

That night Simon did think about it and he decided that what he could was to use his hobby, which was collecting inspirational quotations from famous people. So the next day he arrived at work with a bag full of small strips of paper on which was printed his "Quotations for the Day". In each bag he packed that day he included one and told the customer that he hoped they liked it.

> *Some months later a Regional Manager was visiting the store and became most concerned to see that although the store had dozens of checkouts, all were virtually empty except one that had a massive line of customers, waiting patiently to use it. He soon learned that it was where Simon was packing the bags. Customers liked his "Quotation for the Day" so much that they were prepared to queue to get it.*
>
> *Everyone can make a difference!*

So get to work and start managing all the elements of perception to get your customers into the *"it feels great to be their customer"* state of mind. It can be an incredibly powerful "secret weapon" for any business, one that keeps your customers locked in to you as their supplier, and keeps your competitors locked out.

Recommended Actions	✔
♦ Make your business reliable. Keep all your promises. Don't let customers down. Be a trustworthy supplier.	❑
♦ Be responsive to customers' requests for help. Don't drive them to your competitors by being unresponsive.	❑
♦ Ensure that all staff have confidence in their own and their colleagues' ability to do a good job. Show them how to pass it on to their customers to build assurance.	❑
♦ Hire people who enjoy giving great service to customers. Find any who don't and encourage and help them to change. If they won't change — change *them*.	❑
♦ Don't be let down by the basics in your business. They must be right. But having got them right, don't think that that alone will make you a success.	❑
♦ Continually monitor your customers' perceptions of your products and services. Don't kid yourself into thinking you already know. Develop a programme to focus on and manage the perception-forming things in your business.	❑
♦ Make sure your staff know and are constantly reminded that "everyone can make a difference".	❑

Chapter 8

Getting Customer Feedback

"Any company out of touch with its customers will spend more and more time on things which have less and less importance to customers." — Ron Zemke, Performance Research Associates

"**C**ustomers know what they want? Oh no they don't," I've been told many times. "You have to tell customers what they want. You can't go asking them. They might ask for things you can't provide. That'll lead to them being dissatisfied. No, it's much better to tell them what they can have rather than risk asking them what they want."

That's not a bad argument. And it could work as a strategy so long as your customers are happy about your *telling* them and none of your competitors start *asking*. But if they're not, or one does, then you've got a serious problem!

We see this "we know better" attitude all around us.

Examples of Organisations Out of Touch with Their Customers

♦ *There are car dealers who are forever offering special deals on cars to attract new customers when if they'd just improve the service they gave their existing customers they might find a few more coming back to them for their next new car.*

♦ *There's the city which couldn't even keep its own streets clean but thought it was fit to stage the Olympic Games.*

◆ *There are retailers complaining that business is slow and there aren't the number of customers around that there used to be, yet they still don't seem able to find the time to keep the front of their premises clean and tidy.*

◆ *There's a charge card company that spends a fortune on advertising and promotional campaigns to attract new customers but shows little or no concern about keeping the ones it already has.*

◆ *There are mobile phone companies with so-called customer service staff who act as though customers who complain about the poor quality of transmission and lost connections are a nuisance.*

◆ *There is a fast food operator that boasts about putting more meat in its burgers than its competitor, but if it could only provide speedy and friendly service and a clean environment it probably wouldn't need to.*

◆ *There are hotels that spend an absolute fortune on buildings, decorations, furniture and lavish staff uniforms but won't invest proportionately in the selection, training and rewarding of the people who are going to work in these luxury surroundings and wear those lavish uniforms.*

◆ *There are businesses that are prepared to spend vast sums of money on TV advertising campaigns, brochures, exhibitions, etc., all to attract new custom, yet have a "penny-pinching" approach to dealing with complaints from existing customers.*

◆ *There is an American airline that has a customer loyalty scheme to attract and keep customers but then has air crew who treat long-haul customers like cattle to be herded and fed.*

◆ *One of the new train franchises seems to be more focused on getting its new trains in a few years' time than it is on getting the service right now on the trains it already has.*

These are all indications of organisations that seem to be out of touch with reality. They don't appear to see things in the same way their customers do. They obviously don't invest the time and resources necessary to learn and understand the way their customers think. What they need is to become totally saturated with their customers' thinking. To achieve this they need to generate constant feedback.

Customer feedback enables you to understand your customers and how they think about you, your products, your service, your people, your systems, your competitors, etc. It is gathered by opening up many feedback channels so that you have it coming in constantly and from a variety of sources.

Most Companies Seem to Favour the View in the Rear-View Mirror

When you're driving a car, you need to have the odd glance backwards in the rear-view mirror to keep a check on what's behind. But if you don't want to crash, you'd better spend most of your time looking forward through the windscreen.

It's the same in business. Your main focus should be on the future, yet most businesses seem happier looking backwards. The majority of organisations are generally prepared to invest heavily in resources such as people, equipment, offices, management, etc., for recording, analysing and reporting upon what happened yesterday, last week, last month or last year. Yet few are prepared to invest anything in the equally (I think more) important job of researching, analysing and reporting upon what is likely to happen tomorrow, next week, next month or next year. They are happy to invest in looking backwards, but not prepared to invest in looking forwards. No wonder they so often "crash" into the unexpected!

I've used these quotations already but they're so relevant to this that I'm going to use them again. At a lecture in Manchester Business School, Terry Leahy, the Chief Executive of Tesco, said:

"We've learned that if management will just shut up for a while and listen to what their customers have to say, they'll write their business plans for them."

"When we stopped chasing Sainsbury's and chased our customers instead, we started beating Sainsbury's."

Customer feedback keeps you focused on what matters in a business — the forward view — and the things that matter to your customers. By having many channels you get different information, at different times, about different things. Listed below are the five key customer feedback channels:

Key Ways to Generate Customer Feedback

With every purchase or delivery

Via mailed questionnaires

By telephone research

By a third party

In person (face-to-face)

The key is to have as much of this customer feedback as possible. If you can, you should use all of these channels to provide numerous opportunities for customers to feed back to you their thoughts and views about your business.

Let's therefore consider each of these channels and look at examples of how they are used.

With Every Purchase or Delivery

Hotels — Most hotels have some form of feedback card in the room.

Restaurants — A growing number of restaurants are trying to generate feedback with every purchase — more than the simple "did you enjoy your meal?" question that we are often asked.

Retailers — Many retailers are asking for feedback with every purchase to learn more about our experience of using them as a supplier.

Motor service — Some motor dealers now provide a feedback opportunity each time a car is serviced or at regular intervals.

Utilities — The utility suppliers now often ask for feedback each time they provide a service.

Manufacturers — Many manufacturers now provide opportunities for feedback by including a feedback form with every product supplied. Sometimes this is included with guarantee registration cards.

Holiday Companies — It's now normal for holiday companies to request feedback from every customer.

Health Service — Even some state institutions now ask for feedback from customers with every purchase.

Financial Services — It's now becoming more common for financial service providers to be more intent on listening to customers.

Through Mailed Questionnaires

Could you write to your customers to ask them for feedback? Many companies do. If you were to write to 10 per cent of your customer base every month for 10 months a year (miss out the holiday months), every customer would have the opportunity of providing feedback, by mail, once every year.

They wouldn't all respond. That doesn't matter. They would all have the opportunity to respond. That *does* matter.

One way to increase the response from questionnaires is to make them look interesting and quick and easy to complete. Don't send your customers a questionnaire that looks like the type of thing you might get from the Inland Revenue (even it is now trying to make its questionnaires look better and be simpler to complete) or an exam paper.

Viking Direct, the direct office supplies company, has a good one. At the top of the form it says:

> **If we've goofed lately please let us know.**
> **You'll get it out of your system and then**
> **we'll get it out of ours.**

I particularly like this bit at the top. It's written in a way which makes you smile and it adds a bit of fun.

There are plenty of books about questionnaire design. I've listed a few in the recommended reading list. They give lots of good examples of questionnaire styles. Yet none of them go as far as I think that you can to make questionnaires more fun and interesting.

There are lots of ways in which you can create interesting questionnaires that provide customers with the opportunity to record their views of your business, and have a bit of fun at the same time. There really is no need to fill the form with the usual barrage of boring boxes for them to tick or write comments in.

For example, here are just a few examples of different styles of questions that have a fun look. If you give the design of your questionnaires a bit of thought, I'm sure you could come up with many more ways of making them look more interesting and more fun and thereby get a bigger response.

1. How fast are we at _____?

Tortoise   **Supersonic**
Pace

> Please place a cross at ↑
> the appropriate point

2. How do you rate us for _____?

☺   **Excellent value**

☺   **Good value**

☺   **Neutral**

☹   **Poor value**

☹   **Awful value**

Please draw what ↗
you think is the
appropriate smile or
frown

3. How would you place us for _____?

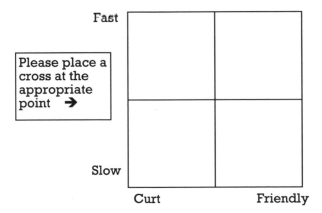

Please place a
cross at the
appropriate
point →

4. How many stars do we deserve for _____?

☆☆☆☆☆ Fantastic

☆☆☆☆ Pretty good

☆☆☆ Very average

☆☆ Pretty bad

☆ Lousy

Place your star rating in the box below.

↓

5. Circle the words that apply to our _____?

Brilliant	Awful	Lousy	Slow
Fantastic	Good	Bad	Quick
Friendly	Miserable	Caring	Curt
Off-hand	Helpful	Knowledgeable	Great

Please write below any we missed:

6. How do you rate the overall quality of _____?

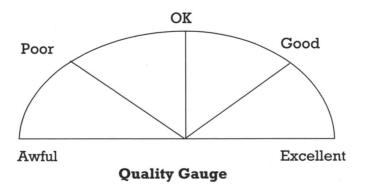

Quality Gauge

Some people comment that questionnaires like these will be difficult to analyse. That may be true, but I've always found ways to do it. The point is that questionnaires like these are easier to complete. You therefore get a bigger response. They also create a different image of your business, one that is more friendly and human. These two benefits make it worth the extra bit of effort necessary to analyse the responses. Remember, customers are people, not machines, so send them questionnaires that look as if they were designed by and for people. (If you've had any really successful ones I'd be interested to learn about them, so please send me a copy.)

By Telephone Research

If you're a director or a manager, and you don't often meet customers, it's easy to become isolated from the really important issues and get out of touch with reality. One way of making sure this doesn't happen is to give yourself "a daily dose of reality" by making contact with a customer, every day (not the same one), to find out what they think of the products and services you are providing. Simply telephone a customer every day to say:

"How do you think we're doing?"

Ron Zemke calls this "having the guts to ask and the patience to listen"

You need both. It does take courage to do it. Most people haven't got it and invent all manner of excuses to mask the fact that they haven't the "guts" for it. Then you need patience. Patience to listen without defending or justifying things a customer may complain about. Patience to listen carefully enough to understand fully what the customer is telling you. Patience then to put right anything that is wrong and to check back with the customer to make sure that they agree that you've put it right.

If you're really serious about this then do it more than just once a day. Do it throughout the day. This may mean that, as well as (not instead) doing it yourself you also have some people whose job it is to do this daily.

Some examples of companies that use telephone feedback systems are:

Hayley Conference Centres —— Hayley Conference Centres have some great conference and meeting venues throughout the UK. We use them a lot and I am always impressed by the way we are telephoned after a seminar or meeting to ask how things went and whether any improvements could be made in future. These calls have helped to keep the centre busy, the staff on the ball and the overall package competitive.

Jaguar — One of the main elements of the recovery programme instigated by John Egan, when he was chief executive at Jaguar, was telephone contact with customers at various intervals following the purchase of a new car. This enabled them to track the reliability of the cars and their dealer network and to quickly fix any problems they found. It also did wonders for their reputation with customers.

British Telecom — BT has a continual programme of telephone monitoring of customers' views of activities such as new installations and service visits.

Interprint — Interprint follows up selected deliveries with telephone calls to check the customers' views of the service provided.

J M Computing — J M Computing is a computer dealer in Manchester. It contacts customers by telephone every week to establish their views on a product or service provided the previous week. This feedback is used to improve its services generally and to determine an overall "customer satisfaction" rating. This rating is then used as one of the elements that determine quarterly bonus payments for all employees.

Kwik-Fit — Kwik-Fit has a team of people who follow up on everyone who uses the service but doesn't complete the written questionnaire handed to them in the depot. By this process they find those few customers who were not completely happy with the service but didn't report it at the time. This of course enables them to fix and recover the situation, keep the customer and perhaps even create an advocate or Raving Fan who will bring them even more customers.

Through a Third Party

It's a good idea to occasionally engage a third party to ask customers, on your behalf, what they think of your organisation. You often need a third party to get at the "brutal" truth. Whether the news is good or bad, some people are not comfortable telling you directly. In these instances the indirect, third-party route is necessary.

You could use an independent specialist research organisation to gather this feedback for you. If you're a reasonable-sized company you should be using a third-party specialist research company once or twice a year.

Alternatively, you could simply ask someone you know and trust, who knows or meets your customers, to ask on your behalf. For example, you could get third-party feedback from:

☞ Another customer

☞ A supplier

☞ An engineer/support colleague

☞ A delivery driver

☞ A journalist/reporter

☞ A trade association

☞ An industry magazine/newspaper

☞ A mystery shopper.

As with the other methods of feedback, the more of these channels you can open up, the better.

In Person (Face-to-Face)

This has been saved until the end because it's the best. In many businesses the majority of feedback is gathered by passive, indirect and rational means (questionnaires, through third parties, etc.). But the best feedback is always active, direct and emotional (face-to-face). You can't beat hearing what your customers think about you directly, face-to-face, seeing the look in their eyes, hearing the tone in their voice and watching their body language as they tell you. It may hurt but it's good for you and you can never have enough of it.

You should therefore be doing this yourself, and encouraging all your staff to do the same. Do it as often as you can. Whether you do it formally or informally (ideally both) doesn't matter, so long as you do it!

Formally

There are various ways you can get face-to-face feedback formally from customers. These include:

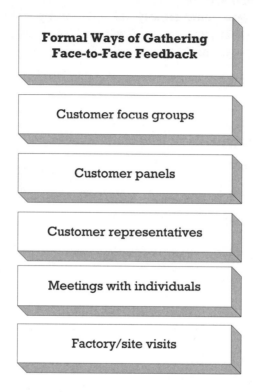

Customer focus groups. These are groups of customers that you bring together as and when needed to provide feedback information on specific issues about your business. At such meetings you should ensure that you are completely outnumbered by customers. Twenty of them to two of you would be great. This way they are more confident to provide you with the brutal truth you need.

Customer panels. These are panels of customers, perhaps with common interests, who meet with you at regular intervals to discuss your products or services and provide you with feedback on how they view you are doing.

Customer representatives. These are customers who have agreed to provide you with a customer's perspective when required. They would be invited to join in company meetings, particularly when new or different things are being planned, to help you see things through the customers' eyes.

Meetings with individuals. These are meetings you have with individual customers to learn how they view your products and services. This probably happens routinely during field sales visits but you should encourage other people in the business also to become involved in these meetings.

Factory/site visits. These are visits by your staff to a customer's site or by customers to your site. Whichever way around, they should be frequent and used to allow customers and your staff to exchange ideas, build understanding and improve relationships.

Case Study — Cardway Cartons

Cardway Cartons has achieved steady growth in profits every year since it began trading 20 years ago. It makes packaging cartons, mainly for the food, pottery and electronics industries.

Gerald Keeler, Cardway's Managing Director, knows that if their cartons are delivered late to the customer, or are poor in quality, it will reflect badly on their customers' reputation with their own customers. They have, therefore, always been determined to provide the highest possible levels of product quality and service to their customers. In order to do this Cardway has devised a number of customer service initiatives that have proved to be most successful. These include:

1. *The whole workforce is involved in regular meetings and training sessions about customer service and product quality.*

2. *All employees are encouraged to get closer to customers by making regular visits to their premises to see how the cartons they make are used and to seek out ways to improve products or services.*

3. *All company information is available to employees and customers. Employees are given training so that they understand the financial information about the company.*

4. *Customers are invited to attend the company sales meetings where they are encouraged to influence the sales decisions being taken.*

5. *Open meetings are held with customers, suppliers and employees at which the latest information about the company and the market is considered and actions agreed.*

Bernard believes that what is considered to be exceptional service today may be seen as only average service tomorrow, so Cardway must continually improve just to maintain its current position. His overall goal for Cardway is "to be recognised by our customers as their best supplier".

Informally

There are also many informal ways of getting feedback from customers. These are often better than the formal ones because the customers are more relaxed and less on their guard about what they say. A few examples are:

Informal Ways to Gather Face-to-Face Feedback

Doing the jobs that get you amongst customers

Wandering about where customers are, listening and watching

Becoming a mystery customer of your own business

Doing the jobs that get you amongst customers. If you want to know how customers think, get out there and serve them. Do the jobs that get you close to them so that you can see things for yourself and they can tell you what they think. Don't let them know your seniority in the business, it may inhibit their frankness. Just be another employee to them and you will gather lots of valuable, uninhibited feedback.

Wandering about where customers are, listening and watching. If you don't feel able to do the jobs that get you amongst your customers, at least spend a lot of time around them, either in your premises or at theirs. Again, try to spend your time with people who aren't inhibited by whatever position you may have so that they feel able to talk freely.

Avoid the "Royal Tour"

There's really not much point in doing the type of "royal tour" that some chief executives seem to favour. This is where they visit the branches or departments of the company, with a loyal entourage of hangers on, and lots of prior notice so that everywhere can be painted, cleaned and tidied in advance, and then ask only the obvious, dumb questions of employees who have been primed to give polite, equally dumb answers.

Nothing of much value is learned from such exercises, except perhaps that the chief executive is the kind of "prat" the employees always thought he or she was. (This brings to mind the Billy Connolly comment that the Queen must think that the whole world smells of paint.)

Becoming a mystery customer of your own business. Make yourself a regular customer of your business. Keep trying it for yourself to learn what it's like for your customers. But don't let it be known that you're doing this or people will make sure you get special service and you'll learn nothing of value.

Case Study — Eurocamp plc

Eurocamp provides camping holidays in France and other areas on mainland Europe. This means that its customers take delivery of the service hundreds of miles from the Eurocamp head office in Knutsford, Cheshire. It is therefore essential that it use all possible means of gathering feedback from its customers so that the staff are always aware of the customers' views of the service it provides. The feedback Eurocamp gathers is divided into two types.

*1. **Statistical information**. This is gathered in two ways:*

- *Questionnaires that customers complete while on holiday*

- *More detailed questionnaires that are mailed to customers when they return home.*

This statistical information helps to identify what improvements are needed.

*2. **Qualitative information**. This is gathered in various ways:*

- *At meetings with site couriers*

- *During telephone conversations with customers*

- *From information gathered at the customer help desk*

- *In letters from customers*

- *From the qualitative answers on questionnaires*

- *During customer focus group discussions.*

This qualitative information identifies how improvements can be made and how important they will be to customers.

Jim Crewe, the Managing Director, stresses that this feedback is viewed as so important to the company that it encourages every employee to play some role in its collection. All the company directors are fully committed to playing their part in this and are actively involved in the feedback activities, along with the staff. Jim says that "the overall goal is to have everyone in the business immersed in the gathering of feedback so that they fully understand our customers' expectations and requirements."

Case Study — Superquinn

Donald R. Keough, President and Chief Operations Officer of the Coca-Cola Company (USA), describes Feargal Quinn as being "one of the world's greatest retailers". Feargal is the Irish equivalent of David Sainsbury. He has built one of the biggest food retail chains in Ireland, called Superquinn, and a worldwide reputation for delivering exceptional levels of customer service.

Feargal is someone who is obsessed with gathering feedback. As with all the top leaders he leads from the front and demonstrates his commitment to the need for feedback by devoting his own time to its generation. For example:

- *He spends afternoons on checkouts, wearing a white coat, packing customers' bags and asking them what they think about the service and products in the stores.*

- *He holds regular evening "focus groups" at which he and his secretary are confronted by groups of around 20 customers whom he asks to tell him, with brutal honesty, what they think about his stores.*

Through these and other ways he keeps himself totally focused on customer needs and able to adapt and develop his offer so that he is continually in tune with his customers and ahead of his competition.

We Surely Don't Need All This Feedback?

Yes, you do. All this and more if possible. If you can find other, better ways of getting the feedback then use them also. You cannot have too much. Almost all businesses have too little — too many have none at all.

In his book *The Customer-Driven Company*, Richard Whiteley says that what is needed is for a business to be "totally saturated" with the voices and thoughts of customers. I like the phrase "total saturation". Being completely soaked in it. Awash with it. Having it come at you every day, from all sources — incessantly. Getting into every department, every meeting, every report, every plan . . . wonderful!

But What about the Statistical Relevance
of the Information Gathered?

I was once asked in a seminar, "But what about the statistical relevance of the information gathered?" It's an interesting question. It would be one to take seriously if you only had trickles of feedback coming into your organisation. Perhaps the odd third-party research project (say once a year), or an annual customer focus group, or just the odd comment from the field sales team. If that's all you've got, then statistical relevance really matters.

But if you have a continual flood of feedback, if you're totally saturated in it, then the statistical relevance is less of an issue. With all this feedback, you will soon see the issues that really matter and need attention. The real problems, the ones that keep cropping up, soon show through. The sheer volume of information you have will outweigh the need to worry much about statistics.

So go for total saturation and to hell with statistical relevance.

Tipping as a Form of Feedback?

My last visit to the US raised some interesting questions about customer service and its link to instant rewards.

Questions of Service

- *Why is it that the service for a $1.99 Denny's Grand Slam breakfast was better than the breakfast service on a £450.00 American Airlines flight?*

- *Why were the bar staff in the Pan Pacific Hotel in Anaheim apparently keener to provide good service than the reception staff?*

- *Why did I get great service from the porter and lousy service from the checkout clerk in Caesar's Palace Hotel in Las Vegas?*

In all these examples the people that gave the better service were paid less than the people that gave the worse service. So wages cannot be the answer and one conclusion from this must be that you don't automatically get better service provision simply by paying higher salaries.

I think that a possible reason for this not uncommon anomaly was tips. A common factor between all those people who gave me great service, that was missing from all those who didn't, was the need for tips. The better service providers all relied on tips to turn their relatively poor wages into good ones. They had all learned the following:

> **Great service = Good tips**
>
> **Poor service = No tips**

So they had to give great service if they wanted any tips.

This links with something I once read about a theory that one reason why American businesses generally give better levels of service than their international competitors stems from the American university education system.

Having to Work While at University May Create Better Businesspeople

Many of the American students have to work while they are at university to help pay the cost of being there. The kind of jobs they tend to get (evening and weekend jobs) are often in the service sector. The basic wages are generally low in this sector so they rely on tips to boost their income. This is where they learn a vital lesson:

Better service = better income.

This lesson then sticks with them throughout their working life. They therefore know, from first-hand experience, that great service is an essential ingredient of business success.

But this kind of learning can go beyond just tips. The most important connection is the one between the service provided and the instant customer feedback about that service. Tips are just one form of instant customer feedback about service. Good service gets tips, poor service doesn't.

I think that this is one reason why employees in smaller businesses, or small teams, often give better service than employees doing similar jobs in bigger businesses or teams. In the bigger units it's easy to feel that you're just a "small cog in a big machine" and that nothing you do can make a difference. In the smaller firms or teams the employees can more easily see the direct connections between the service they give, the customer's satisfaction, whether customers come back and how that links to the wages they get.

So what can we learn from this? I think that the key lesson is the need to create an instant, or at least very quick, means of customer feedback, ideally linked to rewards, for all employees. The shorter the route for this feedback and the quicker it comes, the better.

To Tip or Not to Tip — An Interesting Question

The Brits aren't a nation of tippers. We're often embarrassed to give tips or feel that the people serving us should do their job well enough without the need for tipping. We're also not a nation that's renowned for great service. The places that do have such a reputation tend to be few and far between.

I think the two things are linked. It might therefore be better if we became more like the Americans in our tipping habits. Then, more British service staff would see a direct link between the service they give and the rewards they get and, I believe, service levels would improve. So please, be a bit more generous with people who give you good service. We all should benefit in time.

Good Listening is a Rare Skill

When I was new in sales, a wise sales manager taught me the following about people:

Different Types of People

- A **bore** — someone who talks about themselves.

- A **gossip** — someone who talks about other people.

- An **interesting speaker** — someone who talks about you.

- A **brilliant conversationalist** — someone who listens to you.

There aren't many brilliant conversationalists around. Most people want to bore you by talking about themselves. Few people have developed really good listening skills. But it's no good opening up all these feedback channels if you don't know how to listen properly. You need to ensure that you hear and understand the real meaning and the implications of what's being said.

Listening is a contact activity. It's more than just looking at the other person while they're talking to you. It's something which requires skill. It needs you to engage with the other person. You can't do it properly at a distance and you can't be unconnected with your customers if you want to listen properly.

I've noticed three distinct types of listening which seem to take place when customers are telling their suppliers what they think. I call them offensive, defensive and naive listening.

Offensive Listening

This is where the reaction to a complaint or negative comment is something like:

"How dare you?"

"Do you realise the effort or trouble that we put into this?"

"Well, you obviously don't understand the way this works."

"I'll have you know we're rated by our trade association as the best in the business!"

With this type of listening the supplier "attacks" a customer for complaining. It often results in an argument and/or the customer deciding that telling the supplier about dissatisfaction was an unpleasant experience which they will not repeat. It usually also guarantees a lost customer.

Defensive Listening

With this type of listening the reaction to a complaint or negative comment might be:

"Well, let me explain why we do it like that."

"I think you'll find that it's not actually that bad."

"Oh well, there's a good reason for this. You see ..."

This again results in the customer generally feeling that the feedback was a waste of time. The supplier has simply used the feedback as an opportunity to restate their case, not as an opportunity to listen and learn from customers. But at least this is less likely to create an argument than offensive listening.

Naive Listening

When customers complain or make negative comments a naive listener might say:

"That's really interesting, could you tell me more about it please?"

"I see, and what is it that makes you feel this way?"

"I'm not sure I really understand, will you please expand on this?"

"And what do you think we should do about that?"

Naive listening encourages the customer to tell you more. It helps you to get to the real facts beneath the surface. It's non-confrontational. It's the correct way to do it.

If you or your colleagues are unable to adopt a naive listening style with customers, don't let that be an excuse for not engaging in any face-to-face feedback exercises. You will simply have to employ a neutral, third party to do the face-to-face feedback gathering for you.

Using the Feedback

There's no point in gathering all this feedback if you don't use it. In fact, it's better not to gather it at all than gather it and not use it. At least you will not then have caused your customers to spend time providing you with information that you will make no use of.

Customer feedback is one thing that can help you to form a reasonably accurate view of the future of your business. After all, customers have the final say about whether or not you stay in business. If they like what you have to offer they may buy it and then you're in business. If they don't like it, they won't buy it and then you're out of business.

I referred to this phrase from Philip Kotler earlier:

Figures are your history, *customers* are your present and future.

It's also relevant here. Customer feedback information (the view through the windscreen about your present and future) is at least as important (I think more so) as the historic information (the rear-view mirror details) that you almost certainly already gather. You should, therefore, be prepared to commit the same resources in people, equipment and time to the analysis of it as you do to your figures.

The best way to use customer feedback information is basically to do the same things with it as you probably already do with your financial information, as shown in the diagram below.

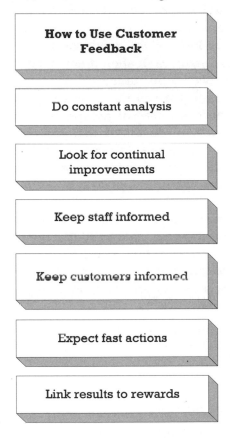

Do constant analysis. Just as you will have systems to analyse the financial information which is being created in your business, you need similar systems to analyse the customer feedback. This could mean investing in computers and software to enable this to be done. You need to track customer perceptions and how your product and service levels are changing, and hopefully improving, to match customer needs. This information should then be analysed and reported, as graphically as possible, at regular intervals.

Ideally, you will provide reports on customers' feedback at the same regularity as you have reports on your figures. So if you have monthly management accounts you should also have monthly feedback accounts. They should really be bound into the same report. One part shows your history, the other shows your present and future.

Look for continual improvements. Just as you are looking for continual improvements in all aspects of the company's finances, you should also be looking for continual improvements in all aspects of customer feedback. It should never be "good enough" — improvements can always be made.

Each improvement that you make puts you into a new position from which you have a different perspective. This different perspective enables you to see things that you could not have seen before. You can therefore see different opportunities for fresh improvements that will help you continue your continuous improvement programme.

Keep staff informed. Staff need feedback too. They need to know what improvements they are making so that they know their efforts were worthwhile. You therefore need to communicate regularly with all the staff so that they know precisely how customers' views of them and their services are changing. Ways of doing this include:

- Company newsletters
- Notice boards
- Staff briefing sessions
- Formal/informal management presentations
- Public praise for individual successes
- Memos about goals and achievements
- Appraisal interviews.

You should use as many of these communication channels as possible to ensure that all the staff are constantly aware of the customers' views of the products and services they provide.

I came across a good example of this during a stay at the Hampton Inn in San Diego:

Instant Praise for Service Success
at the Inn of the Decade

The San Diego Hampton Inn has been voted their "Inn of the Decade" for service. That's quite an accolade when you consider the high level of service generally provided at Hampton Inns. They are committed to delivering great service by their service guarantee:

100% Satisfaction Guarantee

We guarantee high quality accommodations, friendly service and clean comfortable surroundings. If you're not completely satisfied, **we don't expect you to pay.**

Poor service therefore results in lost income. This has been found to be an excellent way to learn how and where they can improve and it focuses the minds of all staff on delivering excellent service. It also shows confidence in the staff and the service they provide.

So to be the "Inn of the Decade" in the Hampton Inns network of over 400 units, the San Diego Hampton has to be an exceptional service provider.

The incident that sticks in my mind happened on the morning we checked out. I was in the reception hallway, having a coffee while we waited for transport to arrive. The manager came to reception to inform the staff that he had just learned that last month they had beaten their all-time record for sales. He thanked them for their efforts and invited them to a small celebration that evening. He then went off to another part of the hotel, I guess to tell more staff the good news.

I was impressed that his first action when he got the news was to relay it personally to the staff. That instant bit of feedback provided them with two rewards. A public pat on the back and a small celebration for providing the good service that had led to sales success.

Keep customers informed. Customers need regular feedback about feedback. It is not sufficient simply to collect the feedback from customers and act on it. You need to communicate back with customers what you have learnt from the feedback they have provided and what actions you have taken or intend to take. Doing this lets customers know that their time and effort in providing you with the feedback was not wasted because you have listened, learned and acted upon their thoughts.

There are many ways of communicating back to customers what has been learnt through feedback. These include:

- Customer newsletters
- Routine customer meetings
- Customer conferences
- Exhibitions
- Road shows
- PR and advertising
- Customer feedback meetings
- Letters about feedback.

You should look for a combination of a few of the above communication channels to ensure that all customers are regularly updated on the ways their feedback is helping you to improve the business for them.

Expect fast actions. Speed is an important element of success when acting on customer feedback. If you don't act quickly, customers find it difficult to link your actions with the feedback they have provided and therefore may not see the worth of the feedback.

Therefore, you should ensure that you and your colleagues understand the need for and are committed to acting quickly on problems or changes that are required as the result of information from customer feedback.

Link results to rewards. If you are serious about delivering high levels of customer service, and want the whole workforce to be committed to it, you will find ways of linking your reward systems to the levels of customer service that are being delivered.

When you mention rewards, people tend automatically to think you mean money. Money is obviously an important reward but it is far from being the most important.

Some of the most comprehensive research into rewards and motivation has been done by Frederick Hertzberg in America. He has interviewed thousands of people to establish what they find the most satisfying and the most dissatisfying things that happen during work. The satisfiers create positive motivation and the dissatisfiers negative motivation. The chart below shows his findings:

Factors Affecting Job Attitudes			
Causes of Dissatisfaction			*Causes of Satisfaction*
Company policy and admin.	36%	42%	Achievement
Supervision	18%	31%	Recognition
Relationship with supervisor	10%	22%	Work itself
Work conditions	10%	21%	Responsibility
Salary	7%	12%	Advancement
Relationship with peers	6%	7%	Growth
Personal life	4%	0%	Salary

Notes: These findings are based on analysis of interviews with over 1,750 people in all types of jobs. The percentages are the percentage of interviews in which the particular item was mentioned.

As can be seen, money is quite low on the list of satisfiers and a little higher on the list of dissatisfiers. It is, therefore, somewhat de-motivational if it is not considered fair, but not very motivational when it is.

The best rewards are linked to things that people value most. Those are the things that people find most satisfying and motivational. Therefore, if we use the Hertzberg research as a guide to how to provide the best rewards, they would be as follows:

Achievement — Create an environment in which everyone is expected to achieve things of which they can be proud. Link these achievement goals or objectives to customer service issues.

Recognition — Give people lots of public recognition when the goals are achieved. Let them and their colleagues know how well they have done and the value of that to the business.

Work itself — Remember that work is as natural as play. Don't, therefore, create systems or routines that start from the wrong assumption that people don't want to work. People do want to work and will apply themselves if the environment in which they work recognises this.

Responsibility — Most people are capable of and would welcome much more responsibility than they are given at work. Find ways to give people more responsibility and their motivation and results will improve.

Advancement — We all want to feel that we are advancing. For some people advancement may mean promotion, for others it may mean working on a bigger project with more responsibility. You should be able to find ways to provide opportunities for advancement for all people that deserve it.

Growth — Growth is personal improvement. Create an environment where everyone is expected to commit to a personal improvement programme involving becoming better skilled and educated, and morale and motivation will flourish.

Salary — Pay people well. Create an easily understood direct connection between customer service success and pay to motivate and reward people for service achievements.

Any or all of the following list of things could therefore be used as rewards for delivering great service to customers.

Rewards for Service Delivery

- Greater income (salary or bonus)

- Promotion to a more senior job

- Recognition and praise for things done well

- Extra training

- Work on interesting projects

- Work in new areas of the business

- More customer contact opportunities

- Extra responsibility

- Travel opportunities

- Time off for study or holiday.

I never like to dwell on negatives, but it's an interesting exercise to use the dissatisfiers to create the following formula for disaster:

The Formula for Disaster

Lots of company rules and regulations

+ Close supervision of everyone

+ Nit-picker type supervisors

+ Poor working conditions

+ Poor pay

+ Awful workmates

+ Problems at home

= A low morale, poorly motivated, underproductive, uncooperative, high-turnover workforce.

So make sure you haven't got a formula that looks anything like this in your organisation.

Using Feedback to Create Competitive Advantage

Feedback can also be used to develop strategies that will give you an advantage over your competition. This is done by establishing your customers' key purchasing criteria. These are the things that have the most influence on a customer's choice of supplier.

These criteria can then be grouped into the four categories shown in the diagram below:

Key Customer Purchasing Criteria

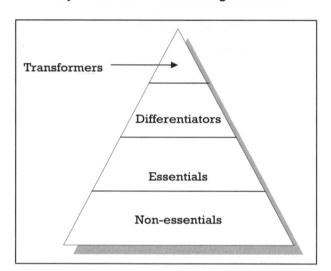

Non-essentials — These are the things that customers would like but are not essential to make or keep you as a supplier.

Essentials — These are the things that you must have to be a supplier.

Differentiators — These are things that other suppliers don't have or do that cause customers to perceive you as being different from and better than your competitors.

Transformers — These are things that have the power to transform the relationship and cause customers to become "advocates" or "Raving Fans" of your business. When this occurs customers tend to rely totally on you for whatever it is you supply and you become their only, or at least their first-choice, supplier.

Another way to decide what the most important issues or items for customers are would be to use a matrix like the one below. It shows how you could break down the overall requirement to deliver exceptional customer service into the components that must be delivered by each part of the business.

Components of Service Excellence

Once you know what the key customer purchasing criteria are, the relative importance of each one and the components that must be delivered by each part of the organisation, you can then analyse them using a chart like the one on the next page.

By placing each key customer purchasing criterion on this type of chart you can see where you have opportunities to improve your competitive advantage.

Quadrant 1 is where you want to be. This is where you perform well in the areas that are important to customers. I call this the "winners" quadrant.

A key quadrant is obviously quadrant 2. These are the things that are important to your customers, the essentials, differentiators or transformers, that you are not performing well at. These, therefore, present the opportunity to improve your customers' perceptions of your business and gain competitive advantage by improving your performance in these areas. I call this the "improvement" quadrant or, if you don't act quickly, the "losers" quadrant.

Key Customer Purchasing Criteria
Performance Analysis

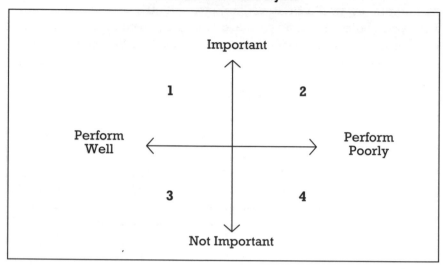

Quadrant 3 is always worth attention. Here you are performing well in areas that are not important to customers. You therefore need to find ways to make these areas more important to your customers. But if you can't, you should perhaps divert some of the resources being used here to the items in quadrant 2. I call this the "questions" quadrant.

You could also analyse the items in quadrant 4 to identify whether there are any that you could use to create a new competitive advantage. If you were able to make improvements in the delivery of a particular service and then promote this to customers so that it became important to them, this could give you a substantial lead over the competition. That's why I call this the "opportunity" quadrant. There are examples of this in many markets where a particular benefit one company is promoting is something that wasn't important to customers until the company made customers aware of it through strong promotion. Here are good examples of this:

One Hour Spectacles — Who Needs Them?

Our eyes don't deteriorate suddenly, it happens gradually over the years. So we rarely have a desperate need for spectacles that we didn't have a few hours before. Yet many retailers have developed the ability to provide spectacles in one hour. I'm sure that most of us couldn't care less whether we can have our new spectacles in one hour or one week. But these companies have created a market niche for themselves by developing the ability to provide this service and then advertising it extensively to create in people's mind the need to have it.

Instant Mortgages — What For?

There are some organisations that are offering virtually instant decisions on mortgages. Why? I doubt whether many house purchases are the result of an impulse decision, so why do we need mortgages that can be arranged almost instantly? After all, who ever heard of the solicitor who could arrange the instant conveyance? (Maybe there's another market niche waiting to be exploited.) But a number of firms have created a nice little niche for themselves by offering mortgage quickies.

Another way to consider these purchasing criteria could be to analyse them along the lines of the diagram on the next page.

By analysing your performance in the various service elements, comparing it with your competitors and then deciding where it fits on the above chart, you will have a guide as to what you should do to maximise the potential to create customer delight without overspending on items that are unnecessary.

Your Performance	Non-essential	Essential	Differentiator	Transformer
Better than the Competition	You may be investing in something that is providing little or no worthwhile return. If you find you are, make your performance the same as the best competitor.	It's good to be ahead of the competition and/or customers' expectations in this area. But don't go too far, just be ahead enough to be noticed by customers.	This is a good position to have. Try to maintain it by constantly introducing new and better ways of delivery.	This will be a major source of loyalty and referrals from customers. Capitalise on this by looking for ways to sell more things to and get more leads from these customers.
The Same as the Competition	This is the best point to be unless you can make this a more important thing to your customers.	Try to develop a small lead over the competition, as suggested above.	You're missing out on a real opportunity to create competitive advantage. Make yourself perceptibly better than the competitors in ways that customers value.	Improvements here could transform your relationships with customers. Find as many ways to improve as you can. Involve everyone in it. Do it now!
Worse than the Competition	Try to become at least as good as the competitors in this but only if you can do so without major expense.	You need to improve here. You should perform no worse than the competition but not a lot better.	This will be a cause of great dissatisfaction and lost customers. Correct all problems as soon as possible.	Correct all problems urgently and at any cost. You are losing substantial business as a result of this.

Recommended Actions	✓
◆ Decide which feedback methods will suit your business and your customers best. Remember that the more feedback you have, the better.	☐
◆ Involve all the staff in the development and testing of your feedback systems.	☐
◆ Practise *active* and *naive* listening techniques. Find the people in your business who are best at it. If you haven't got any, locate someone externally who can do it for you.	☐
◆ Develop your systems to record and analyse the feedback. Make sure you allocate sufficient resources to this. (Don't be penny-pinching — this is your window to the future!)	☐
◆ Create some methods of communicating the feedback findings to your staff and to your customers. Give them opportunities to comment on your findings, your conclusions and your proposed actions. (Don't be surprised if they don't see it the same way as you do.)	☐
◆ Find ways to link the customer feedback to a rewards system for all staff. (Remember that money isn't the only reward.)	☐
◆ Establish your customers' key purchasing criteria. Analyse them to find the essentials, differentiators and transformers. Monitor your performance in these key areas and use this knowledge to improve your competitive advantage.	☐

Chapter 9

Employees Are Also Customers

"For Federal Express, customer satisfaction begins with employee satisfaction. The bottom line is that, in order to satisfy our customers, we feel we must treat our colleagues like customers first." — Fred Smith, CEO, Federal Express

If you don't care about your internal customers (your staff), they won't care about your external customers. Basically, they will be *incapable* of providing good external customer service if they are not receiving *excellent* internal customer service.

This may seem to be stating the obvious, but it needs stating because there's a lot of hypocrisy around in many organisations. It's not uncommon to find the following:

Treatment of Customers	Treatment of Staff
Staff are expected to be caring and considerate and to treat customers like gold.	Staff are treated like dirt with poor pay and facilities and little or no management care or consideration.
Customers are considered hard to attract and easy to lose, so once attracted much is done to keep them.	Staff are considered easy to attract and replace. Staff turnover is considered unavoidable so no time or effort is put into trying to make them want to stay.
Customer loyalty schemes are created to reward long-serving customers.	Long-serving staff are treated the same as all others. Some companies even treat or pay them worse than new staff.

The service staff give customers, at best, will mirror the service they experience from the company. That's why it is so essential to "treat staff like customers first", as indicated by Fred Smith of Federal Express.

Therefore, if you want your staff to provide levels of service that will WOW your customers, you'll need to start by WOWing them. This means treating them in exactly the same way that you want them to treat their customers.

The following list of a few basic essentials that demonstrate that people matter to you and your organisation will help to get you on the right lines:

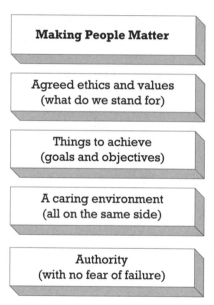

Making People Matter

Agreed ethics and values
(what do we stand for)

Things to achieve
(goals and objectives)

A caring environment
(all on the same side)

Authority
(with no fear of failure)

Agreed Ethics and Values (What Do We Stand For)

People like to know what they can expect from each other. But they don't want this to be prescribed for them by management, they prefer to work it out for themselves. If you ask people how they think they and their colleagues should behave towards one another, customers and suppliers, they will generally set much higher standards for themselves than you would have set for them.

An example of the kind of standards people create for themselves when given the opportunity is shown below. These ethics and values were created by the staff of Solvay Interox R&D

team when they were given the chance to meet and discuss the issues and agree them for themselves.

Solvay Interox

Mission (why we exist)
To deliver the technology that Solvay Interox needs.

Philosophy (what we believe and how we will behave)
To promote a working environment which encourages:
- empowerment, trust, co-operation and teamwork
- continuous growth and improvement in each individual
- initiative and freedom to act
- setting and achieving the highest performance standards
- a "we can" attitude (not "someone should")
- recognition and acknowledgement of individual and team contributions.

The Vision (how we want it to be)
We will be part of a department which:
- is customer-obsessed
- is technically excellent
- has trained, performing management
- has measures of performance
- is well-equipped and maintained
- continually strives for improvement
- is valued by the company
- offers opportunity to individuals
- is safe and environmentally-responsible
- has a reputation for excellence.

Another example comes from Lucent Technologies. Theirs is expressed as follows:

Lucent Technologies

Vision
To be the best business communications company to partner with and work for.

Mission
Our company will partner with customers through excellence in customer service, delivered by a professional team, striving for continuous improvement with profitable growth.

Values
Benchmark in customer service
Partnering with customers
Easy to do business with
A great place to work
Attention to detail
Excellence in everything
Integrity and respect
Measurement to improve

These examples are typical of many that I've seen when people sit, discuss and agree the way they want things to be. So give your people the opportunity to do the same and I bet you'll be both surprised and delighted with what they create.

Things to Achieve (Goals and Objectives)

We've already learned from Fred Hertzberg that achievement is the greatest motivator there is, so provide lots of opportunities for this for your staff. Have lots of projects for them to work on. Agree goals to be achieved in all these projects. Mark their achievement with recognition in the form of public praise, letters of congratulation, small awards, the odd party or trip to a pizza palace, etc.

A Caring Environment (All on the Same Side)

Unless people are all on the same side, pulling in the same direction, you have little or no chance of success. It's amazing how many companies you find where people act as though the competition was in the next office, another branch or at the other end of the factory. The bigger the organisation, the longer it's been established and the more departments or branches it has, the more likely it is that there will be internal conflicts.

It may be stating the obvious, but if people are constantly fighting amongst themselves internally they will never win the most important battles against the external competition. So what are the main causes of these types of internal conflicts and what can you do to avoid them? The following is by no means a complete list — some people and companies seem to have an amazing ability to create reasons for conflict — however, it should help you to spot and cure some of the key causes:

- **Management-led conflicts** — Some managers operate on the "divide and rule" principle. They seek out ways to pit people within a business against each other. Some actually like to have animosity between the people in their department and those in other parts of the company. This is often called the "us and them" syndrome. Healthy competition to do better is always a good thing but internal conflict never is. So if you have managers who do this they must change (or perhaps be changed).

- **Lack of two-way communication** — If people don't communicate regularly and openly with each other, it may not be long before they begin to view their colleagues as "the enemy". So make sure that you provide the opportunities, formally and informally, for people throughout the organisation to meet, exchange ideas and discuss issues.

- **Distance** — The further apart people are, the bigger the problem you could have with internal conflicts. You therefore need to encourage people from different locations to visit their colleagues regularly in other locations to get to know each other better.

- **Walls** — It's amazing how big an impact walls can have on communication breakdowns. I've worked in some businesses where each department views its office as its "safe haven" which it tries not to venture out from. Some even toss "bombs" (problems for colleagues) over these walls with glee. There are different things you could do about this. One would be to expect people regularly to meet colleagues from other departments, as suggested already. You might even get people involved in job sharing or exchange programmes so they get to know the people in other departments of the business and how they work. I have one customer who decided that the only solution was to remove all the walls. He therefore had them knocked down to create open-plan offices for everyone (himself included).

- **Wrong mix of people** — One of the most difficult and important jobs that any manager has is that of recruitment. Most businesses or managers generally allocate far too little time to this. And when they find someone who can do what is wanted they often hire the person without considering a vital question, "Will they fit in and get along with the other people in the team?" The wrong type of person in a team can cause immense damage to the morale and performance of the team as a whole, so it is really important that this is considered. The best way I know of dealing with this is to insist that new people meet the people in the team they will be joining so that the team members may have an input to the choice of all new members.

- **Wrong type of people** — Some people just like causing problems for other people. They get a kick out of it. Fortunately there aren't many of these around, but if you've got one you owe it to the other team members to deal with it. This means that either that person must change the way they act or you must act and change that person.

- **Poor leadership** — People learn from the examples set for them by their leaders. If people see or hear their managers constantly criticising other people or departments in an organisation then they will naturally assume that this is the right thing to do and so do the same. So make sure that the leaders in your business (managers, directors, and you) do not set this kind of wrong example.

Some organisations seem to wage inter-departmental warfare using weapons like the following:

- **Time bombs** — These are things planted by one department or person that later blow up in the face of a colleague. An example would be salespeople promising a customer things to get an order that they know their colleagues won't be able to deliver. The customer then "explodes" with the colleague some time later when they realise that they can't have all the salesperson (who by now is well out of range) promised.

- **Land mines** — These are things that go off only when certain (perhaps rare) circumstances combine. But of course they occasionally do and again, the person who laid the land mine is then generally nowhere to be found. An example of this might be a field service engineer who only partially fixes a problem with some equipment, perhaps leaving faulty something that they think or hope the customer will never use. Or a customer service person who promises something, but then doesn't tell the colleague who has to provide it, hoping the customer will have forgotten by the time it is due.

- **Stun grenades** — These are things created by one department and then tossed into others, knowing they will cause problems. An example of this would be systems that one department creates to make things easier for themselves, which they impose on colleagues in other departments, knowing that they will make things more difficult for them.

Authority (With No Fear of Failure)

Give people the authority to decide and act without needing someone's permission. Referring again to the Hertzberg research, most people are keen to have and are capable of dealing with more responsibility than they are generally given.

Embarrass Yourself — Find Out What Your Staff Do Outside Work

Tom Peters has a great way of making this point. He suggests that you do a bit of research into the kind of things your employees do when they are not at work. You'll probably find that they are involved in activities like organising Scout groups, or PTAs, or church committees, or acting as treasurer to the local political association, or doing voluntary work, or perhaps running a family on a budget which is less than you spend on business expenses each year. All things that require courage, judgment, intelligence, planning, teamwork, organisational skills, etc. Yet often these very same people are treated at work as if they were imbeciles or children and expected not to think and contribute, but to do as they are told by their immediate supervisor or the company procedures manual. What a waste of talent! What a loss of opportunity!

Don't let this happen in your organisation. Keep loading more and more authority on your front-line staff. Give them the responsibility to decide what should be done and how to do it. Give them clear, agreed goals so they know what's expected of them. Provide them with continual training and encouragement to improve constantly, and then sit back and watch them blossom.

A word of warning. Some people give authority to their staff but accompany it with the words "but don't you dare make a mistake or I'll be down on you like a ton of bricks". Others don't use these words but create systems and cultures that make people afraid to make a mistake. Either way the result is the same. People who are afraid of failure never take risks and so never learn anything new or worthwhile.

Banking on Perfection — And Getting it Wrong

I spent some time working with managers from UK banks. They worked in a culture that used to (and in some cases still does) carry a fear of failure.

The result of this was that errors still happened but they were denied, deflected or buried. Decisions were then made by senior management based on the erroneous understanding that no mistakes were being made elsewhere. This meant that these decisions were often wrong, which caused yet more errors to be made and so the cycle continued, often with disastrous consequences.

The fear of failure acts like a brake on the speed of development of any business. Sometimes it creates a dead stop. So remove the fear of failure from your workplace. Allow people to learn by the most effective method there is . . . by making their own mistakes. Create an environment where people aren't afraid to admit their mistakes openly so that they and other people can learn from them. Listed below are a few wise thoughts on the subject of failure:

Wise Thoughts on Failure

"Failure is only the opportunity to more intelligently begin again." — Henry Ford

"The greatest mistake a man can make is to be afraid of making one. There is no failure except in no longer trying." — Elbert Hubbard

"The successful man will profit from his mistakes and try again in a different way." — Dale Carnegie

"The freedom to fail is vital if you're going to succeed. Most successful men fail time and time again, and it is a measure of their strength that failure merely propels them into some new attempt at success." — Michael Korda

"Never accept failure, no matter how often it visits you. Keep on going. Never give up. Never." — Dr. Michael Smurfit

"Good people are good because they've come to wisdom through failure." — William Saroyan

"Success is moving from failure to failure with no loss of enthusiasm." — Sir Winston Churchill

"Go ahead and fail, but fail with wit, fail with grace, fail with style. A mediocre failure is as insufferable as a mediocre success. Embrace failure. Seek it out. Learn to love it." — Tom Robbins

---

I was fortunate in 1998 to hear Ken Blanchard speak in both the US and the UK. (If you ever get the chance don't miss it — he's brilliant!) He referred to this subject by talking about the way his grandson learned to walk. When he first tried he fell down. But he didn't then say to himself "Well I should have got that 'right first time' so I'm obviously no good at this walking stuff. Maybe I'll just stick to crawling." Of course he didn't, he just had a good chuckle every time he fell over and then got right up again for another go. Isn't it a shame so many of us stop learning that way when we get older?

A good way to demonstrate to people that they should have no fear of failure is to show them that you have no fear of it yourself. You can do this by making them aware of all your failures so that they can learn from them.

So set the right example. Show people you care about them. Involve them in all aspects of the business. Provide an environment in which they feel capable of and are keen to give of their best. Then you can expect and should receive the best from them.

Doing What Comes Naturally

However, there is a "but" in all this. It's a big "but" too, because it's so important. The "but" is:

> **But . . . you can't make people do it if they**
> **just don't like giving good customer service.**

If it's not natural to them, if they are naturally unfriendly or uncaring people, no amount of training or supervision will change their nature. So what happens is that while you or their supervisors are around they perhaps do their best and obey the rules or follow the guidelines. However, as soon as your back is turned they revert to what comes naturally and do things the way they think they should be done.

You therefore need to consider the following Daffy's Law:

> **Only hire people who**
> **want to give excellent**
> **customer service.**
>
> **Get rid of any that don't.**

This may seem a bit brutal, but the question you should ask is:

> **"Do you have people who really want to**
> **care for customers and build the types of**
> **relationships that give sustainable success?"**

If you haven't you may have staff who are losing customers and business. The following chart shows the result of research done to find the key causes of lost customers:

How Companies Lose Customers	
1%	Die
3%	Move away
4%	Are natural floaters
5%	Move on recommendation
9%	Find somewhere cheaper
10%	Are chronic complainers
68%	Go elsewhere because the *people* who serve them are *indifferent* to their needs. They just don't care!

This could be interpreted as suggesting that poor service is the main cause of lost customers. It often is, but the word *service* can disguise the real reason. The real cause of lost customers is *indifferent people*. It is therefore important to focus on the key issue this research highlights by remembering the following:

> **The key cause of lost customers is**
> *people — you and your colleagues!*

So, if you're losing customers, you could look at your products (or services), you could look at your prices, but make sure you also look in the mirror. The problem is often there!

The following case study provides a powerful example.

**Case Study — Prophylactic Pamela,
Caesar's Palace Hotel, Las Vegas**

During a recent trip to America we decided to visit Las Vegas for a couple of days. Choosing a hotel was difficult because one is so spoilt for choice in Las Vegas, which has many excellent and interesting hotels at generally very reasonable prices. However, we decided to book into Caesar's Palace because of its reputation for great service.

Caesar's Palace proved to be a lovely hotel with splendid rooms, excellent facilities and friendly staff. We really enjoyed our stay there — right up to the last few minutes when it was all spoiled by an awful experience when we checked out.

As we were waiting to settle our bill I noticed that one of the checkout clerks was acting in a surprisingly awful manner towards another hotel guest. She had a look on her face as if she were standing in something that smelled foul and she was talking to him in a contemptuous manner as if he were a naughty schoolboy or someone who owed her money. She was certainly not providing the "gracious personal attention" that Caesar's Palace claim is their hallmark. I was therefore pleased that she became the next free clerk so that I could personally sample her version of customer service.

She began by beckoning me over to her desk with the type of gesture the animal trainers at Universal Studios use to beckon a performing dog. (However, they usually smile when they do it. Pamela still had her "I don't like doing this" expression on her face.) There was no "Can I help you?" or "Who's next please?" from Pamela.

Then she ensured that her main attention was devoted to her computer screen that was positioned at right angles to the desk. This way she was able to keep looking away and avoid any eye contact with me. She actually spoke out of the side of her mouth rather than turn and face me.

Next she demanded $461 as though it were overdue tax. No "Here's your bill for you to check" from Pamela. When I requested a copy to check she gave me one of her scornful looks as she passed it over.

I decided to confront her about her attitude to give her a chance to explain or change her manner or perhaps even to apologise. When I did so her first response was one of those questioning "Excuse me?" phrases used by Americans. So I again explained my disappointment with her attitude, this time in more detail. She then totally ignored what I had said, made no reply at all and resumed her concentration on her computer screen.

Finally, when she passed me my receipted bill, I politely said, "Thank you". She replied by grunting, "Uh huh". There was no customary "It's my pleasure" or "You're welcome" from Pamela.

I've nicknamed her Prophylactic Pamela because up until meeting her we would have stayed at Caesar's Palace during our next visit to Las Vegas. But because of her we decided to stay in another hotel during our next stay. She was therefore very effective in preventing any second visit.

> *The point to take from this example is that in spite of the massive investment in building and fittings, all the superb facilities, all the good service given by Pamela's colleagues, our overriding and lasting impression of Caesar's Palace is the awful service she provided. Her one negative outweighed all the other positive ones.*
>
> *It works the same way in most businesses. People's actions create the most important and lasting impressions and just one negative can outweigh many positives.*

I decided to practise what I preach and give Caesar's Palace Hotel a chance to recover from this. The next part of the story explains what happened.

> ### Marvellous Michael, Caesar's Palace Hotel, Las Vegas
>
> *I decided to write to Caesar's Palace with details about my experience with Pamela to give them an opportunity to comment. Their reply, from Michael D. French, Vice President of Hotel Operations, was excellent.*
>
> *He began by apologising for the experience with Pamela. He explained the problem they have with over 2,000 employees and 500,000 guests per year of ensuring that every customer contact is of the type they would like. He agreed with my comments about the effect such an incident can have. He explained how they were determined to learn from the situation, and he asked me to return to give them a second chance! I shall. I'm keen to sample the "special accommodations" he promised to arrange for me. This is a superb example of recovery from Michael D. French of Caesar's Palace.*

Unfortunately, most businesses don't have a Michael D. French to recover for them, but many have their versions of Pamela. People who just don't want to give customers the type of service you wish your customers to receive. You must therefore make sure that these people know about and understand the gap between your expectations and their performance. You perhaps also need to encourage them to find an organisation that better fits their ideas of service. I've heard this described as "de-cruitment". This may be a silly word but it is just as important a management skill as recruitment. If just one person who gives bad service can outweigh the efforts of many who give good service you need to be just as keen about your de-cruitment policy as you are about your policy for recruitment. Remember:

"One rotten apple can spoil a whole barrel of good ones."

This is an old adage with a message that relates perfectly to the Pamela-types of this world. They can also create low morale amongst your good employees who may eventually develop a "what's the point?" attitude if their good efforts are regularly ruined by the actions of a Pamela-type. So you need to be vigilant in ridding your business of all Pamela-types if you are serious about consistently giving excellent customer service.

There are two final and important points on this.

1. **Your good staff will generally thank you and respect you for strong management and vigilance on this issue.** So, although you may not like being the person who has to ask people to leave the business, if you have management responsibility it's part of your job. You can also take heart from the fact that the remaining good staff will be pleased that you have accepted and acted upon your responsibility to deal with this issue.

2. **You don't have to pay any more to get people who are caring, friendly and have a sense of humour.** So take the time to look for the right kind of people. It won't cost you any more to employ them but they'll bring you a lot more business.

Training

Having got the right type of people the least you can do is ensure that they are fully equipped to deliver the type of service necessary to keep customers coming back. This means that you should be prepared to provide them the best training possible.

During the 1996 Manchester Business School study tour of UK service excellence we visited Royal Mail North West and met Eric Logan, the Operation Performance Director. He said:

"We should be developing our people so they could leave the operation but then motivating them so that they stay."

I really like this expression of commitment to training. Training people to the extent that they could get a job anywhere, and then creating an environment so that they choose to use their skills with you.

It's regrettable that there are so few businesses that are prepared to adopt this attitude. I regularly find organisations with the belief that there is no point in training people because they will only then leave and take the training to a competitor. What a sad attitude that is! And what a reflection on the management of a business if as soon as people have any skills worth having, they use them as their passport to a better business.

The best businesses always lavish training on people. They view it as investment in their greatest assets. (For many businesses, people are the only assets that have been appreciating over the past few years). They never fear people leaving to join others because they realise that people who do leave are potential ambassadors for their business.

It's interesting to note the scope of the training that takes place in the best organisations. The following list shows the breadth of training that is common amongst the top service providers:

- **Job skill training** — people obviously need to be trained to be skilled at the job(s) they do. This training should be continuous and involve regular refresher courses because we all go blunt and/or develop bad habits.

- **Cross-training** — the more jobs a person is trained to do, the more flexible and valuable they are to the business. In the best businesses this is recognised and people are therefore given training to enable them to do a range of jobs and work in a number of departments.

- **General business training** — You don't have to be a director, manager or supervisor to understand the basics (or even the intricacies) of how a business operates and makes money. The best businesses know this and therefore provide training for all staff in general business subjects such as finance, strategy, quality, marketing, etc.

- **Peer training** — Too few employees have the opportunity to learn from their peers, yet this is some of the best training we ever get. I was lucky to have an engineering apprenticeship in the 1960s which gave me the opportunity to learn from people who were older, wiser and more experienced. This gave me a great grounding and helped me to avoid the mistakes that had been made by my teachers. You should also allow this to happen. Let new recruits spend time with your best and most experienced staff to learn from them. Give them access to some older and wiser people who can put them on the right lines for success. These "mentors", if wisely chosen, will also ensure that the right work ethics are passed on to your new recruits.

- **Off-the-job training** — It's not enough just to provide on-the-job training. No matter how good it is, your people need to have the opportunity to mix with people from other organisations to compare ideas and learn how other companies do things. You should therefore encourage your people to attend external training courses, seminars and conferences.

- **Self-improvement training** — The more knowledge and skills a person has the better person they are. Whether or not those skills are relevant to your business or their job does not always matter. Therefore, it is also a good policy to encourage and support people to build knowledge and skills in any subjects, even hobbies that may have no direct relevance to their job.

The point of all this is simple, it's another Daffy's Law:

> **The better the people,**
> **the better the business.**

Caesar's Palace Revisited

We went back to Caesar's Palace in 1997, so I thought you might like to know how the story ended. I contacted Michael D. French, just as he had requested in his letter, so that he could organise the "special accommodation" that he had promised. The room we had booked for ourselves on our last visit was pretty good. We were therefore really looking forward to seeing the "special" room he would arrange.

It turned out to be a bit of a disappointment. The room was exactly the same as the one we had stayed in at our last visit so there was nothing special about it at all. That's not to say it wasn't a very nice room — it was. It had a king bed, a Jacuzzi in the bedroom, mirrors on the ceiling (I think they're there so the ladies can do their make-up in bed) and a beautiful bathroom. But it was not what we'd call "special", because it was the same as before. I guess he hadn't made the effort to check which type of room we'd stayed in during our last visit and assumed that that room would be perceived by us as "special". He did, however, arrange a discount off the normal price for me so maybe that's what he meant by "special".

I took a copy of my book for Michael and left it at reception for him one morning. When I spoke to him that evening, he hadn't received it. I was a bit concerned by this but he wasn't at all bothered. It surprised me that he wasn't concerned by the inefficiency of his staff. ("What if it had been something urgent?" I thought.) He excused it by the fact that they get very busy at weekends. (Surely if this is predictable, more people can be around to maintain the proper levels of service?) During our conversation he asked if I would be returning to Las Vegas. I told him I might but had no plans. He then invited me to visit Caesar's again to sample their new Tower, which was opening in 1998. He also later wrote to my office with a note of thanks for the book and another invitation to return. I've thought about this since my return and decided that I shall be going back to Las Vegas, but it's unlikely that I shall be staying at Caesar's Palace when I do. The reason is that during my last two visits they have displayed the same disappointing traits that many London hotels have. Las Vegas, like London, is a major world tourist attraction and it is therefore not too difficult to fill hotel rooms. (I guess this is especially so when you have a name that is as well known around the world as Caesar's Palace.) This often gives rise to a complacency phenomenon that reveals itself in subtle ways. I wasn't impressed by this last visit. There was a lack of attention to the important little details that I think differentiate the great from the merely good in hotels. I also felt that many of the staff showed too much arrogance and too little genuine care. All signs of the complacency phenomenon! (See Chapter 12 for more on this.)

However, although Michael blew his opportunity to live up to our expectations and turn us into advocates of Caesar's Palace, all is not lost. The Forum shopping mall, which is attached to the hotel, is an incredible place. We shall definitely pay it a visit every time we go to Las Vegas.

Recommended Actions	✓
♦ Create some internal discussion groups for people to debate and agree the things about work that are important to them. Make this something that happens at regular intervals.	❑
♦ Make sure that every employee has things to achieve through work. Go looking for their successes rather than their failures. Make sure they know you notice and appreciate their achievements.	❑
♦ Develop systems to ensure that all people are on the same side and aiming for common goals. Be on the lookout for any signs of internal conflict, seek out its root causes and remove them.	❑
♦ Remove fear from your workplace. Create an environment in which people feel free to express themselves and to experiment, with no worry about learning through the odd error.	❑
♦ Don't abdicate your responsibility to remove any people who don't fit. You owe it to the other employees to act quickly on this.	❑
♦ Be prepared to lavish training on people. Do everything you can to help them to develop their knowledge and skills.	❑

Chapter 10

Customer Care Strategies, Systems and Standards

You cannot give excellent customer service if you don't have the right strategies and systems to allow you to do so. You also need agreed standards of performance and ways to measure yourself against them. The following elements are the keys to getting started with the right strategies, systems and standards.

Success Strategies

Most quality and customer service programmes fail to achieve the goals set out for them. The current success rate seems to be about 20 per cent. So 80 per cent or so result in failure. This is obviously an appallingly high failure rate and much research has recently been done to try to establish the key reasons for this. As always, there appears to be lots of reasons, with different ones being the key ones in different situations. However, there are a number of elements that seem to be present in either the successes or the failures. These are as follows:

Getting the Strategy Right	
Elements Common to Failures	*Elements Common to Successes*
Top-down thinking	Bottom-up thinking
Inside-out systems	Outside-in systems
Focus on product or process	Focus on people

Top-down vs. Bottom-up Thinking

Top-down thinking is the type that is composed in a boardroom, gets exposed to senior management and is finally imposed on the workforce. It stems from the "we're the bosses so we always know best" beliefs and attitudes that are common in many organisations. Yet these beliefs and attitudes are often wrong. The people who know best are the people closest to the issues: the workforce.

Bottom-up thinking recognises this. It stems from the "we may be the bosses but that doesn't mean we always know best" beliefs and attitudes. This creates a situation where the people closest to the issues, the workforce, are kept informed and are expected to contribute to most, if not all, decisions.

Inside-out vs. Outside-in Systems

Inside-out systems are designed purely to serve the business or a particular part of it. They usually are created with no involvement from the people they are ultimately inflicted on, and the people who create them are normally oblivious to the damage that they cause. In many of the businesses I've worked with, most of their systems were inside-out and needed changing.

It's a shame that many so-called "quality" systems are like this. Even some that parade under the grand banner of ISO 9000 fit the inside-out description. I've come across far too many of these systems that seem to have been designed on the principle that bigger, thicker, heavier and more complex is better for quality manuals. I've also seen reporting systems that require people to record all kinds of useless information that, once it is gathered, is never used.

The problem with these types of systems is that they often impact directly on customers and/or the people who are there to serve customers. They may then slow down service delivery, make it impossible for front-line staff to fix things for customers (recovery), make the purchase process unnecessarily cumbersome, or even cause sales or customers to be lost to competitors with better, quicker, simpler systems.

Your goal should be to have outside-in systems. These are ones that are designed first and foremost to serve customers or the people who serve customers. These people have been involved in their design so that they are quick and easy to use. They are designed to improve rather than impede the sales process. For most businesses, to achieve this will need the reappraisal of every system to make it outside-in and not inside-out in design.

Focus on Product or Process vs. Focus on People

Having the best product or the most efficient process is obviously important to success. However, in a drive to improve service many businesses wrongly focus attention on these. This kind of focus tends to ignore the fact that great products and processes are created by great people. Therefore, if the focus is not on them, they may believe that they are not important to the creation of great products or processes, and so not contribute.

The successful organisations are the ones that recognise that all great things in business stem from great people doing great things. They therefore focus their attention on the recruitment and development of great people and the creation of a great environment. They then get their great people to focus their attention on the creation of the best products and the most efficient processes.

PTA Groupings

The way people are organised will affect the success of any customer service programme. The best way to organise for maximum speed and success is as follows:

PTA Groupings
Projects + Teams + Authority
= Speed + Success

I've given this way of working this title so that it will stick in your mind. I guess that PTA is already there for Parent Teacher Association, so hopefully whenever you need to get something important done you will remember PTA groupings. This is how they work:

Projects (or Programmes). Try to create projects or programmes for as many things as possible. Projects for things that have a timescale and an end point; programmes for things that will be continuous. For example, you could have the following:

- +1 project

- Feedback programme

- Recovery programme

- Cross-training project.

Projects and programmes tend to give "life" to important things that need to be done in an organisation. Give each one a name, then go about recruiting a team to work on it.

Teams. Having created a project or programme, it needs to be handed over to a team for action. People should be invited or volunteer to serve on the team. No one should be forced into it. A well-constructed team will contain people from different parts of the business and with varying levels of authority. However, once people are in a team they must understand that having a more senior position does not give them any more authority in the team. They have just one vote, the same as everyone else. Nor does having authority give the right to elect oneself as team leader. The best teams elect their own leaders. (And sack them if they don't do a good job!) A good team size is three to eight people.

Once the team is formed and has elected its leader, the members need to make sure they understand clearly the objective(s) of the project. Then they must agree (sometimes negotiate) the scope, parameters, budgets, time scale, etc. When this has all been agreed the vital last element can be added.

Authority (and responsibility). The vital ingredient is authority. Without it the team will never become the type of high-performing team that is capable of achieving stunning results. With it, the team is transformed into a unit that is capable of great things.

The kind of authority the team needs is as follows:

- The right to select its own leader

- The right to select and dismiss its own members

- The right to consult expert advice with no obligation to use it

- The knowledge that so long as the team's solutions meet the agreed criteria, then whatever the team decides should be done, will be done.

With this authority go some obligations and responsibility, as follows:

- The duty to treat all team members fairly

- The duty to keep fully informed all people who need to know progress

- The duty to advise promptly all who need to know if the project looks likely to fail or not to meet any of the agreed objectives or criteria

- The duty to consult all people who will be affected by team decisions before making them.

If you can create this type of team structure, be prepared to be surprised by the results they achieve. My experience of working in this environment and talking with lots of people who have, too, is that it is one of the most exhilarating and rewarding there is. It is also one that generally enables things to happen quickly and successfully.

The sad thing is that very few people have ever had the chance to work in this way. They have, therefore, missed one of the best experiences it is possible to have in the work environment. So don't deprive your colleagues of this opportunity. Get some PTA groupings formed now.

Systems and Standards

All your systems and standards of performance should be measured against the following criteria:

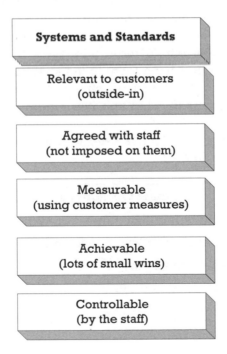

Systems and Standards

Relevant to customers
(outside-in)

Agreed with staff
(not imposed on them)

Measurable
(using customer measures)

Achievable
(lots of small wins)

Controllable
(by the staff)

Relevant to Customers

If you look at the systems that are used within your organisation you will probably find that most, if not all, of them were designed to serve some internal purpose. (We touched on this in the section about "Success Strategies".) This usually means that at the point where the system interfaces with the customer it is friendly to your organisation and staff but not so to customers. These systems I have described as inside-out systems.

The best systems are outside-in. These are systems which are designed from the customer's viewpoint back into the company. They begin by looking at ways of providing the most simple and service-oriented link with customers. Once this has been established the links with other internal systems are then created.

You should therefore look at all your systems from the customer's point of view and change any that are inside-out to become outside-in.

Agreed with Staff

It's no good imposing customer service rules or regulations on people. This may get their compliance but it will not achieve commitment. If you want people to be committed to a customer service initiative you need their full commitment to it. You will only get their full commitment if you involve them in all stages of the programme. This means letting them take part in the gathering of customer feedback, involving them in the analysis of the feedback, collecting and using their ideas on what to do about what has been learned, and letting them plan and implement the agreed strategies and systems.

There is an acronym which is used to describe the elements of good objectives — SMART:

Smart Objectives
Specific rather than general or vague
Measurable to allow monitoring
Agreed with all parties
Realistic and realisable
Time-related — by when?

These same five elements can be used to describe good customer service systems. So make sure that yours are all SMART and that you don't have any that are SMIRT, where the "I" stands for Imposed. Imposed objectives are not owned by the people they are imposed on, so those people have no real commitment to their achievement.

Measurable (Via Customer Measures)

One way of knowing what an organisation views as important is to look at the things that it measures. Companies only measure what they view to be important. Therefore, companies that view customer service as important measure the levels of customer service they are providing.

But what is most important here is that you measure things from the customer's point of view. You need to measure what is important to customers. It is all too easy to measure things that you think are important but that don't matter to customers. That way you may kid yourself that you are achieving success when you are not.

A good example of this comes from research done in the US into what matters to people attending seminars and conferences. The researchers first asked the venue staff what they thought was important. They listed things like:

- Good quality coffee

- Good china

- Hot coffee

- Friendly staff

- Fresh biscuits.

The researchers then asked attendees at seminars and conferences what they viewed as important. The things listed at the top of their list were:

- Access to toilets with no queues

- Plenty of telephones around

- No queues to get tea or coffee

- Places to sit.

As can be seen these lists are very different. The list that was created by the staff obviously covered key things that they viewed to be important. However, if they were to measure them they would get a false picture of their service performance because they are not the things that the customers viewed as important.

Another example comes from the Marketplace Performance Unit in British Airways.

Checking the Right Things at Check-in Time

When Sir Colin Marshall became chief executive of BA he realised that it was vitally important to see things from the customer's perspective. He therefore created a Marketplace Performance Unit that had the job of measuring and benchmarking operating performance. Their job was to find out what the customers really want, rather than what the management thought they wanted.

A good example of this came at check-in time. The management view had always been that what concerned passengers most was the time it took to get to the front of the queue. However, when the Marketplace Performance Unit asked passengers, they found that they were far more concerned with the length of the queues and the rate at which they moved.

This obviously meant a different approach was needed than had been adopted before.

It is therefore vital that you learn from customers what they think is important. You need to see things from their perspective and then measure what's important to them.

Achievable

One sure way to demotivate people is to set goals and targets which they cannot achieve. By doing so you create a team of failures. It is therefore important to make sure that any targets set are challenging but also achievable. My simple Daffy's Law is as follows:

> *Most* targets or goals should be
> achieved *most* of the time

Experience and research has shown that 100 small steps get people there much quicker than one large step. Therefore, if you can find lots of little steps that will lead to an overall major goal, that approach is more likely to create success than going for one big step.

This also applies to systems for implementing customer care programmes. A "wild fire" approach is much better than a "grand slam". The grand slam is trying to achieve major steps in one big swoop. This generally fails. Most success is achieved by having lots of small initiatives, all started at once, some of which may fail and some that will succeed. Don't worry about the failures, concentrating on the successes is what's important. Fan the flames of those that succeed and spread them to other departments and teams so that the success gradually spreads throughout the organisation. This approach provides lots of positive examples that show what can be achieved and encourages others to do the same. (This is covered in more detail in Chapter 14.)

So go for the little-by-little approach, have lots of rewards to match the successes and you will find that the overall goal is achieved more easily and quickly.

Controllable (and Simple)

Just as bottom-up ideas work best in the overall planning of a customer service strategy, bottom-up control works better as well. This means it is not a good idea to create an elaborate system of inspection to check that people are doing what they are supposed to do.

With product or production quality, you know you've got it when you don't need a team of inspectors to check other people's work. It's just the same with customer service quality. You will know you are succeeding when there is no need to check whether people are doing what they are supposed to. When they do it because they want to, when they measure and control their own quality of service and correct anything which is wrong without having to be told to, you have achieved real success.

The key, therefore, is to build in this level of trust at the beginning. Help people to develop their own systems of checking and control. Let them know that you expect them to monitor their own performance. Then, once the system is agreed, let them get on with it. Let them know that you are interested to help with problems and keen to reward successes. But don't sit on their shoulder, watching everything they do and picking on them when they make a mistake. Hand the monitoring and the control over to them.

The systems must also be simple for front-line people to use if they're going to help them in delivering high service. The simple rule is that all the best things are simple, and simple things are always best. So if your systems are complicated they must be wrong — so change them.

Above all, make the measurement and analysis of all systems and standards positive. Measure and report what's been done *right*, not what's been done *wrong*. Measure and recognise progress towards the goal rather than the achievement of it. Remember the purpose of these systems and standards is to motivate people to strive to do better. They are *not* there to make them feel guilty when they get things wrong. The Daffy's Law is:

> **In the best systems the staff are involved in setting their own standards of performance. They also create and operate their own methods of measurement and control.**

Make Sure You're Not Rewarding the Wrong Customers

There seems to be a strange logic in what many companies are doing regarding their treatment of customers. Some appear to be more interested in attracting new customers than in keeping the good ones they've already got. Others seem to be more keen to reward the small or infrequent purchasers than they are to reward their large or regular customers.

You can find examples of these practices in all types of business. The following are just a few I have noticed recently.

Holiday Companies
Buy early and pay top prices — leave it until the last minute and get a great deal!

The holiday companies are notorious for selling at the maximum prices they can until they have lots of holidays they can't sell which they then have to discount. Perhaps if they began by offering good discounts to existing, regular customers they would not be left with so many unsold holidays each year.

Supermarkets
Small purchasers get dealt with quickly —
big spenders can wait in line!

Most supermarkets have express checkouts for people with just a few purchases while their better customers, who have spent many times more, have to wait in a queue. Why can't we have express checkouts for the big spenders?

Mail Order Catalogues
The quicker you become a customer — the worse
the deal you will get!

Most catalogue sales companies have big budgets for attracting new customers — and for keeping the worst ones. Once a catalogue has been sent to a prospective new customer, the longer that customer waits to place their first order, the bigger the discount they will be offered to do so. Good customers, who order quickly, aren't offered discounts. Also, if an existing customer stops spending or starts spending less, they will be offered special deals that are not offered to the good, regular spenders, to resume or increase their spending. So the worst customers get the best deals!

Banks
While you are a customer we will charge the highest price we can
— if you threaten to leave we'll suddenly give you a great deal!

A colleague recently decided to take advantage of offers to people who moved their mortgage to a new lender. There's a lot of hassle associated with remortgaging but some lenders are trying to make it worthwhile.

He therefore applied and was accepted by a new lender. When he then advised the bank that provided his existing mortgage of his decision it suddenly found it possible to offer him a rate equal to that being offered by the new lender.

He was really annoyed by this. It appeared to him that they were happy to keep charging him a high rate as an existing customer, so long as he didn't notice, and only offer him a lower, more competitive rate when he threatened to leave.

In the short term the bank may get more interest from existing customers with this policy, but in the long term it stands to lose them and will then have to spend massive amounts on marketing and offer big discounts to attract new ones. It must make more sense to have policies that ensure that it keeps the customers, like my colleague, who it already has.

Clothes Retailers

Regular customers pay full price — sale-only customers get discounted prices!

I really like the clothes from one British retailer but hardly ever buy from them during the normal trading year because they tend to be too expensive for me. However, I'm on their mailing list so they always tell me when their sales are due. I then rush in to purchase the same clothes at sale prices. I'm therefore not a very good customer because I only shop at sale times. If they were to provide special offers for being a regular customer throughout the year, I would become a more regular customer and shop at non-sale times as well.

Insurance Companies

If you've never spent a penny with us before you can have a gift — if you've spent a fortune over the last few years you get nothing!

Many insurance companies offer gifts to attract people who have never been customers before. Why aren't similar gifts offered to the existing, good customers as a bonus for loyalty or renewing a policy?

Mobile Phone Companies

If you're a new customer you can have the latest phone at a give-away price — if you're an existing customer you'll have to pay a lot more!

Most mobile phone companies offer the best deals on new phones to those potential customers who have never contributed anything to their profits. I think that even better deals should be offered to the existing customers who create the profits that allow the silly deals to be offered to new customers. (Maybe this will happen when we get the right to keep our telephone numbers if we change suppliers.)

Building Societies

New customers get a discount — existing ones don't!

The recent drops in mortgage interest rates have yet again shown that building societies seem to value new customers more than existing ones. They all seem to have offered the reduced rates to new customers instantly while existing customers have to wait a month. Surely this is the wrong way around.

These are just a few examples that come to mind. I bet you could think of some from your own experience. But isn't this really daft? Surely it makes more sense to invest in keeping the good customers that we've already got rather than spending a fortune on trying to attract new ones. It also seems silly to provide incentives and rewards for the small spenders and nothing for the bigger, better customers.

I've discussed this topic with many of my customers and attendees at my seminars. They often justify these practices with one or more of the following:

- Offers are the best way to attract new customers from competitors.

- We need to encourage the smaller-spending customers to become bigger spenders.

- It's more cost-effective to take defensive actions to keep the few good customers who threaten to leave.

This all makes sense, so long as it is not adding unnecessary expense to the business, it doesn't damage relationships with existing customers, and it's sustainable. But often it is, it does and it isn't!

In most instances of offers for new customers the competition is making similar types of offers. So what happens is that the least loyal customers move around to the company with the best offer at the time. Existing, good customers soon notice when new or low-spending customers are getting better deals. They then conclude that being a good, loyal customer means little or nothing and look for an alternative supplier. These types of campaigns are constantly having to be changed or improved to react to the latest moves from the competition. They are therefore not sustainable and do not appear capable of providing a worthwhile long-term return.

In Edward de Bono's book *Sur/Petition* he explains how he believes it is possible to move out of the rat race of competing with others in the same marketplace and onto a higher level where you are in a race of your own. He calls this sur/petition as opposed to competition.

I work with many companies that seem able to do this. They have a clear long-term vision of where their business is going. They have a loyal customer base and steady growth through recommendations, repeat purchases and referrals. They are relatively untouched by recessions or volatile markets. They are able to attract and retain high-calibre staff who look forward to Monday mornings.

These organisations reward the right customers and provide them with sound reasons to stay, no matter what the latest deals or promotions are from the competition. They provide great service and the best value *all the time*, not just at the times they wish to attract new customers or when they think they could lose existing ones to the competition. They take the trouble to listen to and learn from their customers so that they know precisely what they want and expect. They are then prepared to exceed these expectations with products and services that go beyond those of the competitors. This enables them to sur/pete, rather than having to compete. It is, to my mind, the best strategy for building a successful business.

The Systems Behind the Magic

During a visit to Orlando I was able to go on a Disney behind-the-scenes tour to see some of the systems behind the magic of Disney. It was amazing to see the way everything was systemised to ensure that the right things always happened at the right time. (They even have what they call "understudy" plants and trees so that if one on the park is damaged or not looking at its best it can be replaced overnight with the understudy.) This got me thinking about how magic is created by anyone. There obviously needs to be a strict system and then hours of rehearsal before anyone can perform the kind of tricks we call magical. Then, if the performer adds that little bit of sparkle in the performance, the magic happens.

Well, it's obviously the same with service. There needs to be some really good systems in place, which serve the front-line people well, so that they can then add the magic that creates a world class customer service experience.

Benchmarking Your Strategies, Systems and Standards

We have seen that there are a few critical strategy, systems and performance standards issues that will determine your success in adopting the policies recommended in this book. This is now a good time, therefore, for you to check how well-placed you are in these issues. The following list of questions will enable you to assess your current position quickly. Simply place a tick in the box that is closest to the description of where your organisation is at present and then add up your scores.

Wrong	1	2	3	4	5	Right
Customer-facing people are the bottom of the pile in status, advancement and pay.						Only the best people are placed in contact positions with customers.
People are promoted away from customers.						Promotion does not bring reduced contact with customers.
Customer contact is generally avoided (it means trouble) and is confined to customer service personnel.						Interactions with customers are encouraged with people responsible for and dedicated to individual accounts for long periods.
People are recruited for their experience and knowledge of the organisation's particular business.						It is knowledge about the customer base and an understanding of each customer that matters. Technical aspects of the business are considered simple enough to learn.
Employees are chosen and trained on the basis of technical skills and needs.						People are sought with the "softer" skills — judgment, flexibility, problem-solving, intuition, team player, etc.
People are motivated through fear or loyalty.						People are motivated through shared vision(s).
People tend to say "it's really *their* problem".						People tend to say "it's really *our* problem".
Decisions are based on assumptions or judgments.						Decisions are based on accurate data and facts.
Staff act as though everything begins and ends with managers or directors.						Staff act as though everything begins and ends with customers.
There are departmental barriers with independent decision-making.						There is cross-functional cooperation with joint decision-making.
The business is improving at crisis management and recovery.						The business is improving at getting things right the first time.
Number of Ticks						
Multiply by:	1	2	3	4	5	
Totals						
Grand Total:						

What Does It Mean?

♦ **46 to 55** — You're amongst the best in the world — keep it up.

♦ **36 to 45** — You're doing well, but there's room for improvement.

♦ **26 to 35** — You're about average and need to improve.

♦ **16 to 25** — You're below average and need to refocus the business.

♦ **Below 16** — You're amongst the worst in the world — worry and change things . . . fast!

Recommended Actions	✓
♦ Turn all the elements of your customer service programme into projects. Hand over the projects to high-performing teams. Give the teams full authority to do what is necessary to achieve success. Then keep out of their way unless they ask for help.	❏
♦ Check all the systems in your organisation. Are they inside-out or outside-in? Revise all the inside-out ones to make them outside-in.	❏
♦ Discuss and agree with your staff all the plans for improving customer service. Encourage their involvement in the planning. Elicit and use their ideas.	❏
♦ Agree with all colleagues the things that should be measured regarding customer service. Remember always to use the same measures that customers use.	❏
♦ Create lots of small steps that will chart your course to the levels of customer service you want. Celebrate each step that you successfully climb.	❏
♦ Hand over the running of the programme to the staff. Trust them to get it right and to get it back on course when it goes wrong.	❏
♦ Benchmark yourself against the checklist. Keep doing this at regular (6-month) intervals to chart your progress.	❏

Chapter 11

Customer Care and Leadership

"One of the biggest challenges facing management today is to be worthy of the people we manage." — Jack Welch, CEO, GE

This phrase should be on the wall of every manager's office. There are far too many managers around who aren't worthy of the people they manage. They act as though having the title is enough — as if once you're called a manager (or perhaps a director, a supervisor, an executive, etc.) you automatically inherit the skill and knowledge required to do the job that carries the title.

Consider this. If you were to bring together a group of people who work for the same company and ask them:

"How would you like things to be around here?"

Do you think they would say this?

☹️   We want to produce goods and services that aren't very good.

☹️   We want to make things that go wrong a lot.

☹️   We want to be off-hand and uncaring towards customers.

☹️   We want to treat one another like enemies.

We want to scheme and contrive ways to make each other look foolish.

  We want to love Friday evenings and hate Monday mornings.

I'm sure you'd agree that it would be very unusual if people said this. Yet these are precisely the things that are happening in many businesses. So if these are not the things that people want to do, why do they so often do them? There must be lots of answers to this question, different ones in different businesses, but the most common answer is:

THE MANAGEMENT

I find this usually happens because the way people are managed forces them to act unnaturally.

What is needed is a lot less management. The word manage infers control, manipulation, commands, instructions, rules, regulations, checks, etc. Instead of management, lets have some leadership. Have you ever heard people talk about a great church manager, an excellent scout group manager, a brilliant military manager or a charismatic political manager? Of course not, they are all leaders. And it's leaders who are needed in the business world if you are to create the type of company that is capable of delivering world class customer service.

The word leader infers guiding, coaching, suggesting, inspiring, encouraging, conferring, empowering, etc. These sound much more like the kind of things that will encourage people to give of their best. So what we need today are fewer managers and more leaders.

I have been involved in many exercises with people, in all types and sizes of companies, where they have actually been asked the question:

"How would you like things to be around here?"

I can tell you with confidence that these are the types of things they actually say:

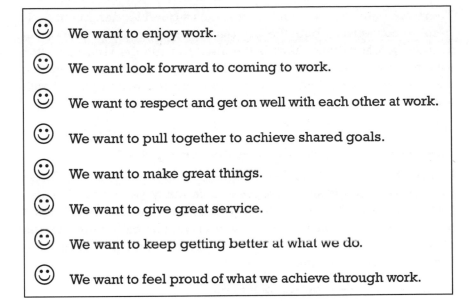

☺ We want to enjoy work.

☺ We want look forward to coming to work.

☺ We want to respect and get on well with each other at work.

☺ We want to pull together to achieve shared goals.

☺ We want to make great things.

☺ We want to give great service.

☺ We want to keep getting better at what we do.

☺ We want to feel proud of what we achieve through work.

With good leadership, people tend to organise themselves in ways that enable them to achieve these kind of ambitions. But when someone imposes *management* on them, things often start to go wrong. So if you want a team that will provide world class customer service, you will need to learn and use the skills of leadership.

The Elements of Leadership

I heard the following phrase awhile back and it's stuck in my mind ever since. I think it's a really good way to explain what is the essence of leadership:

What is Leadership?
R & D designs *it*
Production makes *it*
Front line delivers *it*
Finance accounts for *it*
Service maintains *it*
Management organises *it*
but
Leaders decide what *it* is.

There are many views about what makes a good leader, but there is general consensus about the key issues. One of the most important abilities a leader must have is the ability to see the right direction for an organisation to follow and then to get everyone going that way. This is often called "vision" and when it is accompanied with the ability to communicate effectively that vision to all concerned, the results can be dramatic.

The Use of Paradigms — A Core Leadership Skill

I've been an advocate of Dale Carnegie ever since I read his book *How to Win Friends and Influence People* many years ago. I've also been on Dale Carnegie training courses. One of the things I learned on a Dale Carnegie course was what he called the triangle of success. It suggests that success occurs when a person combines three key elements. These are:

- Knowledge — knowing *what* to do

- Skill — knowing *how* to do it

- The right attitude — *wanting* to do it.

Of these three, the most important is attitude. This is because when you have it the other two are enhanced, yet without it the other two are often wasted.

But I've now come to realise that there is another, fourth element, one that is much more important and powerful than Dale Carnegie's three for success. This fourth element is nowadays often called a paradigm. A paradigm is something that helps us understand *why* things need to be done. The diagram below shows the paradigm in the centre of the triangle of success. I've drawn it this way to indicate its power to influence the other three elements.

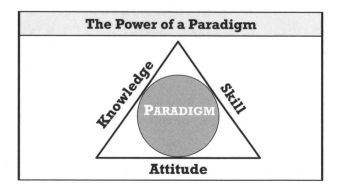

I must admit that when I was first introduced to the concept of paradigms I found it difficult to understand the context in which it was being applied to businesses. But I heard Stephen Covey explain it in the tape about his book *The Seven Habits of Highly Effective People* and then I understood.

Stephen talks about paradigm shifts and the power they have to change people's habits. A paradigm shift occurs when something happens to a person that gives them a completely new and different perspective about a particular person or issue.

A Paradigm Shift for a Shopper

Imagine you were waiting to be served in a shop or restaurant. You'd been there some time yet were being totally ignored by one of the staff who was close to you. He or she was simply staring into the distance and acting as though you didn't exist. Your attitude towards that person is likely to be one of impatience and irritation.

Let's say you therefore decide to confront this person and complain about the poor service they are providing. But what if they then said, "Oh, I'm sorry. You're right, my mind was elsewhere. You see I've just learned that my mother has been taken seriously ill and I was thinking about how I could get to see her. But let me attend to you, what was it you wanted?"

Wouldn't your attitude towards that person instantly change? I guess it would become one of sympathy and concern instead of impatience and irritation?

That change of attitude would be the result of a paradigm shift. The new information you received gave you a totally new and different perspective that could affect your attitude and your actions.

This works in business too. A paradigm shift is often a necessary precursor to a major change in the way people think and behave. Just think about it. You may be able to get people to work *harder* and apply themselves more to a task. That will probably have some effect, but generally only minor and it may not be sustainable without your constant attention. You could perhaps train people to work *smarter* and use more skill. It too will have an effect, but all too often this also provides few lasting results. You may even be able to change people's *attitudes* and get them to be more positive about what they are doing. But even this often has limited effect. The fact is that if we want major changes in people's habits, ones that will be sustainable, we must find a way to change their paradigms. In other words, we must help them to see things from a totally new perspective.

Great leaders usually have the ability to create the type of business paradigms that help people to see things from a new perspective, which then causes them to think and act differently.

Examples of Corporate Paradigm Shifts

Renold

Renold plc is one of the world's biggest chain manufacturers. It makes all types of chains from tiny thin ones for motorbike ABS systems to enormous fat ones for the anchors of supertankers. When David Cotterill became the new chief executive he was concerned to find that one of their best customers, who accounted for about 3 per cent of sales, was treated as a nuisance by many staff. There was an "Oh no, it's them again" attitude amongst some of the people who dealt with them.

He therefore set about the task of helping them to see this customer in a new light, not as a nuisance company that made unreasonable demands but as a valued customer making perfectly reasonable requests of its supplier. He organised special staff training and meetings with the management and operatives of both companies to build a new, better working relationship.

The result of this has been of benefit to both companies. The customer now has much more co-operation from the Renold staff and service levels have improved. This means that Renold has become a better supplier and sales have grown. In fact, they are now approaching twice their level from before this paradigm shift.

Travel Industry

I spend a lot of time working in the UK travel and tourism industry. Due to overcapacity and price-cutting policies of the big tour operators over recent years, many of the smaller, independent people have been having a pretty lean time. I therefore try to show them that "it doesn't have to be like this".

There are many excellent examples of businesses that have used service as a differentiator and been able to create a new, less price-conscious, more profitable market niche for themselves.

A couple of phrases seem to have a real impact. The first relates to the practice of working longer and longer hours for less and less return. I call this becoming a "busy fool". It's a pretty blunt phrase but it's true of many self-employed and small business people.

The second phrase is to consider having "fewer, better customers". This gets people thinking about the fact that sales is not the only goal and perhaps if they switched the goal to profit or margin, they could find ways of getting more from less. Many people from the industry have told me that these ideas have created a paradigm shift for them (they may not use these words) and that they now see how they can create a new, better future for themselves in the industry.

Tesco

For many decades Tesco was the high-street food retailer that "stacked it high and sold it cheap". That all changed when Sir Ian MacLaurin came along. Under his leadership Tesco rapidly moved to the quality and service end of the spectrum. Now they are one of the best service food retailers in the UK, they sell quality products, they are the biggest in the business and they are making the profits that go with it. A major paradigm shift would have first been necessary in the minds of the Tesco staff for this to happen and it has now created another, in the UK population's perception of the kind of store Tesco is.

More Leadership Skills

Great leaders also tend to practise the following (they are in alphabetical order because there is no one element that ranks much above another):

- **Agreement** — Leaders generally look for agreement. They don't tend to impose things on people.

- **Autonomy** — Leaders give people autonomy and tend to let them decide what and how to do things for themselves.

- **Clear goals** — Leaders establish and agree clear goals with people. These will usually be challenging but achievable.

- **Continual self-improvement** — Leaders believe in the principle of continual improvement; for the business, for all employees and, of course, for themselves. I once heard the phrase *"leaders are readers"*. I've used it a lot ever since in training sessions I've run for leaders. If leadership means "I go first", which I think it does, leaders must demonstrate a commitment to improving their own skills and knowledge before they can expect others to do the same. Reading and then sharing the knowledge gained is one obvious way to do this.

- **Emotion** — Leadership is an emotional activity. As we've already learned, it is controlled by the right half of the brain, the creative half. Management, however, is more of a scientific activity. It is controlled by the left half of the brain, the logical half.

- **Empowerment** — Leaders understand that the people closest to things always have more power than people distanced from them. Therefore, they don't try to control from afar but pass control and empowerment to front-line people. This does not mean that they abdicate responsibility or accept anarchy. It simply means that leaders set direction, minimum standards and acceptable parameters and then let the people closest to the issues get on with the rest.

I saw the sign below hanging behind the counter in a bar. It was meant as a joke but, as the old saying goes, *"many a true word is spoken in jest"*. Leaders recognise that in most cases these words are true and so act accordingly.

> **Do you want the person in charge or would you rather speak to someone who knows what goes on around here?**

- **Involvement** — Leaders realise that the good implementation of plans is more important than the plans themselves. To get good implementation needs the full commitment of everyone to the plan. To get full commitment needs everyone to be involved in the planning process. Therefore, leaders always involve people in the planning of things that require great implementation.

- **Love of change** — Leaders always love change. In fact, they are usually the people who help others realise and appreciate why change is necessary.

- **Mutual respect** — Leaders understand that respect is something which cannot be demanded, but something that is earned. They also know that the best way to earn respect is to show it.

- **Partnerships** — Leaders seek to work in partnership with people — colleagues, customers and suppliers alike.

- **R I P — P I P** — This stands for:

Reprimand In Private — Praise In Public

Great leaders know this, but it's a shame how many managers don't. I'm always saddened by the actions of those awful managers who seem to believe that admonishing someone in public, embarrassing them in front of their colleagues, is the way to create the right attitude and behaviour. It's as if they believed that something like the following would work as well:

> **Sackings will continue until morale improves.**

I first saw this in a book on sales management and have referred to it many times in my seminars. It always gets people laughing because it is so stupid. But reprimanding people in public is just as stupid, yet that doesn't get people laughing. In fact, it's more likely to create the exact opposite reaction in a recipient. So never do it!

- **Setting direction** — The key thing that leaders do is to set a direction for an organisation. They have the ability to see how things could be, and then to get others to see it the same way. We covered this in the section about vision and paradigms.

- **Teach** — Leaders take great pleasure and pride from being able to pass on their skill and knowledge to others. They view the job of developing others as one of their most important tasks. They therefore are prepared to commit large amounts of their time to the job of teaching others. The following are examples of the commitment to their role as a teacher of others that great leaders make:

Jack Welch — CEO, General Electric

For the past 18 years, every two weeks, Jack Welch has gone to GE's leadership development institute to interact with new employees, middle and senior managers. He has not missed a session.

John Neil — CEO, Unipart

John Neil's commitment to the teaching of his colleagues is exemplified in the Unipart University he created a few years ago. It now teaches people from throughout the organisation the skills they need to compete in today's markets. John Neil presents many of the courses himself.

Roger Enrico — CEO, PepsiCo

For the 18 months before he became the CEO of PepsiCo in 1996, Roger Enrico spent about a third of his time teaching around 100 of the company's leaders his ideas for how they could survive and thrive in the 21st century. It is estimated that this resulted in ideas that added $2 billion to the top line.

- **Trust** — One of the greatest motivators of people is trust. Leaders know this. They also know that the only way to make people trustworthy is to trust them. They therefore build organisations based on the principle of recruiting trustworthy people and then trusting them to act for the good of the organisation.

These are just a few things that separate leaders from managers. Management is about getting work done through people. Leadership is more about developing people through work. Somebody once said:

> **If you want one year of prosperity, grow grain.**
>
> **If you want ten years of prosperity, grow trees.**
>
> **If you want a lifetime of prosperity, grow people.**

Leaders grow people.

Recommended Actions	✓
◆ Instigate a programme to train everyone (especially yourself) in the practice of leadership.	❑
◆ Don't be afraid to ask people how they want things to be. Be prepared to be surprised by their answers.	❑
◆ Start work immediately on key issues that will change the business from what it is now to how you, and they, want it to be.	❑
◆ Be prepared to invest heavily in your key asset — your people.	❑
◆ Discuss and agree on the things you value. Draw up a list of these things and let everyone have a copy to serve as a constant reminder.	❑

Chapter 12

From Success to Failure: The Danger of Complacency

Success creates arrogance — arrogance creates complacency — complacency leads to failure.

I first heard the above phrase used by Tom Peters at one of his seminars. At the time it really made me think and because it's so true it has stuck with me ever since. He went on to say that the old saying "success breeds success" has been proved wrong by so many businesses that it perhaps should be rewritten as "success breeds failure".

He's right. There are numerous examples of how easily it can happen to organisations that achieve success through customer service. There are many companies that once had reputations for being leaders in service delivery and have been overtaken by competitors or are under such severe attack that they are likely soon to be beaten. A few examples of these are listed below.

Dixons and Comet

For many years Dixons and Comet have been the UK's top retail names for electrical and electronic goods like hi-fi equipment.

However, companies like Richer Sounds, which is now the UK's biggest hi-fi retailer, have used innovative ideas to show what can be done to raise standards and results. This has created more loyal customers and about ten times more turnover and profit per square foot of shop space.

Marks & Spencer

Marks & Spencer has for many years been thought of as the top service provider in UK clothing retailing with perhaps the best UK returned goods policy. However, I find an ever-increasing number of people who say that M&S nowadays is not as good as it used to be, or maybe that it doesn't seem to be as good as it used to be.

Yet the M&S policy hasn't substantially changed for the worse over the past few years. However, this is possibly the key reason for the change in people's perceptions. Whilst M&S has stood relatively still, other retailers have developed ways to provide even better service levels with superior returned goods policies. So by comparison, M&S now seems worse than it used to be. (Their financial performance now also seems to be reflecting this.)

IBM

There was a time when IBM was considered to be the world's top company for service in computers. It once even ran advertisements that suggested "nobody ever lost their job for ordering an IBM".

I'm sure it still provides excellent service, but it doesn't seem to have retained in people's minds that top slot for service. It appears now to have lost that position to new companies such as Dell, which have won numerous awards for being the world's best service provider in computer supplies and services.

Sainsbury's

For many years Sainsbury's has been considered the UK's best food retailer for service.

But now companies like Asda, Safeway and Tesco have driven up service and improved returned goods policies. They have really listened to their customers' needs and so found ways to provide improved service levels. This has resulted in substantial growth in their turnover and profits to the point that in 1996 Tesco overtook Sainsbury's as the UK's biggest food retailer and has stayed there ever since!

So yesterday's and today's winners can easily become tomorrow's losers. It's all too easy to find that the road that led to success can also lead to failure. It is, therefore, important to ensure that the success–arrogance–complacency–failure cycle is not allowed to run. The way to do this is not to allow the first step. Never let success create arrogance.

You will know that you are on that path to arrogance, or have gone beyond it and reached complacency, if you start hearing yourself or your colleagues using phrases like these.

The Verbal Signs of Corporate Arrogance and Complacency

"... we get by."

"... we have our own little niche."

"... we just keep going from day to day."

"... we are doing as well as anyone else."

"... we cannot see what more can be done."

"... but we are the world leaders in this field."

"... we are very successful so we must be doing things right."

"... we have nothing to learn from others, we do the teaching."

"... we'd take some convincing that we should be doing something else."

If phrases like these are common in your business they indicate that you are allowing arrogance and complacency to exist. The business can then slip into a slow drift and decline, where potential is unused and opportunities are missed. Failure is often then the result.

You therefore need to take the actions listed below (probably swiftly) to get yourself off this path. For those who don't think that they're on it, these same actions can also ensure that you never are.

Keep comparing yourself with other companies that have a reputation for delivering high service levels. This exercise is nowadays called benchmarking. It is where you study and compare yourself with other organisations in your industry and others to see how you compare against them, what you can learn from them and which of their best practices you can adopt in your business. It is a practice that should never end. It is also something that should engage the whole company. This is not an exercise just for managers and directors. It is an exercise for everyone.

Turn your whole workforce into a team of researchers, analysts and consultants. Get them all engaged in the activity of studying and learning from other companies' best practices. Teach them how to analyse what they see and then decide how to incorporate other people's best ideas in your business.

This constant striving for new and better ways of doing things will help to ensure that arrogance never takes root.

Instigate a continuous education programme for every employee. Don't ever allow any employee to think that they know enough. Help them to recognise that they can always get better and that you expect and will help them to do so. Make it core in your business that every employee is constantly involved in a personal, continuous improvement programme. Help them to find ways to improve themselves and their performance at work.

It's really important that you lead this by example. Let them see that you are constantly improving your own knowledge and skill, through reading, attending seminars, going on training courses, engaging in study visits to other companies and industries, etc. Your example will show that you consider it to be important enough to do yourself so they will then more readily accept how important it is for them.

Never let things settle. Don't let things get too organised and rigid. Once they get that way people tend to assume that they have reached the ultimate goal and therefore cannot get any better.

If you keep things moving, constantly changing and forever improving, people realise that there is no end to the path of continuous improvement. As many people are aware, it is a journey with no destination. There is *always* a way of improving *everything*. Every step that is taken moves you to a new position from which you have a new perspective which enables you to see fresh opportunities for the next improvements. So keep stirring the pot.

Bring in lots of outsiders. Keep getting fresh and objective views of the business and its different parts. Use external consultants, business schools, friends in other businesses, customers, suppliers, people from one department looking at or working in another, etc. All these new and objective views, with different perspectives, help you to see the way things are in a different way. New perspectives enable things to be seen that have previously been missed. This can open your eyes to new opportunities for improvements.

And don't ever let yourself or your colleagues believe that somebody who isn't trained in, say, engineering can't see a better way of engineering something. The best ideas often come from non-specialists. So bring in the amateurs and expect some great new ideas to result.

Set goals for creativity and innovation. If people know that they are expected to create new, better ideas, and they actually have targets and goals to achieve in this area, they are more likely to do it. You should have various rewards for these innovation programmes to encourage people to take part. These rewards could be financial but often the best ones are psychological. So don't just pay people for good ideas, praise them as well.

Some examples of organisations that do this are as follows:

3M Corporation

In the 3M Corporation all divisions are mandated to have at least 30 per cent of all the products that are sold at any one time to be products that were created within the previous five years. This requirement guarantees that there is a constant regeneration of old products and ideas and a constant creation of new ones so that the business is continually renewing itself.

Milliken

In Milliken, the textile manufacturer that won the European Quality Award in 1994, the average employee now generates 50 suggestions for product or process improvements per year. That is one per week per employee on average. I don't know what the current UK average is but I'm sure of one thing — it's a lot less!

But just imagine if every one of your employees was generating one idea per week to improve the business. What a difference that would surely make to your performance and results.

Have plenty of people around who disagree with you on lots of issues. If you surround yourself with enough people who refuse to be "YES" merchants, but will disagree with you, often and strongly, you will be forced to keep reassessing all that you are doing and so should keep finding ways to improve. This may be a lot more uncomfortable than having a "team" that always see things the same way as you, but it is essential if you want to avoid collective complacency through group thinking.

The following quotation expresses this idea really well:

> **"When two men in business always agree,
> one of them is unnecessary." — William Wrigley, Jr.**

These are just a few ideas of things that you can do to break the success-to-failure cycle. You can probably think of others that would suit your particular organisation. The key is to have lots of new thinking and a general attitude that no matter how good we may become . . . we can always get better!

If It Ain't Broke . . .

I can't end this chapter without referring to another phrase that is, I believe, a precursor to failure in today's markets. It's the phrase *"if it ain't broke — don't fix it"*. It was used a lot 10 or 20 years ago. What bothers me is that you still hear people using it today. I don't know where it came from (it sounds American), but I'd really like to know so that I can strangle whoever it was that first introduced it to standard business language. This seemingly innocuous little phrase has provided people with a plausible excuse for inaction or poor results. Too many businesspeople use it to hide laziness, or a fear of change, or to justify incompetent thinking, or simply as a feeble excuse for mediocre business performance.

The key flaw in the phrase is that it assumes a "competitor-free zone", that the competition will be just as stupid by adopting the same approach and not trying to continually improve things. But I've not yet found a market where that happens. (If you're in one then I guess you're lucky.) All the ones where I work tend to be fiercely competitive, with rivals keen to find anything that will out-manoeuvre a competitor and create competitive advantage.

So this phrase and the type of thinking it supports is really daft. And it's especially daft in the area of customer service, where the climate is getting ever more competitive and where things can *always* be improved. So if you wish to win a competitive battle for supremacy in customer service, you will need to find some endings that are very different to *"... don't fix it"*. Here, therefore, are a few that you may like to consider.

1. If it ain't broke — maybe you just aren't looking hard enough. I just don't believe that you can't find things to be improved. I've never yet found anything in customer service that can't. Continual improvement is an attitude of mind. If you believe that everything can always be improved you will find ways to do it. It's just a cop-out to give yourself the excuse for doing nothing by saying "that will do" or "it's OK".

So look harder. I'm sure that if you do you'll find lots of ways that things can be improved.

2. If it ain't broke — find something that is broke and improve that. If you've read number 1 above, and the warning about complacency, yet you're still convinced that there's nothing you can do to improve the item you're focusing on, then widen your search to find something else that you can improve. There will always be something, so when you've found it, get to work on that.

The Danger of Not Improving in Competitive Markets

Back in the 1960s the UK had a thriving motor, shipbuilding, electronics, motorcycle and other such industries. Now, just 30 years later, there is little or nothing left, or industries are dominated by foreign-owned businesses. There are obviously many things that caused this to happen but I'm positive that a major contributor was the "if it ain't broke..." attitudes that were rife then amongst the management and workers in those industries. They resisted or were slow to change and ultimately had their markets taken from them by foreign competitors, who found it easy to outpace them in product and service improvements.

So beware. Complacent attitudes can cost a lot more than a few customers. It has already cost the UK some important industries.

---

3. If it ain't broke — break it and start again. In many organisations or markets, the best way to create major improvements is to go back to the beginning and start again. This means using approaches like the following.

- If we didn't have what we've got now, and could begin again from scratch, what would we then create, that would be exactly what our customers want, that no competitor yet has? Once you've worked this out (you'll probably need to involve lots of customers in this to come up with the right answers), your goal should be to change, as quickly as you can, from where you are now to where this indicates you should be.

- If a new competitor came into our market, what would they have to do to get most of our customers to switch to them? This could be your worst nightmare. You should know your weaknesses so you should also know best what a smart competitor would have to do to win business from your customers. Once you've worked out what that would be, why don't you do it first, before a competitor does?

I hope these few ideas will make sure that you never use the *"if it ain't broke — don't fix it"* phrase. Also that if you hear colleagues using it, you will suggest to them that there might be a better approach which is much more likely to lead to sustained success.

Recommended Actions	✔
◆ Keep a constant eye out for the signs of arrogance or complacency. Let others know the signs so they can help spot them.	❑
◆ Decide on the tactics you can use to ward off the temptations to become arrogant or complacent.	❑
◆ Lead from the front and let others see that you are involving yourself fully in the agreed programme for continual improvement.	❑
◆ Strangle anyone who says "if it ain't broke" before they can get to "don't fix it"!	❑

Chapter 13

Bottom-line Benefits of Customer Care

You don't generally improve quality or service by reducing costs, but you do usually reduce costs (and increase profits) by improving quality or service.

I f you were like me, when you were younger and your parents were doing all they could to persuade you to eat what they believed was a good, healthy diet, you would sort out the things on your plate that you liked most and put them to one side to eat at or near the end of the meal as a kind of reward to yourself for eating the rest. Well, I guess I must still be a kid at heart because in the same manner I saved what I think are the best bits until the end.

The first "best bit" is that on top of all the other benefits that I have outlined so far, there are also the type of financial rewards for success that should delight you, your investors, shareholders and bankers.

Just as a short exercise, list on the following page ten companies you know of that deliver great service. (If you can't think of ten yourself, ask some colleagues for suggestions.) Try if you can to have businesses in different industries.

Now consider the list of companies you have made and compare their financial performance with their competitors. I've done this exercise lots of times and often find that we have created a list of the top financial performers across a range of industries.

10 Great Service Providers
1.
2.
3.
4.
5.
6.
7.
8.
9.
10.

There has been a lot of research into the differences in performance of companies in similar industries that offer superior levels of service compared to their competitors offering average or inferior levels of service. What has been found is that in most industries, the companies that are recognised as superior service providers make better use of their resources, attract and keep better people, and make more money than their competitors.

There are plenty of videos around on the topic of customer service. I guess I have seen most of them and I have two favourites. My overall favourite is one called "Famous for Service". It's by some fellow called Chris Daffy. (I had to get the plug in somewhere — details can be found at the end of this book.) My second favourite is called "Managing Customer Service" and it is produced by the BBC. A lot of the background material used in this video comes from Ron Zemke of Performance Research Associates. Ron provides details of his organisation's research findings into the noticeable differences between companies in similar businesses that are recognised as being high- or low-end service providers. His findings suggest that the key benefits experienced by top service providers are the following.

The Key Benefits
Improvements in morale (reducing staff costs)
Lower staff turnover (reducing recruitment costs)
Longer customer retention (can be up to 50% longer)
More repeat business (creating 20-40% lower selling costs)
More referrals (creating 20-40% lower promotional costs)
Higher prices (often a 7-12% premium)
Increased margins (usually 7-17% more profit)
A business to be proud of (this affects all stakeholders)

Improvements in Morale

It's not surprising that people would generally rather work in a company that has a reputation for providing high levels of customer service than in one that doesn't. It's usually more fun and less stressful in the high-service companies. This tends to create high morale amongst the workforce. More gets done when morale is high. Therefore, a high-morale workforce is more productive than one with low morale. So when morale is high you can get the same or better results with fewer people.

If you have fewer people producing more, you should be able to pay them more without adding to your labour costs. This in turn further increases the morale of those people. So the high-end service providers have fewer people, producing more and earning more, but with a lower overall labour cost than their competitors.

Lower Staff Turnover

People like working for companies where customers are treated like family or friends and morale and pay is good. They therefore tend to stay longer. This will then result in:

- Lower recruitment costs

- Lower new recruit training costs

- More people with skill and experience in the business.

Over the past few years I've hosted or attended four of the Manchester Business School study tours of Service Excellence, both in the UK and the US. During those tours I have visited and learned about over 100 best-in-class service providers. It's interesting to note that in almost every case, when questioned about their staff turnover, these organisations have been able to claim that they have the lowest that they are aware of in their particular industry.

Longer Customer Retention

Customers of suppliers that provide high service levels tend to stay customers longer. Research suggests that this can be up to 50 per cent longer. So whatever were the number of years you used in the calculation of potential customer Relationship Value, just consider what difference it would make to that value if customers stayed your customers for 50 per cent longer. You would have to increase your average Customer Relationship Value by 50 per cent!

More Repeat Business

Customers like buying from companies that provide them with high levels of service. They often look for ways of spending more with such suppliers and less with their competitors. It's therefore not unusual to find customers choosing such suppliers as single-source supply contractors and then trusting them to provide all of their requirements for whatever that supplier does.

There is evidence to show that it can cost five times as much to sell something to a new customer as it does to sell the same thing to an existing customer. (I've done this calculation in some businesses and found cases where the differential is ten times.) Therefore, if more business is coming from existing customers (through their choosing to spend more with you), this inevitably will reduce the overall selling costs. The research suggests that the overall selling costs can be 20–30 per cent less than for similar companies which are low-end service providers.

More Customer Referrals

We have already seen that delighted customers tell many other people about their delight with a particular supplier. They therefore act as unpaid salespeople and generate new business from referrals. New business generation is always a very expensive activity. If customers are undertaking a lot of this work for you, at no cost, it will obviously reduce the amount of money you have to spend on promotion. Research suggests that companies at the high-service end spend between 20–30 per cent less on promotional costs than those at the low end, yet still grow at the same or a better rate.

**Customers Pay to Become Top Sellers
in the Travel Industry**

I've done a lot of work in the UK travel and tourism industry. One of my favourite customers from this industry is one called Alternative Travel, which organises very special guided walking holidays throughout Europe.

The company is growing at over 20 per cent a year, yet it spends drastically less than the industry norm on advertising or promotional materials. The reason for its sustained growth, and the reason why I like working with them so much is that they treat their customers so well that they go back on holiday after holiday and they recommend it to family, friends and colleagues.

One of the things that they do which really impresses me is holding annual get-togethers around the country. Customers pay to come (yes, they pay to come) to these reunion events at which they meet the Alternative Travel staff, the people they were on holiday with, and other customers and discuss the wonderful times they had and their plans for future holidays.

These events are always fully booked and become a great selling vehicle as customers learn about the fantastic holidays others have had on different tours and so want to go on them themselves. In this way existing customers become the top sellers of the next year's holidays.

Higher Prices

There are many people who are prepared to pay a premium price for high service. In other words, they will pay more for a product from a company that wraps a high level of service around it than they will for the identical product from a supplier that doesn't. Here are a few examples of this:

- **A can of beans** — You can buy branded baked beans from many different retail outlets. Yet although the product is obviously exactly the same wherever you buy it, the price you pay can vary as much as 10 per cent. So why is it that people are prepared to pay so much more for an identical product? The only reason can be for the extra value that comes with it — the service in that store.

  It's also interesting to note that some of the biggest sellers of branded baked beans are the outlets that charge the highest prices. So there seem to be more people prepared to pay a higher price with great service than those prepared to pay the lower price if this means a poorer service.

- **Car insurance** — I buy my car insurance from my local independent insurance broker. I've been a customer of this fellow for about 26 years. I'm sure that if I wanted to phone around I could get a cheaper quote and save a few pounds. But I also get great service from him and his staff so I'm not bothered about the small premium I probably pay for it. By the way, he has thousands of customers so I can't be the only one who thinks this way.

- **Air travel** — In a recent article in the *Harvard Business Review*, Sir Colin Marshall commented on the fact that although BA uses the same aeroplanes as their competitors, fly from and to the same airports, in the same time, with roughly the same numbers of crew, they can command a 5 per cent premium on many of their flights. So people are prepared to pay a premium to fly with "the world's favourite airline" and enjoy their unique style of service.

- **Computers** — I like Dell computers. I've always found them to be good computers, at competitive prices, with great service. I could easily get cheaper ones that have exactly the same specification from other suppliers. But I know that with Dell I have no worries if anything goes wrong and that's something I, and thousands of people like me throughout the world, are prepared to pay that bit more for.

- **Precious metals** — This rule even applies with things like precious metals (gold, silver, platinum, titanium, etc.). I was doing a seminar for Noble Metals, which is part of the Johnson Matthey Group. When we got to the stage in the workshop where I talk about this I must admit I was expecting to find that there was no premium for service available in this industry. But here again I found that there were some customers who were prepared to pay more than the quoted price for gold or silver when it was supplied through a particular high-service part of the business.

- **Cars** — I've been working with Toyota GB for several years. During that time I've spoken to dozens of their dealers from the UK and elsewhere in Europe. They all have confirmed that if you can develop a service that gains you a reputation for being better, then customers will be prepared to pay you a higher price for a car than they would pay to a dealer who did not have such a reputation.

So in most industries, customers will pay more for a product when high service levels surround it. The research suggests that you can typically get a premium of between 7 and 12 per cent for being a high-end service provider.

Higher Margins

If a business is making all the savings detailed above, and is able to charge a premium price, this must have a substantial cumulative effect on the bottom line. The research backs this up and shows that high-end service providers are typically making 7 to 17 per cent more profit than the low-end service providers.

A Business to Be Proud of

There is understandably and justifiably a lot of pride found in companies that have a reputation for being high-end service providers. People are proud to work for the company, proud of the reputation it has and of their contribution to that reputation. This pride also spreads to suppliers and customers. Suppliers are proud to be associated with such a company and find it provides a good reference for them with their other customers. Customers also feel a sense of pride in doing business with a supplier that is renowned for delivering high service levels.

Evidence from the PIMS Database

The PIMS (Profit Impact of Marketing Strategy) database has been operating now for over 25 years. As its title suggests, it's a database of information that looks for the connections between business profitability and various marketing strategies. One interesting bit of their findings is the correlation between strategies based on delivering high customer service levels and the return on investment and return on sales it provides compared with companies with different strategies. The diagram below shows the findings.

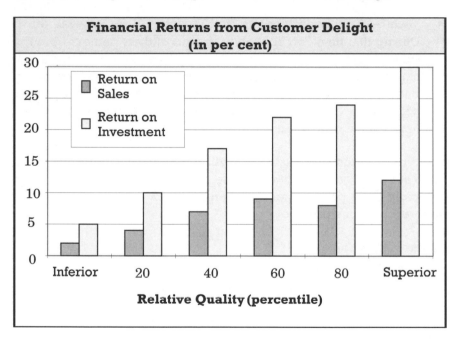

As can be seen, there is a definite correlation between profitability and service levels. The higher the service levels the better return on investment and the better profit on sales. So here is further evidence that there is money to be made from delivering high service levels.

Evidence from Harvard Business School

Michael Porter of Harvard Business School is considered to be one of the world's leading experts on competitive strategies. He suggests that there are three basic competitive strategies that a company could consider. They are simply explained as follows.

Strategy	Explanation	Examples
Cost supremacy	A cost supremacy strategy means that you try always to be the business with the best control of costs in your market. This usually results in you offering the lowest prices to customers.	Examples of well-known UK companies that have lowest cost strategies are Kwik Save (according to their adverts they still "stack it high and sell it cheap") and the Orange mobile phone company who claim to undercut all their competitors.
Focus	A focus strategy needs you to focus the business on a particular product or service or a specific market sector. The focus could be broad or narrow.	A good example of a narrow product focus is Tie Rack (they only sell neckware and associated items). A good broad, market focus example is Mothercare (everything for a mother and her baby).
Differentiation	This needs you to find a way to make your business noticeably different from your competitors. The best differentiation strategies usually involve a collection of many things that make a business different.	Good examples of companies with strong differentiation strategies are Marks & Spencer (try to name a national UK retailer that has a similar offer) and Body Shop (it's mainly soap and scent after all, but they surround it with other things that make the total package very different from anything else).

Some companies have found it possible to develop an overall strategy that combines two or more of the above.

First Direct Bank

First Direct Bank is a very successful part of Midland Bank. It was the first UK telephone banking service (differentiation). They also launched with lower service charges than conventional high street banks (cost supremacy).

Viking Direct

Viking Direct has captured a large share of the UK office supplies market in a relatively short time. They have monthly sales, free gifts and special offers (cost supremacy). They direct their promotional activities at small companies and targeted individuals in large companies (narrow focus). They sell by direct mail and telephone only, with monthly mailings, telephone sales lines open from 7.00am to 8.00pm, free next-day deliveries and a 100 per cent, no quibble, money-back guarantee on all their products for 12 months (differentiation).

Malmaison Hotels

Malmaison Hotels is the latest venture from Ken McCulloch, the founder of One Devonshire Gardens. In Malmaison he has combined a focus on the business traveller (focus), with very high service levels and great style (differentiation), and tremendous value for money (cost supremacy). (They've recently won the award for the best hotels in Europe for less than £100 per night room rate.) It's therefore no wonder that as each one opens it's almost immediately full and they are all maintaining extremely high occupancy levels.

Carphone Warehouse

Carphone Warehouse is one of the UK's most successful mobile phone retailers. They only sell mobile phones. They are one of a very few retailers that can offer their customers a connection to every single service provider they have on site, while-you-wait repairs at many of their shops and they have some of the best trained staff in the business (differentiation). They also provide the lowest prices (cost supremacy).

Direct Line Insurance

Direct Line Insurance is another good example. They charge less than their competitors (cost supremacy), they are only really interested in providing motor insurance for low-risk drivers (narrow focus) and they were the first to provide a direct, instant telephone service (differentiation).

John Lewis Partnership

John Lewis is an excellent retail example of a successful mixed strategy. They provide great service and many own-branded goods (differentiation). They stock everything (except food) for the home in one store (broad focus). They have a "never knowingly undersold on price" policy (cost supremacy).

In some markets it may be difficult, or perhaps unnecessary, to mix cost supremacy with differentiation. For example, if you have the lowest prices, you may not be making the profits to offer the best service. Conversely, if you are offering the best service, you probably don't need to have the lowest prices. However, the focus strategy will generally work well with either cost supremacy or differentiation.

There are two key requirements for a strategy if it is to provide competitive advantage:

Key Strategy Requirements for Competitive Advantage

1. The chosen strategy must be based on something(s) that the customer(s) will value. It's no use offering things that customers don't care about.

2. The chosen strategy must be based on something(s) that is/are sustainable as an advantage. There is little point building a strategy around something(s) that the competitors could quickly and easily copy.

It's interesting to note that some of the examples given above do not meet both these requirements.

- There are now a number of telephone banking services. It was easy to copy so this is no longer a source of differentiation for First Direct.

- Direct Line now has lots of competition for instant, telephone car insurance. It, too, was relatively easy to copy.

- Many other retailers now have a "never knowingly undersold" policy of some description so this is no longer a source of differentiation for John Lewis.

These examples therefore further confirm the point that the best differentiation strategies are often based on a number of things, rather than one single item that can easily be copied.

Research has shown that the choice of strategy can have a marked effect on a company's long-term financial performance. The graph below shows the findings.

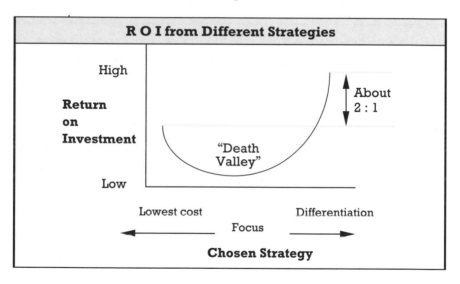

What this shows is that the best return on investment seems to come from differentiation strategies. There is also a reasonable return on investment from cost leadership strategies. However, the return from differentiation is about twice as good in the long term.

The diagram also clearly shows that the strategy to avoid is one that is neither one thing nor the other. This middle ground, where you aren't the cheapest or the best but about average is very risky. I often refer to it as "Death Valley". Just think back to when you last opened the Yellow Pages. Were you looking for an average supplier? I guess not. You were probably looking for something in particular. Maybe a good price, maybe great service, perhaps a different approach, but rarely do we look for something that's kind of average. So make sure you avoid the low-return quicksands of Death Valley — the average, middle ground. They can be very easy to slip into but very hard to get out of!

As we have learned throughout this book, one of the best differentiation strategies is to be recognised as a top service provider. This work by Michael Porter suggests that this is also a strategy that is likely to lead to a top return on capital (and effort, emotion, etc.) invested. So here we have yet more sound evidence of the good sense in this type of policy.

What Does It All Mean?

All this research indicates that if you want the best return on your investments in a business, if you want to get the maximum possible results from your resources, you should focus on delivering levels of service that your customers recognise as being superior to those of your competitors. My Daffy's Law, therefore, is:

> **The bottom line is that delivering exceptional levels of customer service is good for your bottom line!**

Recommended Actions	✔
◆ List the potential benefits to your business of getting your service strategy right.	❑
◆ Do your own investigations and research to be sure of your facts.	❑
◆ Broadcast your findings throughout the business.	❑
◆ Set up a monitoring system to measure and report on the actual benefits you are experiencing.	❑

Chapter 14

From Words to Action

"The problem in my life and other people's lives is not the absence of knowing what to do, but the absence of doing it." — Peter Drucker

"I have not the shadow of a doubt that any man or woman can achieve what I have, if he or she would make the same effort and cultivate the same hope and faith. What is faith worth if it is not translated into actions?" — Mahatma Gandhi

In an article about the success of Federal Express, its CEO Fred Smith explains, "There is no secret to whatever success Federal Express has enjoyed. What we do is in all the business books. Our secret, if there is one, is just doing what they say."

This simple message from Fred Smith gets us to the essence of whether you can make a difference. Reading books like this is all well and good but it doesn't change anything. You have to do something about what you have read — and that's easier said (or written) than done.

If you try to do something there will be resistance against the changes you are trying to make. That resistance can be very strong.

People's Natural Resistance to Change

I believe it was Machiavelli who first observed that when you try to change things you may get weak support from those people who believe that they could benefit from the way things might become, but you will get strong resistance from those people who are benefiting from the way things are now.

Most businesses have a kind of auto-immune system that is triggered when anything new or unusual comes along. People know that many of the new initiatives that are imposed on them by management are simply fads that will soon pass. They therefore often adapt the *"appear to agree and look as though we're trying to make it work, it will then soon go away and we can get back to normal"* technique.

In many instances they are right to adopt this attitude because many managers do seem to adopt a "flavour of the month" approach to business initiatives. But if you're serious about this you will have to find a way to help them realise that this is here to stay. Forever! Or at least as long as the business exists. This leads me to what I think is another of the "best bits".

Grand Slam vs. Wild Fire

The type of approach you adopt to implement these ideas can have a massive effect on their success. In my experience, a "wild fire" approach is much better than a "grand slam".

The grand slam approach is based on trying to achieve success in one big swoop. This generally fails. It often starts with the senior management team going away for a few days to create the new grand strategy. There's nothing wrong with that but there's often a lot wrong with what follows. What typically follows is that the management, having decided upon the new master plan, keep it a closely guarded secret until they are ready to launch it, with every little detail prepared. It is then generally launched at a mass meeting at which everyone is "sold" the new vision and expected to accept it immediately and go along with any changes that it may entail.

As I said earlier, this generally fails. In fact, research has shown that over 80 per cent of the programmes conceived and launched in this manner fail to achieve even half of their original goals.

But why is this, you may well ask? The answer, I think, lies in a quotation from my favourite book on strategy. The book is called *The Grand Strategist* and it's written by Mike Davidson. The quotation is:

"Grade A execution of a Grade B plan always beats Grade B execution of a Grade A plan."

The grand slam approach may create a Grade A plan, but it usually also creates Grade B execution. Grade A execution needs the full commitment of those who will have the biggest influence on it — the front-line staff. They will never be fully committed to a plan that they had no input into. To get Grade A execution, therefore, you need to involve everyone in the creation of the plan who will be responsible for its implementation. "But this will result in a Grade B plan," you may say. Well it might, but my experience suggests that it will not. Yet even if it does, you will have Grade A execution, so who cares?

This is why the wild fire approach is so much more successful than the grand slam. It may begin in the same way, with the senior management team having their few days away to thrash out the general objectives, but then it changes substantially from the grand slam. The next stage of the wild fire is to let in on the general plan straightaway everyone who will be involved in the implementation. You tell them about the outline objectives but admit that you will need some help to hone it into shape and to work out the best approach. You then get as many people as possible working on different elements of the plan. Form them into PTA groupings for this (see Chapter 10). Some of them will be successful, others may not. That doesn't matter. There's no need to worry about the failures. Concentrating on the successes is what's important. You then simply fan the flames of those that succeed and spread them to other departments and teams so that the success gradually spreads throughout the whole organisation.

This approach provides lots of positive examples that show what can be achieved and encourages others to do the same. It also tends to reverse the odds and provide about 80 per cent success. So go out and light those fires now.

Then There is SID

Another enemy of success is SID. This is not the SID that tempted us to buy British Gas shares in the 1980s. This SID is one that can destroy a person's self-image and so ensure that they never achieve what they are truly capable of.

The SID I'm referring to is the one where SID stands for:

Self-
Imposed
Doubt

This can become an epidemic if it's allowed to cultivate itself in a workforce. It begins with people saying and believing things like the following phrases:

"I can't make a difference."

"Things won't change."

"Nobody will notice."

"It doesn't matter."

"No one cares."

I call this "mental pollution", yet we've all done it or heard it. It's as if we have someone sitting on our shoulder whispering in our ear the things we know are wrong but we like to hear because they give us an excuse for failing, or perhaps not even trying.

When I'm working with groups of people I get them to create a mental picture of the person sitting on their shoulder. When I then ask what he or she looks like, they often admit that it looks like themselves. (This is not surprising because it's our own voice we're hearing.) I then show them a picture of what I want them to think of when they hear this voice. A picture like this:

This awful creature is what you should imagine when you hear that voice. It's not friendly advice. It's mental pollution, from a fiend within, that must be ignored.

The common thing about this pollution is that if it's left unchecked it can spread, like a cancer, and infect a whole workforce. People who are affected don't like to be alone so they do their best to infect the other people around them. So if you hear any signs of SID among your colleagues you should do something about it immediately. Explain how to overcome the problem(s), remove the cause(s) of the doubt and provide people with the will and the confidence to succeed.

There's Also MADness

MADness is the management-created version of SID. In this strain of the disease, the pollution comes from the managers. The MAD in MADness stands for:

> **M**anagement-
>
> **A**ffirmed
>
> **D**oubt

This occurs when managers believe and broadcast phrases like these:

> *"We never notice your good ideas."*
>
> *"It doesn't matter what you do."*
>
> *"You can't make a difference."*
>
> *"We won't change things."*
>
> *"We don't care anyway."*

This, too, is a pollutant that can quickly infect a whole workforce. It can turn perfectly reasonable and sensible people into uncooperative antagonists. So never allow any managers or supervisors to practise MADness. If it ever threatens to creep into your premises seek it out and remove it.

This all suggests that we need an overall strategy that will involve everyone in some way and help them to create and then implement a successful plan. The best way I know of doing this is as follows.

Getting Started

When I'm doing open or in-company seminars, the most common question that people ask me is:

> *"This all sounds OK, Chris, but how do we get*
> *something like this started?"*

That's a very good question. It's relatively easy to agree with the logic and general principle of doing things the way I have suggested throughout this book. It's obviously a very different and much more difficult thing to turn it into changes in the day-to-day activities of people throughout a company. I've tried to help this process along by providing checklists at the end of each chapter that suggest things you could do to create actions around the ideas it contains. However, these do not provide an overview of how this should all fit together.

This section is therefore that overview. It is a plan of action, linked to ideas throughout the book, that will get you started on a programme that has the best chance of success.

The Step-by-Step Approach

The order in which things are done is critical. This is because some things have to be in place before others will work. It is also because the elements are interdependent and so work much better together than in isolation. It is therefore important to have a phased, step-by-step approach, which will ensure that everyone moves at the same pace, in harmony, aiming for the same goals.

As we learned in the previous section, we also need an approach or plan that will avoid a grand slam and stimulate a wild fire-type of system. The diagram on the following page shows how this can be achieved in a structured way. As can be seen, there are four key phases or stages to achieving exceptional customer service, with the third phase in two parts.

Phase One: Great Leadership (Showing the Best Way Forward)

The first phase in creating a programme that will succeed is to provide great leadership (ordinary leadership is just not good enough). We've covered this in some detail in Chapter 11 but I will comment on the five elements mentioned in the diagram above.

Strategic Commitment

Staff always know when something is the latest fad of a leader. So if customer service is to be more than this it must be seen as part of the core strategy of the business, something that will always be there, no matter what the market conditions. Something that is non-negotiable. And, above all, something upon which the success of the business depends.

The Key Elements of World Class Service

> **GREAT LEADERSHIP**
> (Showing the best way forward)
>
> • Strategic commitment
> • Uniting vision
> • Shared values
> • Continual communication
> • Alignment programmes
>
> Creates common goals and direction

> **SERVICE CULTURE**
> (Treating colleagues like customers)
>
> • Right people
> • Skilled for service
> • Enabling structure
> • Systems that serve
> • Trusted people
>
> Creates employee loyalty and teamwork

> **CUSTOMER CONNECTION**
> (Treating customers like colleagues)
>
> • +1s and WOWs
> • Dazzling recovery
> • Genuine partnering
> • Manage perceptions
>
> Creates customer loyalty and referrals

> **CONTINUOUS IMPROVEMENT**
> (Never becoming complacent)
>
> • Eliminate waste
> • Simplify processes
> • Constant feedback
> • Benchmark continually
>
> Creates an ever-improving environment

> **WINNING PACE**
> (Out-pacing all competitors)
>
> • Whole company involvement
> • Regular ideas sessions
> • Rewarding the right things
>
> Creates a virtuous cycle

Uniting Vision

"All things are created twice." — Stephen Covey

As you will know by now, I'm a strong believer in the personal effectiveness ideas of Stephen Covey, the author of the book *The Seven Habits of Highly Effective People*. One of these habits is to "begin with the end in mind".

In the context of this plan, the end that needs to be in mind at the beginning is the *vision* for the business. People need to have a clear vision of the type of organisations they are working to create. This vision may be created by the leader or by the staff. That doesn't matter. What matters is that it should be a view of the future that is different from and better than the present.

Vision in the Fish and Chips Business

An excellent example of a business leader who has created a strong vision is John Barnes, the Chairman of Harry Ramsden's plc, the world famous fish and chip restaurants. When he bought the Harry Ramsden's business, John recognised that it had a tremendous reputation and heritage but had lost its way. His vision for the business was based on re-establishing the values that had made it the great business it was in the past, and then building them into the great business he knew it could become again in the future.

He therefore spent the first few months getting to know the business and its staff. He got employee groups together, especially those who remembered the way things used to be, to learn about the best things that were done when "old Harry" was around. He got customer groups together to hear their views. He even found Harry Ramsden Jr., the son of the founder, and got him to work with the business to help re-establish the best of the good old ways.

He then threw out all the existing fryers and had new ones made to the same specifications that were used by Harry. He was determined to be No. 1 in the UK for fish and chips, customer-driven and employee-led.

John's vision has transformed the business. His staff are now proud to be part of it. (You can see and feel this when you're there.) He says, "we now have a business full of driven people, who are driving us".

The second phase of his vision is now underway with expansion into new distribution channels and locations throughout the world. In fact, you can now get Harry Ramsden's fish and chips from the frozen food cabinet in your local supermarket, in motorway service areas and in their own restaurants throughout the UK and Ireland, and now even when you're visiting Hong Kong.

The Sony Vision

We will create products that become pervasive around the world. We will be the first Japanese company to go into the US market and distribute directly. We will succeed with innovations that US companies have so far failed at — such as the transistor radio. Fifty years from now, our brand name will be as well known as any in the world and will signify innovation and quality that rival the most innovative companies anywhere. "Made in Japan" will mean something fine, not something shoddy.

Shared Values

Having established the ultimate goal (the vision), like John Barnes or Sony, you need to discuss and agree your *core values*. These are definitions of, or statements about, the ways you and your colleagues will work together to achieve the goal(s) in the vision. These values differ from organisation to organisation but often encompass such key areas as:

Core Value Areas

- Customer satisfaction
- Environment/community
- Growth
- Image/reputation
- Innovation/creativity
- Market share
- People policies
- Products/services
- Profitability

These values should then become the guiding principles by which the business is operated. They are the things against which all actions and decisions, taken throughout the organisation, should be tested. If an action or decision matches the values, then the right things are being done. If it doesn't then either the action, the decision, or the value is wrong and one will have to change. (What needs to change is generally the action or decision. The right values rarely need any change and should last for many years.)

An excellent example of such values are the following "guiding principles" from Richard Branson for the staff of Virgin Atlantic.

Richard's Guiding Principles

We must meet the passenger on his or her own terms. They are individuals and require different things.

As a rule we should be friendly and informal but always take account of what the individual wants.

Other airline staff are hidebound by rules. We should give ours guidelines and encourage them to solve a passenger's problem.

First to know is best to deal with.

The only way to make our staff trustworthy is to trust them. We must begin to trust people to use their judgement to resolve problems whilst being mindful of any cost to the company.

Mistakes are inevitable; dissatisfied customers are not.

Our staff should be happy, cheerful, smiling, friendly and enjoying their job. It is a manager's job to motivate the staff and create this atmosphere. Their role is to support their people in doing their best for the passenger. Money is not the answer, good leadership is.

We must give our staff responsibility and authority. Responsibility is the obligation to act, not just accept the blame. Authority is the resources to deal with the situation.

We want our staff to bring their personalities to work and put them into their job. Bring individuality, freshness and care to their work.

We need our staff to be comfortable with the exceptions, to think outside the framework and do what is right for the passenger, not just "the job".

We want our staff to anticipate a passenger's problem. Think beyond the immediate, recognise the implications of their actions.

The only purpose in having front-line positions is if the passenger experiences service excellence. Otherwise why not use machines?

We have two competitive advantages — product and service. We invest much money and time in keeping our product different, fun, interesting and high quality. We must now invest in the same way for our service.

We must communicate with our staff. If we change things we must tell them and tell them why.

We must listen to what our staff have to say and act on it. If we can't do it we must say why not.

We must improve in line with our culture, not at the expense of it.

We must never design what we do by assuming the worst in people.

Another example comes from the corporate clothing company De Baer. My son Nick worked for them for a year or so and I was impressed by their document stating their core principles.

De Baer Corporate Clothing Principles

De Baer is a company where there is little supervision of individual staff members. It is up to you to ensure that you undertake your role in a professional manner and to the corporate standards set out below.

The company is successful by being team-orientated, proactive and service driven. It is important that we all understand this philosophy and that the needs of our clients are paramount.

"It is not my job" should never be uttered in this company. It is the responsibility of everybody to 'muck in' and help, ensuring we produce the best possible results for ourselves and our clients.

Considerations of the implications of individual events is essential. It is vital that we all look further than the obvious impact, as often there are implications further than the immediate. It is important that the thought process of "this means that . . ." is considered and other staff are warned about potential problems or time delays.

Think about your fellow workers. Take a little time to work with them and use their best abilities.

If there is a problem, and you can't fix it, tell someone or ask for help. Do not pretend it will go away — it won't. The company is based on a "no blame" culture. If something goes wrong we will look for the reason why we, as a company, failed and we will aim to rectify the root cause. This is much more positive and stronger than searching for someone to blame.

We must have a "can do" attitude. Our market is full of old traditionalists who believe in "it's always been done this way". This is not our philosophy.

When you combine vision and values you have a powerful guide for all staff to follow. Someone once said that it means you can go on holiday without having to keep phoning the office. That's because the real leader (the vision and values) is still there when you're away.

The following example from Sewell Motor Company is an excellent example of the two combined. Reading this helps you realise how Carl Sewell has built his business to be one of the biggest and most successful car dealerships in America.

Sewell Motor Company

Mission

We will provide the best vehicle sales and service experience for our customers. We will do this in a way that will foster the continuous improvement of our people and our company.

We will be a top-performing, thoroughly professional and genuinely caring organisation in all that we do.

Beliefs and Values

We will be at the top when measured against appropriate business standards of performance in every function, in every department, in every dealership.

We will pursue quality and profitability with the aim to stay in business and provide jobs for our associates.

The development of our people is essential to our growth and future success. We will provide training and education to encourage the long-term employment and professional advancement of all associates.

We will strive for constant improvement and innovation in all that we do.

We will earn and re-earn the goodwill, trust and confidence of our customers and colleagues every day.

The highest ethical standards will guide everything we do.

Our suppliers are important to our success. We will establish long-term relationships with suppliers whose values and quality are consistent with ours.

Continual Communication

It's no good having a vision and values if the only people who know about them are the directors and perhaps the senior managers. There should be some means of communicating them to everyone in the organisation.

Visions Are for Everyone

I remember working on one of those senior team "away days" with the board of a UK plc. During the session about vision and values one of the directors said, "I don't see the point of all this, Chris. It doesn't make a jot of difference to how I perform at work". He was right. All this may not make a jot of difference to how a director performs (although I believe it really should). The point is it's not done for the directors. It's done for all the other people in the business who need a reason for coming to work that's a bit better than just to earn a living. Visions and values are for everyone, not just for the directors.

You must therefore find ways to *communicate* your vision and values to everyone and also to provide them with a constant stream of reminders so they cannot be forgotten or ignored. In *The Grand Strategist*, Mike Davidson calls this "managing the mission". Some ways you could do this are:

- Build a session about vision and values into every new recruit's induction training

- Refer to vision and values in memos and newsletters

- Find ways to reward people for doing things that reinforce the vision and values

- Issue memo cards that carry the vision and values

- Build vision and value elements into your appraisal system

- Have posters about vision and values around the workplace

- Find and use opportunities to demonstrate your own commitment to the vision and values through the things you do.

These are just a few ideas you could use. If you try, you should be able to think of many more that would be more suited to your particular business.

Alignment Programmes

Great leaders know that they are best able to demonstrate that they are totally committed to the vision and values of the business through the way they act. I've heard this described as "walking the talk". In other words, the things they do perfectly aligning with the things they say. In fact, they are likely to go out of their way to find things they can do that demonstrate their belief in, and commitment to, their vision and values. Employees are always more influenced by what their leaders do than what they say, so this alignment of actions with words is the way in which leaders show their commitment and employees know that they mean it. There is then a need to spread this alignment process throughout the organisation. People must know that, whenever they come across actions or decisions that do not align with the stated vision and values, something is wrong. They should then question, challenge and change things until an alignment occurs.

The result of these leadership inputs is common goals and direction for the business, and agreed ways of working to achieve them. I once heard Professor John Murphy, of Manchester Business School, describe this output as "a convergence of endeavours."

That's a great phrase. It creates for me a picture of a business where everyone's endeavours come together to achieve agreed, worthwhile goals. And once this has been created, it can then be applied to the five elements in phase 2.

Phase Two: Service Culture (Treating Colleagues Like Customers)

We've already considered that for employees to give great service to external customers, they first have to receive equally great service from their managers and their colleagues — the former being impossible without the latter. This is pretty basic stuff, but it is certainly not the norm so you may need to work at it.

This next phase is therefore all about the internal issues that create a service culture. These issues ensure that employees are provided with a positive example and are treated in exactly the same way that they would be expected to treat the company's best customer. The key inputs to this phase are recruitment, training, structure, systems and trust.

Right People

You will remember the American Express advertisement showing Ken McCulloch of One Devonshire Gardens, in which he is quoted as saying:

"Good service isn't a mystery. Employ nice people."

That's the simplest way I know of expressing the point about recruiting the right people. *Recruitment* becomes strategy if you decide that service must be a differentiator. So if you choose a strategy that involves the delivery of exceptional levels of customer service, you will have to attract and keep the kind of people who genuinely want to give exceptional levels of customer service . . . and you must also be prepared to get rid of any who don't.

Skilled for Service

Training is the next element of this phase. For people to be committed to an organisation they first need to know that the organisation has a commitment to them. One way to demonstrate this commitment is through making worthwhile investments in the employees. The most worthwhile investment that can be made for employees is training.

I find it amazing that when companies find themselves with problems, one of the first things they often do is cut the training budgets. Can you imagine a sports or military team leader doing the same thing?

> *"Listen folks ... we're losing too often to our competitors at present so what we are going to do is cut training and so stop doing the very thing we need to do to help us improve and start winning again."*

What a crazy scenario. You wouldn't stay long in the job of a sports team manager or military leader with that approach. Yet it's common in business. So make sure that you're one of the uncommon businesses that provides continuous training, for all employees, and even more of it when times are hard.

Enabling Structure

The way a company is structured will have a major impact on whether or not high service delivery is possible. It can either enable or disable its delivery. There has to be an organisational *structure* with the fewest possible layers to enable effective communications and efficient working. We have already seen an example of the three-layer structures in Chapter 4.

Another approach to structure is to consider inverting the normal hierarchical pyramid. The diagram on the following page illustrates this.

As this diagram shows, the typical structure for a business is for the boss to be at the top of the chart. The staff, represented by the arrows, all then face towards their immediate boss, waiting for instructions. Customers fit on the chart at the bottom. In an organisation like this, the energy flows in the direction of the arrows, away from the customers and towards the bosses. This is obviously no good for high service.

In the second diagram the pyramid is inverted. Now the customers are at the top. The staff face customers with each successive layer responding to the needs of the one above it. The boss is at the bottom, making sure it all works as planned. In this structure the energy flows the other way, towards the customers. This is the kind of structure that promotes the best kind of service delivery.

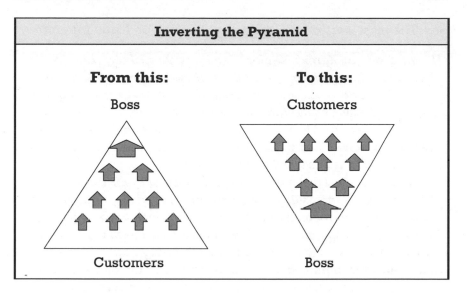

Inverting the Pyramid

From this: **To this:**

Boss Customers

Customers Boss

Systems that Serve

The next element of this phase is the creation of efficient, customer-friendly *systems*. It is no good expecting staff to give great service to customers if the systems they need to support them are not capable of doing so. We covered this in detail in Chapter 10.

Trusted People

The word empowerment is used a lot nowadays in management circles. A lot of managers seem to think that you give things to employees to create empowerment. But you don't, what you do is take things away. You take away things like unnecessary reporting, silly systems, unproductive meetings, top-heavy layers of supervision, etc. The important thing to remember is that front-line people always have had, and always will have, the greatest power to influence customer views of any business. They therefore already have the power. Once that is realised the goal becomes finding ways to ensure that they use to good effect the empowerment they have.

Stupid Sign-offs

I heard one of Xerox's senior managers describing some of the issues they had to face during the critical turnaround they had in the 1990s. One of these issues was that of managers insisting on signing off any expenditure over a certain amount. On face value it seemed reasonable, for budget control reasons, for this to happen. But it slowed many systems down and created a great deal of paperwork, so it was worthy of challenge.

It was decided that it was obviously necessary for the system to be there if, as a result of the sign-off procedure, a substantial number of the recommendations or decisions made by junior people had to be challenged or changed by the managers. This would mean that wrong decisions were being made. However, if very few were being challenged or changed then the system was adding cost but obviously no value and should be scrapped.

When the investigation was completed it was found that the actual number of decisions or recommendations that were challenged or changed was . . . LESS THAN 0.5%. This showed that there was little value at all being added by this process and it was therefore decided that it should be scrapped. This decision was understandably met with much resistance from the managers who previously had the sign-off authority. They argued that costs would go out of control without it. The system was scrapped anyway. Costs stayed the same as they were before. (Except for the substantial reduction in the cost of running the unnecessary sign-off system!)

There are many companies that are prepared to provide levels of freedom for employees that are way beyond mere empowerment. In the best companies, front-line employees are *totally trusted*. But this can seem like an impossible goal for many organisations. It is therefore wonderful to witness the tremendously high degree of trust given to front-line employees in the best service companies. The following are great examples of this, where front-line employees are expected and trusted just to get on with the jobs and decide for themselves what needs to be done.

Total Trust at TNT

A good example of trust is shown at the TNT Hub in Atherstone. TNT is the parcel delivery service that provides guaranteed, next-day delivery times. They have a fellow who is responsible for ensuring that the team has the vehicles they need, where and when they need them, in order to make the deliveries, on time, that have been promised to customers. He explains that, "The deliveries must get there as promised. So if a truck breaks down, I get another. If that breaks down I find another one. And if necessary, I get an aeroplane!"

He's apparently done so, too. He doesn't need to ask permission from anyone. He knows that the deliveries must be made on time. So if he thinks a plane is needed, he simply gets one . . . that's trust.

Total Trust at Ritz Carlton

The Ritz Carlton hotel chain is another great example of trusted employees. Every employee, from the general manager to a porter, waiter or chambermaid, is trained and expected to be able to deal with customer complaints. They also all have the same budget authority when doing so. That authority is $2,000 per complaint.

That's a large amount that is hardly ever used, but the important thing is that every employee knows they don't have to ask permission. They are trusted to use it how and when they think fit.

Total Trust at Alternative Travel

Alternative Travel Group was founded in 1979 on principles of conservation and sustainable tourism. It organises holidays based around journeys on foot or bicycle along continuous routes through the most exciting and beautiful parts of Europe. A guide who is a highly skilled and totally trusted employee leads each tour. These guides are fully trained and expected to be able to deal with any problems or customer complaints during a tour. They have the authority to spend up to £1,000, on the spot, to deal with any problem or complaint.

> *This is obviously a very large amount, which is hardly ever used, but it demonstrates the trust Christopher Whinney, the company's founder, has in the skill and judgement of these front-line people.*
>
> *The company has become famous for the service which these people provide and it's no wonder that over 90% of their bookings each year come from repeat customers and personal recommendations.*

The output or result from this phase is long-term employee loyalty and teamwork. Many businesses seem to think that teamwork is an input. It's not, it's the result of the kind of inputs described in this phase — inputs that create a true team of people, who work together, in harmony, to achieve agreed, worthwhile goals. When teamwork has been created in the organisation, this way of working can then be used to give the maximum effect to the activities in the two parts of phase 3.

Phase Three (a): Customer Connection (Treating Customers Like Colleagues)

The elements in this phase naturally follow when a business has the preceding two phases in place and working. It is obviously much easier to give good service to your external customers when you know that doing so is key to the company's success, and therefore your own success, and that your colleagues will be working with you to help you do it.

+1s and WOWs

These will be natural things for staff to do now that you have the right environment in which they can do them. Their colleagues will notice and praise them for it. They will be recognised by their managers for it. This will make them rightly proud of their customer service achievements. How +1s and WOWs are created was covered in Chapter 6.

Dazzling Recovery

This, too, is natural in the environment you now have. The front-line people will have an empathy with their customers and will therefore be keen to deal effectively with all problems. How this is done was also covered in Chapter 6.

Genuine Partnering

The *partnership* approach to customers (and suppliers) is another vital element of this phase. Customers must be treated as though they are part of the business, rather than outsiders. This has been detailed in Chapters 4, 5 and 8.

Managing Perceptions

Remember that perception and reality can differ so it will be important to manage your customers' perceptions of your service delivery. How this is done was explained in Chapter 7.

The output or result from this phase is tremendous loyalty from customers. It undoubtedly creates the kind of customers who Ken Blanchard describes as Raving Fans of an organisation — the kind of customers that will keep coming back for more and will generate lots of leads and referrals for new customers.

Phase Three (b): Continuous Improvement (Never Becoming Complacent)

Eliminating Waste

No sensible employee wants to be wasteful at work. But many are not clear about what constitutes waste. It's therefore important to provide an easily understood definition of waste. One of the best I've seen was the following.

> **It is our goal to provide the best possible value for our customers.**
>
> **Waste is therefore anything that does not add value for customers.**

This was successful in that people felt it was worth doing. One reason is that it provided a positive goal to aim for. This particular one may not be right for your organisation but something along these lines should help you to keep waste to a minimum.

One thing you could do to systemise waste reduction is to involve every employee, in just the same way as we did for service improvement ideas. As well as seeing the best ways to improve service with +1s, most employees will also regularly see opportunities for cost savings. You could also use the concept of –1s to provide an opportunity for them to put these ideas into practice. –1s are things that will reduce costs for the business, without reducing service to the customers. I call them −1s because the idea is to find things that will save at least $1.00 a day. This may not seem much, but if all employees are coming up with ideas for these savings, every month, they quickly add up.

As with the +1s, −1s should meet a criteria, as follows:

- They must be simple to do

- They must be sustainable

- They must not reduce service to customers.

This −1s concept also works well with staff because it's generally easy to think up lots of ways to save just $1.00 a day. Yet I'm sure you will realise that in considering ways to save $1.00 a day, they will also generate many ideas that can save a great deal more.

Simplifying Processes

Many organisations have found that process mapping and business process re-engineering are good ways to achieve the right kind of customer-friendly systems.

Most organisations are organised into functional departments like sales, accounts, administration, production, etc. Yet for a customer to receive a service a process has to take place that will probably have some input from many of these functional departments. The following diagram shows this clearly:

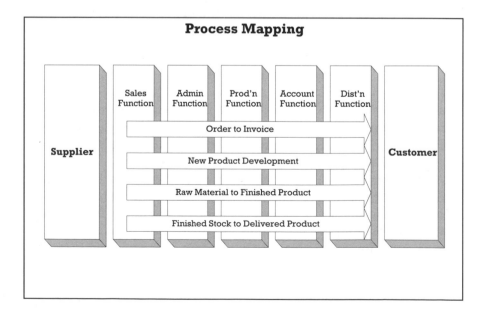

I have instigated many checks into the processes used by my customers and found some really interesting and often daft things, like these three examples:

- One company could make the product they sold in 20 minutes, but found it took three days to raise the delivery note.

- Another discovered that 14 people, in five departments, were involved in the paper flow from an order being received through to an invoice being raised.

- I even had one that found it was impossible to raise an invoice, in a business with over 1,000 employees, if one particular person was off sick or on holiday.

These are just three examples of the kind of things that are often found if you do some process mapping. Process mapping is done by creating a chart, similar to the one below, and then mapping the stages that a piece of paper must undergo or the procedures that are necessary to get something made or to happen in the organisation.

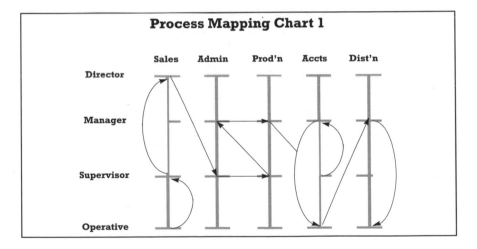

The above process map illustrates just five business functions or departments: sales, administration, production, accounts and distribution. Many organisations have many more than this. It also shows just four levels of authority in the business: Director, Manager, Supervisor and Operative. Again, many businesses have more than that.

However, even with this limited number of functions and authority levels the arrows show how easy it can be for a slow and complicated process to be used to process something. (The illustration shown could be the process of paper from an order to a delivery note.)

Having produced a map like this, and when you've got over the shock it usually creates, you can then begin to untangle the process and create a slicker system. I always find it's best to begin with the goal. For example:

> *"We want this to take no more than one hour*
> *and involve no more than three people."*

You can then work back from this goal to achieve the desired result. PTA groups are a great way of getting this going. Get these groups to understand fully the various processes in your business, decide which of them are key to customer service, look for bottlenecks or unnecessarily complicated systems and create ways to simplify and speed them up.

If your PTA groups were successful they would take the kind of mess from the process map above and make it look more like the much more straightforward and logical process shown below:

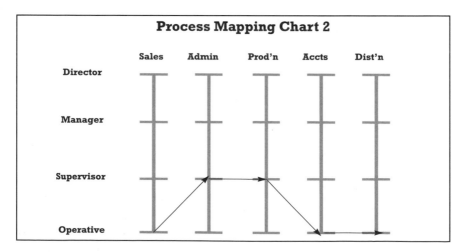

Process Re-engineering in
the National Health Service

An excellent example of how systems have been changed to improve service is the Leicester Royal Infirmary. It has created a process re-engineering team of about 40 people. This team is made up of a few re-engineering experts who work with clinical and hospital management specialists recruited to the team from most of the hospital's departments. The team's goal is to find ways to improve quality, efficiency and customer service.

This team has achieved many remarkable results. For example, in one area of women's health they have completely re-engineered the process. It used to take an average of 79 hours of the patient's time, with 90 minutes of waiting, seeing 16 different people and about 650 yards of walking around the hospital. It now takes just 36 minutes of the patient's time, with only eight minutes of waiting, three people to see and 90 yards of walking. Their new centre is now considered to be the best in Europe. This is just one example, from over 100 similar projects, that they have completed or are currently working on.

Constant Feedback

Feedback will ensure that the customers' views are brought into the business and used to trigger and drive changes and improvements. We covered this in detail in Chapter 8.

Benchmarking Continuously

You need to be continuously looking for best practices and seeing what you can learn from them. This will prevent you from getting complacent. We covered how you can do this in Chapter 12.

Phase Four: Winning Pace (Outpacing All Competitors)

Some experiences awhile ago made me realise the need not just for continual improvement, but for improvement at a pace that outstrips all competitors.

One was being invited as a guest speaker at conferences for different companies that were competitors in the same market. In a number of these instances, the companies had all chosen the same strategy, which was to become *the* business in their industry or market sector that was viewed by customers as being the *one* that is "*differentiated through service*". Yet as they were competing for the same customers, only one of them was likely to succeed in being the organisation so perceived. I therefore gave a lot of thought to the question of what it might be that would determine which one will be successful.

I was helped to find what I believe to be the right answer to this question when I came across the following quotation from Tom Peters.

"Good quality is a stupid idea. The only thing that counts is your quality getting better at a more rapid rate than your principal competitors".

Although Tom was commenting on quality, this principle obviously applies equally well to customer service. So the only way any company in an industry or market sector can become (or remain) the one that is seen by customers as differentiated through service is for it to have a rate of service improvement that outpaces all its competitors. If this pace of improvement can be achieved, it doesn't matter where the business starts from (ahead of or behind the competition — it's all the same), the company must eventually become, or if they already are, always stay, the one that is viewed by customers as having the best service. So the question now is, "How do you do it?"

Here I was helped by a bit of science. (Just to prove I do have some left brain left.) The following equation is from Sir Isaac Newton. It is his formula for calculating momentum, which to my mind is the same as pace:

Momentum = Direction x Mass x Speed

So how does this apply to creating a winning pace in customer service? Here's how:

- **Direction** — This is the result of great leadership. It is vision and values working together to provide people throughout the organisation a worthwhile goal to achieve, one that has key to it the creation of class-winning service levels.

- **Mass** — This means having every employee involved. It's too important to be left to just the customer service or salespeople. Everyone in the business needs to accept a personal responsibility for the attraction and retention of customers.

- **Speed** — This is created through an ongoing cycle of improvement ideas that are quickly implemented to make way for the next wave.

Direction and mass have been dealt with in previous chapters. So let's now turn to speed.

Regular Ideas Sessions

We've already covered this in Chapter 6 but I want to mention it once more to make sure that you understand how important it is. You should involve all your staff (people are always telling me that the best ideas come from the most unexpected sources) in the process of generating ideas for service improvements. The following process is the way to do this.

- **Get every member of staff involved in generating WOW ideas.** I've found that lots of short sessions are best. Using simple brainstorming techniques it's easy to generates dozens of ideas.

- **Test them all to find the best ones.** They may not all work as expected but that doesn't matter. The key is to quickly find the best ones so you can move on.

- **Embed the best ones into your systems and processes to make them habitual.** Having found the best ideas you want to make them a standard part of the way you do business. Spread these ideas around to everyone so that this happens. Every one of these ideas, no matter how small, moves you further away from your competitors and closer to your customers.

- **Repeat the whole process again and again.** Now keep repeating this process as often as possible. The more times you do this, the more ideas you generate, the more motivated your staff become and the more pace you generate.

The number of ideas generated and the frequency at which you repeat this process are obviously what will determine your rate of improvement. If you want a world class benchmark for this, Toyota provides an excellent model. At every factory, every day, every employee is involved for at least 15 minutes in a "quality circle" meeting. The result of this is that they generate an average of 200 improvement ideas per employee per year. That's world class!

The Value of Employee Improvement Ideas

A good example of how valuable and powerful employee ideas can be is the following: Toyota uses fewer man-hours to produce a Lexus than a German competitor uses re-working a comparable luxury vehicle at the end of the line after it has been made!

Rewarding the Right Things

An important element of alignment is the alignment of rewards. I find it amazing how many organisations miss this absolutely vital element. Some state that what matters is teamwork yet only reward individual performance. Others claim they value staff who deliver high customer service yet only reward those who deliver high sales or profits. It is therefore important to develop schemes that link employee rewards directly to service delivery. We considered the many types of rewards that could be linked to service in Chapter 8.

Julian Richer of Richer Sounds does this by linking income to service delivery. The staff in his retail shops therefore get their biggest pay bonuses for delivering service that customers rate as excellent. (They also get fined if customers rate them as poor.)

But pay isn't the only reward for delivering excellent service. D2D, the electronic circuit board assembler, has an award system involving a catalogue of prizes that staff can win for delivering great customer service. TNT and Unipart have days at which people are recognised, thanked and given awards for delivering great service to customers, and Ken McCulloch of One Devonshire Gardens sends his staff to stay in other great hotels, to relax and enjoy the environment and at the same time observe and note any good ideas they could copy and make good use of.

So there you have it. An outline plan of action that takes all the ideas so far and puts them into a logical step-by-step approach. It's one that I have suggested to many of the businesses I work with. It's worked for them. I'm therefore confident that it can work for you.

Making it Habitual

I've liked this quotation from Aristotle ever since I first read it:

**"We are what we repeatedly do.
Success, then, is not an act, but a habit."**

This quotation says what you need to do to make this a success. If you do these things, over and over again, they become your natural habit and part of your culture. They will be so much a part of you that if they were not happening it would be so unusual that it would immediately show and look and feel wrong. It's only then that you can claim that you have developed a natural and cultural service habit.

Recommended Actions	✔
◆ Remember that you need actions to generate results — plans alone can't do it.	❏
◆ Go for Grade A execution and always involve all people in the planning process.	❏
◆ Seek out SID and help people get rid of it.	❏
◆ Seek out MADness and expel it from your organisation.	❏
◆ Decide where you currently are on the four-phase plan. Get everyone involved so that you all agree with the conclusion.	❏
◆ Now start dealing with the issues that come next in the plan. Don't leave any out — you'll only regret it later when you find that something else isn't working.	❏
◆ Work through all the stages of the plan, in a step-by-step manner, agreeing with everyone where you are at all times.	❏
◆ Always be prepared to go back to something that you thought was OK but later find isn't. Remember that the elements are interdependent so it's vitally important that they all work as they should.	❏

Chapter 15

Finding the Funding

I am always being asked where the money is going to come from to pay for the type of programmes that I recommend. The answer is usually quite easy. In most cases the money is already there in the business, no new money has to be found and we just have to reallocate some which is not being well spent at present. Let me explain.

The first thing that must be understood is that it always costs more to get something wrong and then put it right than it does to get it right in the first place. You could express this with my last two Daffy's Laws:

> **You rarely increase quality by reducing costs, but you often reduce costs by increasing quality.**

> **It always costs more to *put* things right than it does to *get* things right.**

Anyone who has worked on quality improvement programmes knows that poor quality always costs more than good quality. It's just that the costs of fixing the results of poor quality are often hidden or lost in other budgets, so they don't seem to exist. Well, it's just the same with service. In my experience it always costs less to give a good service than it does to give a poor one. This book contains plenty of ideas for ways you could take a long, hard look at the costs to your business of poor service. And if you do, the logic of this argument soon leaps out at you.

One way to approach the creation of budgets for service improvement programmes, that I've found works well, is to understand what I call bucket marketing.

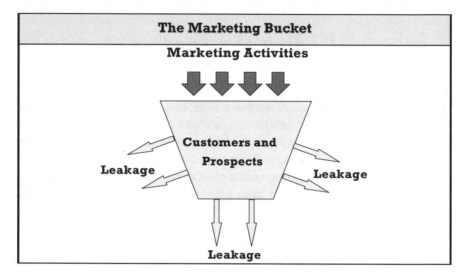

Imagine that all your existing customers were in the bucket in the diagram. I guess that, like most businesses, you are constantly engaged in various marketing activities to keep the bucket topped up.

But what if I were to say that you could no longer commit resources to these activities? What would then happen to the level of customers in the bucket? The normal answer is that it would go down because the number of customers, or the amount they spend, would reduce. In other words, customers and/or orders would be leaking out of the bottom and sides of the bucket.

My next question, therefore, is, "Can you put specific names to these holes that are causing leakage?" The answers I often get naming the causes of these leaks are things like:

- Late deliveries

- Product quality problems

- Poorly trained front-line staff

- Slow or cumbersome customer systems

- Rude or unhelpful staff or management.

Having now identified the causes of the leakage, we can begin to plug the holes. One by one we can remove the causes of lost customers or lost orders. And where does the money for this come from? It comes from the money saved from the marketing expenditure at the top of the bucket.

It usually follows that if we aren't losing the customers we've already got, we can still build the business but with a smaller spend on marketing. So in most cases the necessary budget already exists, the only problem being that it's wrongly allocated. And that is, or should be, easy to correct.

So give your marketing bucket a really close inspection. See if it has any leaks and plug all that you find. Doing so can quickly lead to needing a bigger bucket!

Dotty Logic

I'm often asked to comment on the effect on the business and its profits from customers who abuse the goodwill policies I suggest. It's a fair question and the best way I have of explaining my view is as follows.

In most of the businesses I work with, the actual percentage of returned goods, guarantee claims or complaints that are, or seem to be, a result of abuse is very small. (Many of the people who ask this question don't know what the percentage for their business actually is and so have a false and often far too high impression of what it is.) Usually it is a small percentage of the total returns, complaints or guarantee claims. We could, therefore, express this percentage as a small dot on a sheet of paper, like the dot in the diagram below.

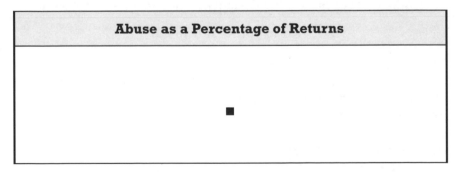

Abuse as a Percentage of Returns

If we then calculate this number of abuses, false claims or complaints as a percentage of the total sales, we would get a much smaller figure that could be expressed by the dot on this second diagram.

Abuse as a Percentage of All Sales

.

I hope you can see this dot. It's really small. Tiny, in fact, in comparison to the total size of the box. It's almost insignificant . . . and that's my point! When you work out the real facts you usually find that the actual amount of abuse is insignificant. Much too small to be worthy of complicated policies to prevent it.

Also remember that any such policies would also be applied to your good customers. So just think of it. You could be creating policies that make your business difficult to deal with — designed for the tiny number of customers who abuse your goodwill (who you probably don't want to keep anyway) — which could drive away the good customers you do want to keep. That sounds stupid to me. That's why I call it dotty logic, I think it would be dotty to do it.

That doesn't mean that you should encourage abuse, or condone it. You should be aware of its potential damage and do all you can to prevent it. But policies that make you more difficult to deal with are not the answer. The best approach is to leave your frontline staff to deal with it within clear guidelines that have been agreed on with them.

A good example of this is the policy I developed with one of the UK's major retailers. We decided on a policy that was based on:

"Fair to you — fair to us."

We told the staff that if there was ever doubt they should always assume that the customer was right. Then when they felt there were unreasonable expectations from the customer they should look for a "fair to you — fair to us" solution.

A typical example of this could be some returned goods that the salesperson thought were not faulty but had been subjected to unreasonable use. They might say to the customer:

> *"I think this problem has occurred because of the way you have used these goods, this means that we really should not change them. But to be fair to you, you have gone to the trouble to bring them back so I will give you an exchange in this instance. Yet to*

be fair to us also, I must point out that if this happens again I
shall not be able to offer another replacement."

We found that with this approach the staff were happy because they were left in control, yet they had clear guidelines within which to operate. They were also happy to know that the company's money was not being wasted on the wrong customers. The customers were also happy because they felt they were being treated fairly, but they also knew the company would not allow repeated abuse.

So you need to work out a system, perhaps similar to this retail example, that will keep everyone happy. The key point is to keep the problem of abuse in perspective. It's usually much smaller than you think, so don't develop any dotty systems that may stop the occasional abuser but will also damage valuable relationships with your good customers.

The Brand Value of Service

The next thing to consider is the value that gaining a reputation for high service adds to a business. I've been investigating this for some time now and it's interesting to note how, once you become interested in something, you tend to discover more things about it than ever before. Someone once explained this to me as "opening new windows in your mind". When you "open a window" by developing an interest in something new, you start to be aware of things you previously would have ignored. So a lot of light has been shining through my newly opened window onto this topic of brand value and how high service can add value to a brand. Only a few days ago I received a mailing from Financial Times Conferences. It was promoting a conference called "Reflecting Brand Value on the Balance Sheet". It was a conference for financial people and was not, therefore, focused on the service element in brands. But I think the existence of such a prestigious two-day event on the subject of brands adding value to a balance sheet does demonstrate how important a topic this is becoming.

I went about exploring this subject by giving myself three key questions to find some answers to. These questions and the answers I found are as follows.

Question 1: Can Service Become Part of a Brand?

There are a few organisations (generally only one or two in any market or sector) that have made themselves different and distinctive because of the service they provide. At the various seminars and conferences I do each year I regularly ask for examples of such organisations that readily come to delegates' minds. It's interesting, but I guess not surprising, that the following businesses, most of which I've referred to already in this book, tend to be mentioned again and again.

Ritz Carlton Hotels. Each year Tony Mosely of Manchester Business School organises the Service Excellence study tour of America's best service providers. He recently admitted to me that when choosing the high-service organisations to visit he always has at the back of his mind a wish to stay in a Ritz Carlton hotel if possible. Most Ritz Carlton hotels are a franchise, so the local owner-managers each add their own style to the hotel. But Tony knows that the Ritz Carlton brand means that the service will be exceptional and that his customers will therefore be delighted with his choice.

Tesco. In the UK grocery sector Tesco is the business that nowadays gets the most mentions as a distinctively high-service provider. I think that's quite an achievement when you consider that not too many years ago they were famous for their founder's motto, "stack it high and sell it cheap". I shall be commenting later on the effect this new "brand image" is having on Tesco's brand value.

Disney. Disney is another great US example. In their theme parks they have an attention to detail and a style of service that is unique, and so forms a part of the added value of their brand.

Virgin. Another interesting UK example is Virgin. The problems they have experienced with Virgin Trains are, I believe, a result of the fact that Virgin has created a core service element that the British public attach to and expect from the Virgin brand. So when the Virgin brand appears on a train, although the service experienced on the train is about the same as from BR, we complain. Letters of apology, vouchers offering discounts off future journeys and promises of "better service when we have our new trains" do not appease us. We understandably and rightly expect a Virgin train experience to be similar to the service that goes with anything carrying the Virgin brand. (This example not only demonstrates the power of a strong brand, it also highlights the problems that can occur if the expectations or promises that go with it are not met.)

Nordstrom. Nordstrom, America's world famous clothing retailer, is another organisation that has developed a level and style of service that can only be experienced in a Nordstrom store. Service is now, therefore, a key part of their overall brand.

Marks & Spencer. A final example must be Marks & Spencer. They only sell own-brand goods so their brand and the values within it are critical to their success. The Marks & Spencer brand has been built on their three core values of quality, value and service. It's a simple but obviously powerful formula that's worked for decades. So if they were to do anything that seriously damaged their reputation in any of these areas, that could also damage the core value in their brand. And that, I guess, would eventually also damage the overall value of the business. (As I write this, recent events make me wonder if they haven't done just that over the past few years.)

These examples prove that service can be a core part of a brand. But secondary questions to this must be:

- How do you define a brand, and

- Where does service fit in?

Terry Leahy, Tesco's Chief Executive, says that a brand is *"something that creates value to the customer"*. I think that's a great definition because it's simple to understand. Another definition I like comes from the ex-Chief Executive of First Direct Bank, Kevin Newman. What I particularly like about his definition is that it specifically answers my question about brands and the place of service within them:

Brand = Value + Values

Value = Product + Price

Values = People + Culture

I think that this makes great sense. Customers will decide the value of something by balancing the actual product (or service) with the price that they have to pay for it. So the better the product or service and the lower the price, the higher the value to the customer.

The first value part of a brand is pretty obvious to most people. But the second value element is one that many organisations seem to have overlooked. There are, however, some businesses, like First Direct Bank, that have worked as hard on the creation of this element as on the value part. A good example of a UK business committed to a strong value component in their brand is the Body Shop.

Body Shop

The Body Shop brand is known worldwide. Its core elements are captured in the following quotation from Anita Roddick: "We produce products that cleanse, polish and protect the skin and hair. How we produce them and how we market them is what is interesting about us. We are innovative in our formulations; we are passionate about environmental and social issues; we care about retailing. The image, goals and values of our company are as important as our products."

This statement clearly demonstrates how values have become a key part of the Body Shop brand. In fact, they are perhaps the only elements that no competitor has yet been able to copy. Boots has developed their "Naturals" range. Other franchise operations have been launched to market similar products to Body Shop. But so far none of them have been able to create the "soul" or values that are a key part of the Body Shop offering.

Sewell Motor Company

An example of service values becoming a core part of a business is Sewell Motor Company in Texas. Carl Sewell has built one of the most successful car dealerships in the world by focusing on value-driven things. This is not to say that he doesn't also get the other things right. He is fanatical about things being clean, efficient and right first time, every time. But he also insists that his staff show a commitment to the business's core values of openness, honesty, being fair to customers and "treating every customer as if they were a member of your own family".

These examples create no doubt in my mind that the answer to question 1 is YES. Service *can* become part of a brand. This then leads to my second key question.

Question 2: Can Service Add Value to a Brand?

In order to answer this question I've been investigating organisations like the ones listed earlier to learn their views and search for evidence of how service has added value to their brands. I've already mentioned the lecture I attended at Manchester Business School given by Terry Leahy, the Chief Executive of Tesco. He had been invited to talk about the key elements of Tesco's success and it was interesting to note how much importance he put on the Tesco brand and what it represented. He suggested that the most important value a brand can have is "the trust of customers" and that the creation of such trust will definitely add value to any brand.

As an example of the value a brand can add, he referred to Tesco's takeover of William Low, a Scottish retail grocer. Just two years after the Tesco brand had replaced the William Low brand, the following had resulted.

- Sales were up by 40%.

- The average prices were around 6% lower.

- £35 million had been spent on store improvements.

- 100,000 more customers were being attracted per week.

- 60% more people were employed in the business.

- Pay had increased by 15% for the average employee.

- Double the business was being done with local suppliers.

- Annual profits had grown from £17 million to £51 million.

Terry explained how, over the past few years, the Tesco management team has been focusing every employee's attention on customer service. Every decision and action in Tesco is first checked against the question, "What's in this for the customer?" If no worthwhile answer can be found, then the decision or action must be changed.

Another example comes from when the Marriott Hotel brand replaced the Holiday Inn brand at a number of hotels in the UK. The hotels were the same as before (apart from a bit of redecoration), the locations were the same and most of the staff were the same. However, with the Marriott brand went an international reputation for high service. These newly branded hotels were therefore able to charge a higher room rate and they now have a higher level of occupancy than before — all because of a new brand.

These examples clearly demonstrate that service can add value to a brand. I therefore have one last question.

Question 3: How Does Service Become Part of a Brand?

This is a more difficult one to answer. However, I think a clue to the answer comes from these words used in my answer to question 1: *"different and distinctive"*.

I think that to make service a part of your brand, the service that your customers experience must be both different and distinctive. Do you remember the quotation from Jerry Garcia from Chapter 6?

"You do not merely want to be considered just the best of the best.

You want to be considered the only one who does what you do."

Well, I think that's it. You need to find a way to deliver a service that makes you the only one who does what you do. You've just read a book full of ideas on how you do this so I hope you now know how to do it for your business.

So if you can make your service different from anything your competitors have, in a way that your customers will value, then like most of the examples I've used, you should have a brand that provides added value and a source of competitive advantage that will last for many decades.

Going for the Jugular

If, after all the things I've already mentioned in this chapter, you still haven't managed to convince whoever it is that you need to convince of the "cost justification" of high service or the "likely return on the investment" — try my "going for the jugular" approach. I referred to this briefly at the beginning of Chapter 13, but I'll go over it again so you know how to use it.

At the beginning of my seminars, if I have time, I like to kill off any arguments about the cost of service. The best way I've found to do this is to do a simple exercise. I ask people to think of well-known companies that other people will have heard of, with no more than two from any one sector or industry, that have become "famous" for the great service they provide. I try to get everyone to aim for ten and have a minimum of five. I then create lists of these companies for all to see. You could guess which ones get chosen — I've been referring to them throughout this book. I then ask people to think where they would place them against their main competitors in term of some standard business performance measures, such as:

- Profitability

- Return on assets

- Market share

- Growth rate

- Ability to attract and keep good staff

- Ability to resist market downturns

- Ability to out manoeuvre competitors.

When I do this we find that we've got an almost 100% best performers list in all these categories. So by choosing businesses that have become "famous for service" we've also chosen businesses that are brilliant performers in the other key categories.

How much more proof can anyone need of the value of becoming a "famous for service" business? So, as a last resort, or maybe it should be a first resort, try this with your "I need financial proof" person.

I hope that these ideas will help you make whatever financial case is necessary. As this chapter suggests, it is not a matter of being able to afford the cost of investment in good service — it's more a matter of not being able to afford the costs of not investing. In other words, you can't afford not to, so please stop hesitating and just get on with it!

Chapter 16

e-Service.com

The Reluctant Author

When my publisher suggested that there should be a chapter about e-service in this latest edition of my book I agreed that it was an exciting and important subject to cover. Yet I've been reluctant to get cracking, which seemed odd, until it dawned on me the other day. The reason is the more I learn, the more I realize that whatever I write, the e-commerce pace of evolution is so fast that even before this book is printed, some things will be wrong or have changed. But it's the same for everyone else and I guess it's also understood by anyone who knows anything about the Internet, so now that I've realized this and admitted it to you, I can get on with writing the chapter.

I'm not going to comment on how to start a dotcom business, or what the keys to success in e-trading are. There are already plenty of books, from people who know lots more about it than me, and there certainly will soon be many more (I shall refer to some in this chapter). What I shall focus on is the effect e-business has on customer relationships and how you can use it to build long-term loyalty. I shall also highlight some of the successful competitive strategies that are being adopted by dotcom traders.

A Massive Shift of Power

I've been in many meetings, especially in large organisations with lots of departments, where the question "who owns the customer?" has been raised and fiercely debated by people trying to represent the interests of their team. I've also witnessed (and been involved in) heated arguments about people poaching "my customer" or "our customers". I guess that similar discussions are still taking place in many organisations today. I'm convinced, however, that these issues are totally futile when we consider Internet customers. It's a medium where nobody owns or controls any customers. A massive shift of power has taken place. The result is that in many respects the Internet customers now own or at least have control over their suppliers — and they know it!

Customers now have fast, easy access to more knowledge than ever before. They can research a product or service, contact other users via user groups, compare different specifications and performance data and see what the competitors have to offer. This means that by the time they're ready to order they could easily know more about it than the supplier's salesperson. But then again — who needs a salesperson? If you know what you want, and can order with a click, why should you bother talking to someone about it?

A Lifetime of Knowledge in a Day — Or Maybe a Click

I remember reading that a weekday edition of The Times contains more information than the average person in 17th century England was likely to come across during their whole lifetime.

Well I guess you could say that the Internet will make it possible to access most of the knowledge that exists throughout the world with just a click.

It's no wonder the sale of headache pills keeps growing!

When the next generation of personal search engines really gets going potential customers will be able to set them working, searching the on-line world for the latest information or the best deals, while they're away from their computers doing something else.

Power to the Customer

People with illnesses can now investigate their symptoms and treatment on the Internet so that by the time they get to see a doctor they know more about it than he or she does.

Suppliers can, of course, use the Internet to send customers or prospects what they hope will be enticing e-mails. (I get dozens of them.) But they can be gone in a click if they are boring, or take too long to download or read (thankfully). And you can even click to delete without ever opening them if you don't like their look. (I do that a lot.)

So what does this power shift mean for business? One thing it means is that the old rules and techniques for sales and marketing don't work the same for e-trading as they work elsewhere. Many of them therefore have to be scrapped to make way for new ones.

For example, the cost of acquiring new customers can be enormous for e-traders. You therefore have to think very carefully about whether you want simply "any" customers or just the "right" customers. Research already shows that the "any" customer approach may improve revenues in the short term, but it can be costly in the long term as these customers flit from supplier to supplier. However, the "right" customer approach tends to make it more likely that a relationship (and referrals) will develop and therefore prove more beneficial over the long term. This is perhaps one reason why many sites and links are developing new kinds of synergistic partnerships to reduce or share the cost of new customer acquisition.

The New Net Partnerships

I read an interesting article on the subject of Net partnerships in the November/December 1999 issue of Customer Service Management magazine written by Peter Fisk of PA Consulting Group. In it he suggested that one way the Internet is likely to develop is by segmenting into what he called "customer gateways" and "content providers". His point is that most customers already have more relationships than they want and would therefore not wish to add more via the Internet. They'd rather use it to reduce the number. He suggests that this is beginning to happen now via "customer gateways". These are sites or suppliers that we know or have learned we can trust and will therefore allow to select on our behalf, or at least recommend, the "content providers" we shall use.

Examples of such existing or potential "content providers" include American Express, Cosmopolitan magazine, Disney, First Direct, Reuters, Tesco, Virgin and Yahoo!. These tend to be lifestyle or "trust" brands that would not only offer their own products and services but also partner with "content providers" to make available a range of offerings that we could buy via their Internet site.

Examples of "content providers" include Apple, Blockbuster Video, BMW, Chubb Insurance, Dixons, Nestle, Rank Xerox and Thomas Cook. These are brands that have a reputation for value, reliability, quality and service in a specific sector or for a particular product.

> *We're already seeing many of these new Net partnerships de-veloping. They should create synergy, so everyone gains. Peter Fisk is therefore convinced we'll see many more in the future.*

The above is just one example of how things are changing at the sales and marketing end of customer relationships. There are many other models being developed and I'm sure there will be even more in the future. But these examples are about acquiring cus-tomers. This book is supposed to be about keeping them. So what about that?

New Medium, Same Rules

The more I learn about and experience Internet usage, the more I realise that when it comes to customer service and loyalty, the ba-sic rules are the same as with all other means of communicating with customers. The rules that apply to face-to-face, telephone and mail communications apply equally to the Internet.

In Patricia B. Seybold's book *customers.com* she explains this very simply. To the question, "What's the secret of a successful e-business initiative?", she answers, "It's the customer, stupid!". I think that says it about as succinctly as possible. It's not the tech-nology, or the advertising or the whizzy home page, or the links from every conceivable location. Important though they all are, the key to success is a focus on the customer and a commitment to de-livering what *they* want.

I've also learned that the organisations that are succeeding in using the Internet to create customer loyalty haven't created new techniques to do this. They're simply applying the existing, well-proven techniques to this new medium. So how do we apply the basic rules of customer service to the Internet?

I know that people from all types and size of business will read this book. Therefore, to answer the above question in a way that should be relevant to you all, I've decided to do it with reference to the basic findings from the SERVQUAL research (see Chapter 7). This research identified the elements that determine a customer's perception of any service. It also indicated how much influence each element was likely to have over the overall perception. I be-lieve its findings are as relevant to e-service as they are to any other form of service delivery. I therefore think it will be the best way to consider how you can use the Internet to create the type of customer service perceptions that will lead to sustainable loyalty.

The basic SERVQUAL findings can be expressed by the following diagram:

Customer Perceptions of Service Are Determined by:				
32%	Reliability	⇨ *Trust*		
22%	Responsiveness	⇨ *Help*		
19%	Assurance	⇨ *Belief*	+	Intangibles
16%	Empathy	⇨ *Care*		*Feel*
11%	Tangibles	⇨ *Basics*		

As I explained in Chapter 7, the relative weightings may not be spot on for your particular type of e-venture (although my research suggests that they are pretty close for most), but they do serve as a good guide. So let's consider how these basic rules of managing customers' perceptions of service are applied to e-business.

✎ e-Reliability — Your ability to perform the promised service dependably and accurately (32 per cent)

"Price does not rule the Web; trust does."

This quotation is from an article in the July-August 2000 edition of *Harvard Business Review*, written by Frederick F. Reicheld and Phil Schefter of Bain & Company. It was based on their research into Web loyalty, which clearly demonstrated that the key to long term e-business success is customer loyalty, and the key to loyalty is trust.

Do you remember the TARP (they now call themselves *e-satisfy*) research I referred to in Chapter 5? It suggested that if you're unreliable and so create dissatisfied customers, they are likely to use word-of-mouth advertising to tell 9 to 10 other people about it. Over the Internet, with its growing number of user groups, that same single dissatisfied customer could use word-of-mouse advertising to tell 9 to 10 *thousand* other people about your poor service. So reliability becomes even more critical with this medium, and unreliability can quickly become terminal!

It should therefore be no surprise that the Internet businesses that are most successful are the ones that we know or have learned we can trust to deliver consistently against their promises.

- I know I can rely on Dell to deliver any computer I order when they promise — and also to fix it if it ever goes wrong.

- I've learned I can rely on Amazon to deliver any books I order within a day or so — or if they're a gift, to deliver them to someone else when promised. (I even trust them to store my credit card details so I can use their 1-click ordering system.)

- I've also learned I can rely on Easyjet to supply my airline tickets on time — and to give me a small extra discount for booking on-line.

e-Reliability, which creates trust, is therefore a must for success. I think the basic e-Reliability rules are:

- Make sure that the "back-office" people act as if they were front-office. Don't let them hide behind the anonymity that Internet trading allows. Make sure they take personal responsibility for all promises made to customers.

- Agree minimum operating standards and monitor your performance against them (e.g. Dell technicians must respond to customer queries within four hours; Land's End staff must take no longer than three hours to reply to customer e-mails).

- Make sure that you use suppliers (e.g. carriers) that are equally able to live up to any promises you make.

- Ensure that you have adequate stocks to satisfy demand within promised delivery dates. If you do ever face problems caused by over-demand, make sure your customers know immediately. Offer them a full refund or a new delivery date you can guarantee you *will not* miss. (If you're serious about recovery you'll also need to do something more to compensate for your failure to honor your original promise. Refer to Chapter 6 for ideas on this.)

- There is a phrase used by many successful retailers: "retail is detail". Well I believe that "e-tail is detail", too, so keep a close eye on all the little details. They may not seem important to you, but they could reflect your trustworthiness and so have a big impact on the customers' perception of your business.

---

e-tail is Detail

There is a dotcom trader called Zercon that sells discounted de-signer clothes. Not long ago their site was inaccessible and a no-tice was posted saying it was "closed for maintenance" and would re-open on a certain date. That was OK, but days after the promised re-opening date the site was still closed but no one had thought to apologize for the delay and update the notice. I there-fore guessed they were another e-trader that had gone bust so didn't try to access their site again.

I've since learned that I was wrong and they're now open for business again. I wonder how many other potential customers made the same assumption that I did and stopped visiting them as a result of this foolish little oversight?

Remember that with these things accounting for around 32 per cent of customer perception, and according to Bain & Company's research being the most important aspect of Web trading, nothing is more important to get and keep right.

✎ e-Responsiveness — **Your willingness to help customers and provide prompt service (22 per cent)**

Perception of service is partly driven by expectations. The medium of the Internet tends to set customer expectations high. It should therefore be no surprise that when customers have 24-hour shop-ping they expect 24-hour service too. When they can place orders in a few minutes, they expect responses to queries in a few minutes as well. And when they see advertisements that claim how easy and quick it is to shop on-line from one e-supplier, they expect the same ease and speed form all e-suppliers.

It's therefore understandable that my research, reading and dis-cussions all indicate that good responsiveness is even more im-portant for on-line businesses than it is for their off-line equiva-lents.

e-Responsiveness requires many things. Some will be specific to particular organisations. Some that I think are common to all include:

- Fast access to all parts of the site. All too often the site design-ers get carried away with their whizzy technology and graphi-cal design skills. It's all too easy to forget that speed of access and navigation are essential to keep customers online. Fancy graphics may look good, but if they slow down access or usability customers will become frustrated and click off.

Site Designers vs. Site Users

Site designers usually have mega-memory, ultra-fast machines to work with. They're generally doing the job because they're "turned on" by technology or graphics.

Customers usually have pretty basic machines for access. They're more likely to be "turned on" by speedy access and simple usability.

Make sure someone in your e-business has the job of constantly reminding the site designers that they're doing it for the customers — not for themselves.

- Easy telephone access for the times when customers need to talk to someone. (The best sites offer either an 800 number or the option to request someone to call you.)

- One-click navigation that gets you straight to any information you need. No multi-click tunnels that result in dead ends.

- Simple-to-use order forms. Don't expect your customers to waste time answering superfluous order form questions. (I've abandoned many attempts to buy online because of onerous order forms — I'm sure many other people do the same.) You may want to build detailed information about your customers, but you can do this gradually, as you build their trust. Don't try to get all the information you want at once by giving them a "third degree" interrogation with their first order.

- Practice dazzling recovery techniques (see Chapter 6). This is even more important with e-business so make sure you have developed recovery techniques and systems that will WOW your customers.

These things determine 22 per cent of customer perceptions so they, too, warrant detailed attention and carefully planned systems to ensure proper implementation.

❧ e-Assurance — The knowledge and courtesy of your employees and their ability to convey trust and confidence (19 per cent)

As I write this, most of the start-up e-businesses are still making massive losses. (Amazon.com still seems to have a business model where the more they sell the more they lose.) Some are achieving e-burnout (annual expenditure grossly exceeding annual income with no indication of it ever changing) and therefore going bust. I'm sure many more will follow. This obviously creates uneasiness with existing and potential dotcom customers so it's important to ensure that your site conveys the trustworthiness and builds the confidence necessary to turn the interest of a prospect into the action of a buyer.

If you already have a known and trusted brand, like Virgin, IBM, BA or Federal Express, it's easy. You can simply transfer the reputation and goodwill your existing brand has to a new e-business with the same name. But if you're a previously unknown start-up, with a catchy dotcom name you thought up in the pub with some friends, you've got a much more difficult job to convince potential customers that you can be trusted to deliver what you promise.

The Dottiness of Dotcoms

Someone recently told me that some e-business start-ups have found it more difficult to convince customers to spend £20.00 to buy something from their new website than it was to convince investors to spend £20,000,000 to enable them to create it!

Some of the ways you could do this include:

- Aligning yourself or partnering with well-known people or existing brands that are already trusted by potential customers.

- Offering service guarantees that commit you to minimum performance standards.

- Having clear and customer-friendly returns policies.

- Subscribing to trusted e-business verification organisations like Which Web Trader, Trust on-line, ePubliceye.com, or VeriSign.

- Entering (and winning) the respected awards for service and reliability that are currently being won by companies like Dell, Amazon, and eBay.

At 19 per cent of customer perception this is only marginally less important than e-Responsiveness so it's vital you get this right, too.

✍ e-Empathy — The caring and individualized attention the organisation provides (16 per cent)

It is possible to provide a personal attention "feel" to a Web-based transaction. I experience it every time I shop for books with Amazon. This can make a big difference to whether I feel like a "special and valued" customer or just "another" customer.

There are many ways to create this. Here are just a few:

- e-Feedback — It's just as important to gather feedback from your e-customers as it is from any others. You could therefore have e-Feedback forms that customers can complete to tell you about their experience of doing business with you. It should also be possible to use all the design opportunities that the Internet provides to make these forms easy and fun to complete.

- Rapid responses — Set up your systems to provide rapid responses to customer communications. Acknowledge receipt of e-mails and orders instantly (even if you can't provide instant replies). Send e-mails to keep customers regularly updated with information about the progress of their order or request.

- Customization opportunities — Allow customers to customize your site or the way it works or responds to suit their particular preferences. The more they feel it works "for them", the more they will visit and use it.

- Continual learning about customer preferences — Every time a customer visits and uses your site they provide valuable information. Click by click they tell you about themselves — the pages they look at, the information they download, the things they purchase and even the things they reject. All this information should enable you to create an ever more useful profile of each customer's preferences and habits.

Yet research has shown that very few e-traders are gathering and making use of this valuable data. Bain & Company's research showed that less than 20 per cent of e-traders even bother to track customer loyalty, instead they have a fixation about visitors, hits, sales and general Web capacity. They believe that the average Website achieves only 30 per cent or less of its full sales potential with each customer. So be one of the few to use this customer information, get to know their habits and preferences, adapt your offer to match them and then see how much of that potential 70 per cent you can attract.

Amazon

Amazon keeps a record of my purchases so that whenever I visit the site they have a list of any new titles that are related to past purchases.

L. L. Bean

L. L. Bean keeps detailed records of their customers' purchases and clothing sizes. Their site also contains valuable information about how to care for and get the best use from the products that they sell.

- One-click order opportunities — I think the Amazon one-click order system is great. So far it's the easiest way of buying a book I know. I'm sure this idea has potential for most e-traders, so look into how you can develop something similar that will make it as easy for your customers to buy.

- 🔖 **e-Tangibles — The performance of the products, and the appearance of physical facilities, equipment, personnel and communication materials (11 per cent)**

There are e-Tangibles with e-business just as there are with others. The e-Tangibles include things such as:

- The initial appearance of the site (especially the home page)

- The performance of the products and services provided

- The advertising and PR materials used

- The paperwork customers receive such as letters, invoices, delivery notes, etc.

With only 11 per cent influence over customer perception this is the least important aspect. Yet for most new dotcom businesses these are the things that seem to get the most attention!

The point to remember is that although they obviously matter, they're much less important than the preceding items. So ensure that you spend your time and resources appropriately and don't allow these items to soak it all up. (As so many e-business start-ups seem to have done.)

New Medium, New Strategies

I thought I should end this chapter by considering some of the competitive strategies that are being used to gain e-market share. Different organisations are using different strategies but the key ones seem to be based around whether the e-business is a start-up or an existing business. There are many in each of these sectors and there are elements of cross-over between them but I think the following are the most prevalent in each category.

Business Strategy 1 — Cutoutthemiddleman.com

This is a strategy used to bring direct supply to the customer without the need or the cost of a middleman trader. Examples of this include:

- Easyjet — their website is one of the easiest to use that I know of and it now accounts for over 50 per cent of their bookings. BA forecasts that they will be in the same situation by 2003

- Dell — Dell built what is now one of the world's most successful computer businesses by going direct to customers and only building to order.

This strategy works well, particularly when the savings made from cutting out the middleman are passed on to the customer.

Business Strategy 2 — Attacksomeonesmarket.com

This strategy is based on using the Internet to attack a traditional market, such as retail. Examples of this include:

- Amazon.com — Amazon began by attacking the retail and mail order book markets. Now they have their sights set on others.

- The UK car market has seen an attack from e-traders offering imported cars, such as Carbusters, Virgin Cars and JamJar.

Amazon has shown how successful this strategy can be if you get in first and establish a dominant position as the No.1 Internet supplier for the product or service you select.

Businesses Strategy 3 — Createanewmarket.com

The Internet has proved to be an excellent medium for new business ideas that are suited to this fast means of communication. Examples of this strategy include:

- Lastminute.com — Lastminute created a new market for existing products and services by focusing on the time-deprived people of today and offering them last-minute purchases.

- Clickmango.com — Clickmango has created a new market by focusing on the interests and needs of people who want to be healthier and are interested in natural and wholesome products.

I'm convinced we will see many more such e-ventures establish new types of Web-based businesses. And many of these will then use their Web success to branch into and succeed in other traditional markets.

Business Strategy 4 — Destroyyourbusiness.com

Jack Welch of GE has done it again. He's had the foresight and courage to show those of us that are less bold (or perhaps less sensible) one way it can be done. He's issued a directive to all the divisions of GE to create new business units to "destroyyourbusiness.com".

What this means is that they must create a properly resourced separate new business. It must be given access to all the knowledge and arrangements of the existing core business, but then set free from the parent company with the task of creating an Internet-based business that will attack it. The job of the existing business is then to do all it can to prevent this new e-business from doing serious damage.

If this sounds like a recipe for self-cannibalisation, it is. But the argument is that if an e-business is possible, it's surely better to cannibalise yourself than it is to let a competitor do it to you. Sooner or later everything that is traded via other channels will be traded via the Internet (or at least someone will have a go at doing it), so it must make sense to be first at trying it in a sector you know and understand.

Jack Welch isn't the only person demonstrating this courage:

- Wal-Mart has created an Internet business to rival their existing retail empire. They've given it independent management and located it in Silicon Valley, far away from the parent commercial centre in Bentonville, Arkansas. Its mandate is to seek its own global destiny.

- The UK's most successful Internet flight booking site, eBookers.com, was formed by the owner of one of the UK's most successful telephone flight booking businesses, Flight Bookers. (At the time of writing this, eBookers.com has 1 million hits per month. It took them 39 months to grow from zero to ½ million hits per month, but then only 39 weeks to grow from ½ million to 1 million!)

This is the most courageous of the existing business strategies. It's also likely to be the most difficult to get approval for, but it's the one that I think that will create the best long-term results.

Business Strategy 5 — Expandontothenet.com

This is another type of existing business strategy. It's based on bolting e-business on as an additional marketing channel for the existing business. It's less bold than the destroyyourbusiness.com strategy because it's designed to build the new e-business channel without causing serious damage to the existing business. It is, however, working well for many organisations. Some examples include:

- Jungle.com, the computer equipment supplies company, was formed by the owners of Software Warehouse, an existing and very successful direct supplier.

- Tesco, the UK's biggest retail grocer, has an e-business operation through which it has become Europe's biggest Internet grocer.

Business Strategy 6 — *Provideabucketloadofinformation.com*

- Fed Ex — The Fed Ex site allows you to track the progress of your parcel right through from collection to delivery. (Why you should need to know this when they guarantee delivery the next day I fail to understand.)

- Vanguard Group — Vanguard has used their Website to provide the type of detailed investment information that they know is of interest to the customers they serve.

This strategy works on the principle of using the net to build general customer loyalty and trust. As such it's a winner when combined well with all other means of communicating with customers.

Business Strategy 7— *Bethemiddleman.com*

This is based on the concept of being a "customer gateway" site as referred to in the previous "momentous shift of power" section. There are many examples of this strategy, but the most common ones fall into the categories of:

- Travel sites

- General shopping sites

- Compuserve, AOL, Virgin, Freeserve, etc.

- Information sites like Yahoo!, AltaVista, Lycos, Ask Jeeves, etc.

The growth of these sites suggests that there's a big market for them. I guess we'll see many more start up before the fall-out when, as with most markets, lots will go leaving a few strong ones that will remain to dominate the sector.

Business Strategy 8 — *Justbeonthenet.com*

This is, I believe, a flawed strategy. In fact, it's wrong to even call it a competitive strategy, or even a tactic. It's simply a manoeuvre, and it's a really pathetic one at that. Yet it's one that seems to be the choice of many organisations that should know better. I guess it results from the board of a business not understanding the potential of e-business yet feeling they "must have a website". A site is then created, with keeping the cost down being a prime driver, which becomes a collection of some existing promotional material posted on the website pages that offers no new worthwhile information, retains no interest, is boring to look at with too much text and provides no incentive to ever visit the site again.

There is no shortage of organisations that seem to have this approach to e-business. I will not mention any but I'm sure you've come across (and quickly left) many.

If you're considering this approach, my advice would be — don't. It's better not to bother than to have something this bad. It would be better to simply reserve your dotcom name and then wait until you're ready to do it properly. But don't wait too long or someone with a proper e-business strategy could steal your market.

e-Conclusions

One of the best books I've found on the subject is *Futurize your Enterptise* by David Siegel. It's packed full of sound advice from someone who obviously knows what he's on about. Here are a couple of short gems.

The Golden Rule

In business, the Golden Rule is seriously flawed. Rather than treating people the way you would want them to treat you, treat them the way they want to be treated!

The Eight Cs of the Web

Community *— I want to meet and interact with people like me.*

Continuity *— I want to go from one session to the next easily, no matter how much time has elapsed.*

Convenience *— I want to get what I'm looking for quickly and intuitively.*

Commerce *— I want the Web to make transactions easier.*

> **Customisation** — *I want to see what I want, I don't want to see what I don't want — most of the time.*
>
> **Content** — *I want very deep content, and I want to be able to mine it to get what I'm looking for.*
>
> **Commitment** — *I want to know that you will help me in the future. If you don't have what I'm looking for you'll go get it for me.*
>
> **Control** — *I want to control our relationship. I want to turn it on or off, and anything you do with my information should be with my permission.*

There are some excellent basic rules for success contained in this list.

One final thought. Most e-enterprises lose money during the first year of trading, break even (if they're lucky) over the second year and move into profit (if they're even luckier) in year three. Add to this the fact that currently 40 per cent of e-business customers are defecting before the break-even point is reached and this all adds up a serious conclusion about e-service. Keeping e-customers loyal is a business imperative that will have a dramatic effect on the survival of many e-traders. So if you're one already, or are intending to become one, make sure that service and loyalty are at the top of your list of key strategic goals.

Chapter 17

Conclusion: Just Do It!

"Even if you're on the right track, you'll get run over if you just sit there." — *Will Rogers*

My hope is that this book has done a number of things for you, things like:

- Helping you to realise how easy and natural it is for people to provide great customer service.

- Making you impatient to have a go yourself.

- Showing you where to get started and how to keep the enthusiasm levels high.

- Encouraging you to involve all your staff in more (all!) aspects of the business.

- Making you want to read it again and perhaps get some of your staff to read it too.

If I've achieved just one or two of these objectives I'm satisfied. Any more and I'm delighted.

I often end my seminars by telling people that one of the best things in all this is that, although most people can understand and accept the logic in my arguments, they still will not do anything about it. I guess that a major reason for this is that it's easier to leave things as they are than to go changing things. But this means that there is a tremendous opportunity for those of you who do put these ideas into practice. It means that in most markets, you'll find that you become one of a very small, elite minority of organisations, with plenty of customers to choose from who are eager to move to and stay with a high-service supplier.

Remember that to make this work it cannot be just your latest fad. These are not quick-fix ideas to be considered only when you have business problems. To work, it must become a way of doing business that is embedded into your very culture. So don't start if you're not committed to seeing it through, staying with it when some things go wrong and making it a core element of your organisation. I've stated above that the concept is easy. It is. The hard bit is getting it to work for you.

But I'm convinced that it's worth it, and I hope you now are, too. If you can become one of that minority of organisations which cracks the challenge of differentiation through service, I know that you and your colleagues will be glad that you did. You will have created a rare business that will be respected and held in very high esteem by employees, customers and suppliers alike.

I thought I'd leave the last word on this to Dr W. Edwards Deming, the American quality guru whose ideas have helped to transform the quality of both Japanese and American manufactured products. He used to end many of his lectures by saying:

"BUT YOU DON'T HAVE TO DO THIS.
SUCCESS IS NOT COMPULSORY!"

This is true, you don't have to do this, but I hope that you will and I wish you good luck and great success in so doing.

Epilogue

Let's Talk

This topic of customer service is one that continually intrigues and inspires me. I get a real kick out of finding new examples of simple things that people do to delight their customers. I've asked in the book for examples of things that you do or that you've come across that impressed you. I really would value hearing about any that you have, so please write or telephone if you have the time.

Also, if you like what you've read in this book, you might like to hear and discuss it during a live presentation. I'm told that I'm at my best in front of an audience, ranting and raving about this subject. This results in invitations to speak at dozens of conferences and company meetings each year. So please contact my agent, Carol Jones, if you want details of my next appearance or if you think that I might be a suitable speaker for your next event. My repertoire of talks ranges from 45 minutes to three days and covers all aspects of customer service strategies and tactics. I should, therefore, have something that would suit whatever you have in mind.

I also value feedback (one of my customers has nicknamed me "the feedback freak"), so please also feel free to let me know what you think of this book. I can usually be contacted at the address below:

Chris Daffy, The Marketing Group, 23 Alder's Road, Disley
Stockport, Cheshire SK12 2LJ. Tel: 01663 766300
Fax: 01663 765057. E-mail: Chrisdaffy@compuserve.com.

Agent (for speaking engagements): Carol Jones
Select Business Speakers
PO Box 57, Monmouth, Gwent NP5 3AN.
Tel: 01600 712387. Fax: 01600 716738.
E-mail: Caroljones@enterprise.net.

Bibliography

Albrecht, Karl and Ron Zemke (1985), *Service America!* Homewood, IL: Dow Jones-Irwin

Blanchard, Ken and Sheldon Bowles (1993), *Raving Fans*, New York: William Morrow

Carlzon, Jan (1987), *Moments of Truth*, Cambridge, MA: Ballinger

Carnegie, Dale, *How to Win Friends and Influence People*

Covey, Stephen R. (1992), *The Seven Habits of Highly Effective People,* London: Simon and Schuster

Davidson, Mike (1995), *The Grand Strategist*, London: Macmillan

de Bono, Edward (1992), *Sur/Petition*, London: HarperCollins

Freemantle, David (1993), *Incredible Customer Service*, Maidenhead: McGraw-Hill

Freiberg, Kevin and Jackie Freiberg (1996), *Nuts: Southwest Airlines' Crazy Recipe for Business and Personal Success*, Austin, TX: Bard Press, Inc.

Gerson, Richard F. (1993), *Measuring Customer Satisfaction*, London: Kogan Page

Handy, Charles (1989), *The Age of Unreason*, London: Business Books Ltd

Hofmeyr, Jan (1998), "Loyal Yes, Staying No", *Management Today*, May.

King Taylor, Lynda (1993), *Quality: Sustaining Customer Service*, London: Century Business

Leppard, John and Liz Molyneux (1994), *Auditing Your Customer Service*, London: Routledge

Martin, David M., *Dealing with Demanding Customers*, London: Pitman

Murphy, John A. (1993), *Service Quality in Practice*, Dublin: Gill & Macmillan

Newell, Frederick (2000), *loyalty.com*, New York: McGraw-Hill

Peters, Tom (1992), *Liberation Management,* London: BCA

Popcorn, Faith (1996), *Clicking*, London: HarperCollins

Porter, Michael E. (1980), *Competitive Strategy*, New York: The Free Press

Prokesch, Steven E. (1995), "Competing on Customer Service: An Interview with British Airways' Sir Colin Marshall", *Harvard Business Review,* November-December 1995

Quinn, Feargal (1990), *Crowning the Customer*, Dublin: O'Brien Press

Reichheld, Frederick (1996), *The Loyalty Effect: The Hidden Force Behind Growth, Profits and Lasting Value*, Boston, MA: Harvard Business School Press

Richer, Julian (1995), *The Richer Way*, London: Emap Business Communications

Seigel. David (1999), *Futurize Your Enterprise*, New York: Wiley

Seybold, Patricia (1998), *customers.com*, New York: Random House

Whitely, Richard C. (1991), *The Customer Driven Company*, London: Business Books Ltd

Zeithmal, Valeria A., A. Pararusaman and Leonard L. Berry (1990), *Delivering Quality Service*, New York: The Free Press

Index

"Famous for Service"

Presented by Chris Daffy

Chris Daffy, now acknowledged as one of the UK's leading speakers on customer service, challenges you to become *Famous for Service*. In this new four-video set, Chris will show you how to apply 21st century concepts to create and keep customers for life. He will take you on a journey that will inspire and motivate you to provide levels of customer service excellence that turn one-off customers into raving fans of your business. Through vivid case studies and clear examples of customer service at its very best, this video package will help you and your colleagues discover the techniques and strategies that will create life-long customer loyalty!

Each Service Video Package contains:

- Four videos, including the "Famous for Service" lecture, an in-depth interview with Chris Daffy, six case studies of Mansell plc, Manchester Airport, Aberconwy Park, Brittania Building Society, Co-op Travelcare and Toyota UK — all of whom have achieved phenomenal success applying Chris Daffy's ideas.

- Trainer's Guide and Exercise Workbook

- Photocopy Masters and a Powerpoint Presentation on a floppy disk.

- A money back guarantee (see order form for details).

Mobilise all your staff and teach them how to differentiate through service; learn the relationship between service and loyalty; how to "WOW" your customers; and win with pace. This value-packed programme is an essential purchase for anyone who has responsibility for customer service!

How to Order

✉ By mail — Post this order form with your cheque or credit card details for immediate dispatch, or post without payment if you wish to be invoiced.*

🖳 By fax — Fax order form to +353-1-676 1644.

☎ By phone — Telephone your order to +353-1-676 1600.

Please send _____ copy(ies) of the **"Famous for Service" Video Package** at £995.00 each, plus £15.00 for postage and packing.

☐ Cheque enclosed ☐ Please invoice me/my company*

Please charge my ☐ Access ☐ Visa

_____ _____ _____
Credit card number   Exp date   Signature

Please note that no videos will be dispatched until full payment has been received.

Name_____

Title_____

Company_____

Address_____

_____

Telephone_____ Fax_____

*Send order form to: Oak Tree Press, Merrion Building,
Lower Merrion Street, Dublin 2, Ireland.
Telephone: +353-1-676 1600. Fax: +353-1-676 1644*

Money Back Guarantee
If for any reason you are not happy with your purchase, for up to 90 days after its receipt, we will refund the cost of the video in full on return of the product in its original condition . . . Cheerfully, immediately and with no quibble!